Washington in New York

George Washington and the First Congress of the United States

Richard Nisley

WASHINGTON IN NEW YORK:
George Washington and the First Congress of the United States

Library of Congress Control Number: 2018966351
ISBN-13: Paperback: 978-1-64398-556-5

Printed in the United States of America

LitFire
PUBLISHING

LitFire LLC
1-800-511-9787
www.litfirepublishing.com
order@litfirepublishing.com

Washington in New York

George Washington and the First Congress of the United States 1789-1791

by Richard Nisley

"My object has been, and must continue to be, to avoid personalities."—George Washington

"A new scene opens. The object now is to make our independence work. To do this we must secure our union on solid foundations. It's a job for Hercules for we must level mountains of prejudice. We fought side by side to make America free. Let us hand-in-hand struggle now to make her happy."—Alexander Hamilton

"If men were angels, no government would be necessary."—James Madison

With much love and affection

I dedicate this book to my two sons,

William David Nisley

and

Scott Gerald Nisley

Special thanks to illustrator

Dea Lenihan for her illustrations,

particularly the cover illustration of

George Washington.

For more, check out her website:
www.dealenihan.com.

Illustrations appear following page 133

CONTENTS

INTRODUCTION

A GATEWAY TO THE WEST

George Washington must have had an exceptional imagination. How else to explain his decision to lead an army of green farm boys against an army of trained professionals, and expect to win? At Trenton, after a summer of devastating loses, Washington saw a way to turn the tables with a series of unexpected maneuvers and actually win a battle—and did so. Coupled with a second victory a week later at Princeton, Washington's ragtag army regained the upper hand. Five years later, at Yorktown, they delivered the coup de grâce. "If you can dream it, you can do it." Long before Walt Disney said it, George Washington lived it.

After the war, Washington resigned as Commander-in-Chief and returned to Mount Vernon, only to discover he was broke. Yes, he had 200 slaves, but that didn't mean he was rich. As Adam Smith wrote about slavery in "The Wealth of Nations": "The experience of all ages and nations, I believe, demonstrates that the work done by slaves, though it appears to cost only their maintenance, is in the end the dearest of any. A person who can acquire no property, can have no other interest but to eat as much, and to labour as little as possible."

Washington began looking beyond the Allegheny Mountains to the nation's interior as a way out of his economic predicament. He owned property there which under the current state of affairs was worth next to nothing. If he could somehow link up the Potomac River with the Ohio River it would open up a vast new empire for economic growth. How? With a canal. Such a canal would make Virginia the nation's economic center, and make his land holdings—on both sides of the Alleghenies—extremely valuable.

Washington had been dreaming of just such a waterway since boyhood. Before the Revolutionary War, he secured approval from the Virginia legislature for the formation of a stock company to improve navigation on the Potomac, and to charge tolls. With Maryland on the river's north bank, approval from that state was necessary. However, opposition from Baltimore merchants who saw their city being bypassed in favor of Alexandria, Virginia, scuttled the deal. After the war, the ex-Commander-in-Chief's prestige was such that the objections of a few nervous Baltimore businessmen was easily overcome, and the Potomac Canal Company was chartered by Maryland and Virginia. While investment capital was scarce after the war, Washington's name attracted enough money to get the project started.

Washington brushed up on his surveying skills and spent a good part of 1784 exploring the Allegheny Mountain range to determine the shortest and most practical route between the two rivers. The more he explored, the more he realized the enormity of the task. Above the fall line, the Potomac was a narrow, fast-moving mountain stream that would have to be opened up for 200 miles. The terrain rose so sharply that hundreds of locks would need to be built, dug out from mostly bedrock. Still, the more he looked the more he dreamed. He foresaw a centrally planned network of canals and improved rivers that would lead everywhere and bring "navigation to almost every man's door." Best of all, it would make Alexandria the gateway to the West. Washington had an idyllic name for his dream water highway—the River of Swans.

The River of Swans called for untold amounts of investment capital and, as more states became involved, the need for a strong national government to regulate interstate commerce became paramount. At Mount Vernon in March 1785, Washington hosted a conference of investors and businessmen from Maryland and Virginia. Talk inevitably turned to the national government's inability to govern effectively. All real power—the power to tax and spend—resided with the states. Under the Articles of Confederation, the states were sovereign entities, 13 independent nation-states that since the Revolution looked after their own interests, bickered and bullied with one another and did absolutely nothing in the national interest. All the while the massive war debt went unaddressed; money was scarce, and the national economy was slipping into recession. If ever Washington's canal was going to be a reality, it would require a strong national government to regulate interstate commerce and to have the wherewithal to restore the nation's credit and thereby free-up investment capital. Before adjourning, Virginia proposed a convention of delegates from all 13 states "to see how far a uniform system in their commercial regulations may be necessary to their common interest and their permanent harmony."

The result was the Annapolis Convention, held in September 1786. Nothing happened because delegates from only five states actually attended. Before the convention adjourned, Alexander Hamilton proposed a convention in Philadelphia to address the heart of the matter: to "render the constitution of the federal government adequate to the exigencies of the Union."

George Washington did not attend the Annapolis Conference nor did he plan to attend the Philadelphia Convention. He reminded friends that he was retired from public life. He was getting restless, however, and frustrated by states such as New York that were regulating commerce to their own advantage at the expense of smaller neighboring states such as New Jersey and Connecticut. It had to be stopped, if the young republic was to survive.

"We have probably had too good an opinion of human nature in forming our Confederation," he wrote a friend. "Experience has taught us that men will not adopt and carry into execution measures the best calculated for their own good, without the intervention of a coercive power. I do not conceive we can exist long as a nation without having lodged somewhere a power which will pervade the whole Union."

In April 1787, with the Convention a month off, Washington decided he must attend. Without him, nothing of significance would happen. The prestige of General George Washington was that crucial to future of the United States, and he knew it.

THE PHILADELPHIA CONVENTION

No rioting in the streets, no smashing of windows, no bricks thrown, no public officials being dragged from their homes in the middle of the night to be publicly executed in the town square. All that long hot summer of 1787 the streets outside the Philadelphia State House were remarkably quiet. Inside, a new government was taking shape.

In a sense the Philadelphia Convention was a shadow government plotting in secret the overthrow of the existing order.

The existing order was the United States government under the Articles of Confederation. The Articles granted the real power—the power to tax and spend—to the states, which rendered the national government little more than a debate club.

Under this system, the states argued and bullied one another over boundary disputes, fishing rights, logging rights, and the regulation of commerce, while the national government faced a myriad of problems that went unaddressed, including the Spanish blockade of the Mississippi River; British occupation of the Northwest Territory (in violation of the Paris Peace Treaty); Barbary pirates in the Mediterranean raiding American ships and making slaves of American sailors; non-payment of the massive Revolutionary War debt; and the collapse of public credit. To top it off, money was in short supply and the once-robust economy was in recession. Rome was burning, while the states, like Nero, fiddled.

There were no easy answers. It seemed every republic that governed a large territory eventually succumbed to chaos and tyranny. That was the fate of the Roman Republic. It started out as a republic, but once it expanded its territory it became difficult for the Senate to rule effectively, and a tyrant seized control.

Was that the fate of the United States? Was a country that stretched from Main to the Gulf of Mexico, and inland beyond the Appalachians to the Mississippi, too large to be governed effectively except by a strong man? That had been the fear of the Founding Fathers at the time of the Revolution, so they refrained from appointing executive officers and prosecuted the war by committee.

Later, when they drew up the Articles of Confederation, they purposely spread the power among the states, granting the national government virtually no power at all, and avoided election of a chief executive officer out of fear he might make himself king. This approach seemed like the right thing to do, but by 1787 it clearly wasn't working. The thirteen states were acting like thirteen bickering separate nations while the business of the republic was going unaddressed. A strong central government was clearly needed, but how to create such a government without creating a monarchy?

One answer was to create a government that balanced power evenly among three separate branches of government—executive, legislative and judicial. The French philosopher Montesquieu created the model in his "Spirit of Law," published in 1748, but postulated that it could only perpetuate true liberty in a small country where everyone knew one another. Clearly, that wasn't the case with the United States.

Enter James Madison. He had read a little-known treatise by Scottish philosopher David Hume entitled, "The Idea of a Perfect Commonwealth." In it, Hume broke with Montesquieu by proposing that a large republic, despite its geographical and socioeconomic diversity, might turn out to be the most stable of all. "In a large government which is modeled with masterly skill," Hume wrote, "there is compass and room enough to refine the democracy."

In other words, if the government is set up properly, it will represent all the various factions of the nation more or less equally, so that no one faction, however large, can become too strong and overrule the others. Under such a government, majority rule had little chance of squashing the rights of the minorities, because the rights of the minorities are given equal representation with the majority. With a balance of power among the factions, no one power can dominate the others.

Hume's idea hit home with Madison. He incorporated it in the "Virginia Plan" that became the model for the new constitution. The answer was not unity, which was impossible anyway, but countervailing interests: Federal versus state power, executive versus legislative, and judicial versus both of them; merchants versus farmers, town versus country, commercial-minded northerners versus agrarian-minded southerners. The result is not chaos, but a balancing of interests—and stability—and, most important of all, the protection of individual rights and liberty.

That, in a nutshell, is why our Federal government of checks and balances continues to defy the odds and to survive for 225 years and counting. As one of my college professors once said, the framers of the U.S. Constitution built better than they knew.

THE IMAGE AND THE MAN

George Washington's portrait on the One Dollar Bill—the image most Americans have of our first President—is not an accurate depiction. The portrait was made when Washington was near the end of his life; his jaw line is distorted because he is without all but one tooth, and the artist for whom he sat was, shall we say, a hostile witness.

Washington and portrait artist Gilbert Stuart did not get along. The painter was in the habit of keeping his sitters amused and their faces alive by a flood of showy and outrageous talk. Washington, uneasy at remaining still and being observed from close quarters, was put off rather than amused. Stuart believed that artists were fundamentally superior to all men, including Presidents, and resented the General's formality. He tried to liven-up the war hero.

"Now sir, you must let me forget that you are General Washington and I am Stuart, the painter," he said.

Replied the General: "Mr. Stuart need never feel the need for forgetting who he is and who General Washington is."

Washington sat for a number of portrait artists in his lifetime, each of whom brought more life to the General's face than did Gilbert Stuart. Washington's final portrait (and my favorite) was done during the last year of his life, by an artist with a very long name: Charles Balthazar Julien Fevret de Saint-Memin. The portrait depicts a man who is dignified yet human, intent yet at peace with himself. A profile, it was used for the image of Washington embossed on the silver Quarter Dollar (as depicted on the cover).

As Americans, we are familiar with the image, but not with the man. Washington's wife Martha knew him better than anyone, and she burned all their personal letters after he died. Washington kept a journal most of his life, but it is devoid of his innermost thoughts, and his many letters to friends, business associates, military personnel, and political leaders (often dictated, written and/or edited by others) divulge nothing of his deep personal feelings. Washington was not an easy man to know.

What we do know: he loved to gamble and to play the ponies. He loved military uniforms and fine clothing. He was comfortable in the company of women. He was a superb dancer. He was absolutely fearless in battle. According to Thomas Jefferson, Washington was the finest horsemen in Virginia, where being a good horsemen meant everything. He loved the spotlight, and yet was embarrassed by too much attention. While not a great speaker, he had charisma; when he spoke, people listened.

He was a good judge of character and surrounded himself with the brightest minds of his generation. He left school after the eighth grade, yet was highly competent in directing college-educated men. He loved being a Virginia planter, loved farming and the outdoors, yet had a library where he spent most of his evenings reading. He was a born leader, and while good at giving orders, he was not good at taking them. He was a good listener, was open to ideas that weren't his own, and knew how to delegate. He demanded loyalty, and gave loyalty. He rarely smiled and had difficulty expressing his feelings. He had a terrible temper but learned to manage it and to keep it under wraps most of the time.

Washington was six-feet-two-inches tall, equally broad at the shoulders and hips, had blue eyes and red hair, never wore a wig, and was physically strong and resilient. There was nothing false about him except his teeth, which he began losing after his thirtieth birthday. He was not a flatterer. Actions, not words, defined his character. Washington was what today we would call the strong, silent type. Had he been an actor, he would have been John Wayne. Had he been a football coach, he would have been Bear Bryant. George Washington embodied all that we have come to associate with the classic America hero.

This book is about the completion of the American Revolution and the critical role George Washington played in bringing it about. Americans, most of them farmers and frontiersmen, didn't agree on many things, but they did agree only one man could be trusted to lead them, and that was George Washington of Virginia, who one of his biographers called "the indispensable man," and justifiably so.

THE FIRST CONGRESS OF UNITED STATES

George Washington and the First United States Congress faced what Alexander Hamilton described as "a job for Hercules, for we must level mountains of prejudice." The prejudices of which Hamilton was speaking took several forms. First and foremost were the anti-Federalists who opposed the new Constitution and the new Federal government. Second was the growing division within the new government itself, formed roughly along North-South lines: those states leaning toward free-labor versus slave states.

The First Congress met for three sessions. The first session was dominated by James Madison, who doubled as Congressional leader and Washington's chief advisor. Beginning April 6, 1789 and ending September 30, 1789, the first session completed the work left unfinished at the Constitutional Convention, by fleshing out the federal judiciary system, drafting the Bill of Rights, and creating the executive departments of State, Treasury and War. As important, Congress rectified the biggest failure of the previous government by creating a federal revenue system with passage of the 1789 Tariff Act.

The second session was the most crucial, because it tested the unity of the new government. Beginning January 6, 1790 and concluding August 12, 1790, three issues threatened to divide the nation: (1) Hamilton's controversial provision for resolving the war debt, the Funding and Assumption Bills; (2) the slavery debate; and (3) the Residency Bill: deciding on a permanent home for the nation's capital.

The third session, beginning December 6, 1790 and ending March 3, 1791, dealt almost exclusively with the linchpin of Hamilton's financial plan, the National Bank. After minor debate the Bank Bill passed Congress easily, but was nearly dealt a death-blow when, in a late move, Madison and Thomas Jefferson questioned the bank's constitutionality. The two Virginians wrote legal briefs buttressing their opinion but it was Hamilton's rebuttal that swayed the President to sign the bill into law. Stung by the defeat, coupled with Hamilton's growing influence within the Washington Administration, led Jefferson and Madison to break with the president. The result led to the creation of the two-party system.

Hamilton and Madison figure prominently in the story, Madison as Washington's chief advisor, and Hamilton as Secretary of the Treasury. Because Hamilton's economic policies dominated the second and third session of Congress, I've devoted two chapters (chapters 14 and15) to a discussion as to how Hamilton arrived at these policies and how they worked. Jefferson, who joined Washington's administration in its second year, as Secretary of State, plays a significant role as well. Other Founding Fathers are discussed including Robert Morris and John Jay, both executive officers under the Articles of Confederation who, despite great difficulty, managed to hold the nation together until Washington's election; Oliver Ellsworth, creator of the federal judiciary system; and Benjamin Franklin, whose last public act was a pointed and wicked parody of the Deep South's justification of slavery.

WASHINGTON IN NEW YORK

The idea for this book started with a trip to New York City. It was my first visit to Manhattan. I'd been reading about the Founding Fathers since visiting Monticello, and was intrigued by the idea that the Big Apple once had been the nation's capital. What remains of the time when George Washington and Congress ruled the nation from Lower Manhattan? Quite a bit actually.

Unlike Midtown, the streets of Lower Manhattan are not wide nor arranged in a neat grid. The streets meander much as they did when

New York was under Dutch rule and called New Amsterdam. Were George Washington somehow to reappear today, he might be daunted by the skyscrapers but he would recognize these streets. He walked them many times.

A few buildings have survived since Washington's day. On Broadway there is St. Paul's Chapel where Washington worshipped. A pew bearing his name is kept roped off to this day. On a number of occasions Hamilton spoke at political rallies at St. Paul's as well. A few blocks south of St. Paul's is Trinity Church that dates from the seventeenth century, where Hamilton's body is buried.

From Trinity Church, it's a short walk down Wall Street to the New York Stock Exchange which, according to at least one historian, stands as a memorial to Hamilton. Across the street from the Stock Exchange is Federal Hall where Congress met. It's not the original edifice but a newer building that serves as a museum and shrine. At the top of the steps is a statue of Washington commemorating his swearing in as our nation's first president. Across the street, a few doors down, at 57 Wall Street, is the site of Hamilton's law office and townhouse.

South of Wall Street, where Broad and Pearl Street intersect, stands the Fraunces Tavern where Washington bid farewell to his officers at the close of the Revolutionary War. On the upper floor of the Fraunces Tavern John Jay had his office as secretary of state (and de facto head of state) prior to Washington's presidency. A stone's throw from Fraunces Tavern is the site of the Royal Exchange Building, where animals were sold for slaughter and where, on the second floor, the Supreme Court sat for the first time.

At the foot of Broadway is the Battery and Bowling Green Park, dating from the time of Dutch rule. Up one block, at 39 Broadway, is the site of the Macomb Mansion that served as the second presidential

"White House." A plaque marks the location. The first White House, known as the Palace, located at 1 Cherry Street, is occupied by an abutment of the Brooklyn Bridge. There is a plaque on the abutment to commemorate the site.

There are other landmarks. At 57 Maiden Lane is a plaque marking the place where Thomas Jefferson lived and hosted a dinner party that resulted in the capital moving from New York to its eventual location on the banks of the Potomac. At 19 Maiden Lane is the site of the boardinghouse where James Madison lived. All of these sites are within easy walking distance of one another. I have tried to convey a feeling of how the city was when Washington and the First Congress called Lower Manhattan home.

I titled this book "Washington in New York" as an intended double meaning, although part of the story takes place in Philadelphia when it served as the capital.

The actual writing began as a series of emails to relatives who were not devoted readers of American history. With each email, my goal was to grab their attention in the first few words and to keep it to the last. Each email ran about 200-300 words. This unusual approach helped me clarify what was worth telling from what was not. The result, I hope, brings alive the achievements of a remarkable group of people who transformed a class-conscious society into a pluralistic and mostly tolerant nation that has endured down to our day.

While writing "Washington in New York," I wrote a number of related pieces which I thought would find a place in the book once it was finished—as sidebars.

That didn't work out as I envisioned it. So I created an appendix where they may be read (See the Table of Contents). These pieces are titled: The Great Awakening; Ordering up a New World; The Spirit of Liberty; Thomas Jefferson on Religious Freedom; Jefferson's Holy Trinity; The King James Bible on its 400th Anniversary; The "why?" of American exceptionalism: Rutgers v. Waddington; Washington's Greatest Asset—Character; The Washington Monument; The White House - A Short History; Hamilton, the Musical; and The Two Party System.

A note about footnotes: there are none. This book is intended for any interested reader and not an academic readership. That is not to say that this book does not rely on a vast academic corpus of books and papers. Every book and periodical listed in the bibliography has influenced my account of Washington and the First Congress of the United States. I hope that the authors to whose works I am indebted here will be content with a place in the bibliography and will forgive their every point not being noted individually in the text. Those historians I have quoted I have named in the text. To summarize, this is not an academic discussion of Washington, Hamilton, Jefferson and Madison, and of early American politics—there are plenty of those books already—but simply an attempt to tell their story clearly and sequentially, using a variety of available sources that helped me in this endeavor. It's an incredible story, one I suspect few are completely familiar with.

CHAPTER 1

The Want of Revenue

A morning in March 1789, with the ground frozen hard and the first rays of sunlight beginning to show on the eastern horizon.

At Mount Vernon, George Washington mounted one of his immaculate white horses, shrugged off the icy cold, and set off for Fredericksburg, a journey of about 40 miles. The electoral votes had yet to be counted, but Washington already knew he'd been elected president. He'd received letters from friends of the electors—an exit poll, so to speak—leaving no doubt as to the election's outcome. For some time, in fact, he'd been preparing to take office, by finishing up personal business, arranging for someone to run Mount Vernon in his absence, and with writing his inaugural address.

One of the most difficult things he'd had to do was to ask a friend for money to pay outstanding debts, and to pay for his trip to New

York City to take office; difficult for him, because Washington was a proud man and a self-reliant man, and his beloved plantation hadn't shown a profit since the Revolutionary War. The journey he was taking today, however, was perhaps the most difficult thing he would do prior to taking office.

Washington knew these roads well; he knew the farmlands they crossed, and he knew the people who managed the farms. Fredericksburg was the country where he was born and lived until the age of 16, when he left home to make his way in the world. On this particular morning he was riding there once again, to see his mother. She was gravely ill and not expected to live out the year. Washington was going there not because he could do anything for her; he never could do anything for her. He could never please her, and if he tried, she would never show the slightest gratitude. She was a hard woman, with a hard face that seldom smiled, a face that mirrored his own. He was going to Fredericksburg to say goodbye.

Mary Ball Washington was tall, physically strong, and demanding, traits her famous son inherited. After the death of her husband, she never married again. She made George, at age eleven, the man of the house and substitute father to his three younger brothers and one sister. According to his biographer James Thomas Flexner, George became the passion of his mother's life, "and it was a very possessive passion. Even when he was Commander in Chief, even when he was President, she objected to his occupation, complaining violently that he was ungrateful and neglectful of his duties to her." The first chance he got, at age sixteen, George Washington left home.

There is a letter, written in 1787, that sheds some light on their thorny relationship. It's a letter he wrote in response to her request for money and to come and live at Mount Vernon. It was written at a bad time for George Washington. Mount Vernon was operating in the red and he had very little money. On top of that, he didn't want her living under his roof. He wrote:

"I take the (first safe) conveyance . . . to send you 15 Guineas which believe me is all I have and which indeed ought to have been paid many days ago to another agreeable to my own assurances. I have now demands upon me for more than 500 (pounds sterling) three hundred and forty odd of which is due for the tax of 1786; and I know not where, or when I shall receive one shilling with which to pay it. In the last two years I made no Crops. In the first I was obliged to buy Corn and this year have none to sell, and my wheat is so bad I cannot neither eat it myself nor sell it to others, and Tobacco I make none. . . ."

He offered two suggestions:

"Either let your grandson Bushrod Washington . . . have the whole interest there (Ferry Farm), that its lands and Negroes, at a reasonable rent . . . (or) let him have the land during your life; and hire out the Negroes—this would ease you of all care and trouble—make your income certain—and your support ample.

With regard to her request to live at Mount Vernon he wrote:

"My House is at your service, and would press you most sincerely and most devoutly to accept it, but I am sure—and candour requires me to say—it will never answer your purposes . . . in truth it may be compared to a well resorted tavern, as scarcely any strangers who are going from north to south, or from south to north do not spend a day or two at it. This would, were you (to live here) oblige you to do 1 of 3 things, 1st to be always dressing to appear in company, 2nd to come in (disheveled) or 3rd to be as it were a prisoner in your own chamber. The first you would not like . . . the second I should not like because those who resort here are . . . strangers and people of the first distinction, and the 3rd, more than probably, would not be pleasant to either of us—nor indeed could you be retired in any room in my house, for what with the sitting up of Company, the noise and bustle of servants—and many other things you would not be able to enjoy. . . ."

If she would do as he suggested and rent her farm and slaves, and should the resulting income fall short, he promised to make amends: "I would, most cheerfully contribute more, a man, a maid, The Phaeton and two horses. . . ."

In closing, he offered some philosophical advice: ". . . happiness depends more upon the internal frame of a person's own mind—than on the externals in the world, of the last, if you will, pursue the plan here recommended I am sure you can want nothing that is essential—the other depends wholly upon your self, for the riches of the Indies cannot purchase it."

Now, two years later, he was coming again to see her for what will be—and surely they both knew this—the last time.

No one was there to record their conversation. If Washington had written something about their meeting in his journal, it is not known, as the journal entries for this period have been lost.

What did he say to her? Most likely that he was going to New York to be the President of the United States and didn't know when he would return. What did she say to him? That she was proud of him, proud of his accomplishments and his selflessness and willingness to serve his country, proud that a grateful American people had once again looked to her son for deliverance? Not likely.

DE FACTO HEAD OF STATE

It was to be a day for celebrating in New York City, a time to usher in a new government, and perhaps the beginning of a new age in the history of mankind.

At dawn, cannons at the Battery fired thirteen rounds, one for each state of the union. At 9 o'clock, church bells in the city's 22 churches and one synagogue rang for five minutes. At 10 o'clock, Congressmen took their seats inside Federal Hall and prepared to count ballots. Outside, on Wall Street, a crowd gathered in anticipation of hearing the results of the first presidential election of the United States.

At 10:15, the doors of Federal Hall swung open and solemn-faced Congressmen filed out and headed for the nearest tavern. The celebrating would have to wait. Without a quorum, there would be no counting of ballots and no election results to announce.

For the record, March 4, 1789 was the day the United States Constitution went into effect. Without a quorum, and without a president—without the new government taking office—who was minding the store? Who was running the country?

That would be John Jay.

The old Confederation Congress having disbanded the previous Fall, Jay was de facto head of state until the new Federal Congress took office. Until such time as the new government had a quorum, however, Jay was still in charge. This was not received as good news by Jay. He'd had more than his fill of power, such as it was under the Articles of Confederation, and was eager to step down. Alas, March 4 came and went with Jay still functioning as head of state from his office on the second floor of the Fraunces Tavern on Broad Street. Days passed and then weeks, and still without a quorum. In fact, it would be another month before the new government actually took office.

Where were the leaders of the brave new republic? Holed up in taverns and inns up and down the east coast, trapped by sleet, and heavy rain that had washed out bridges and rendered roads too muddy for travel.

For Jay, it was yet another month of frustration under a system that for four years had kept him politically impotent. What good was having the responsibility of running the nation without the power to get things done? As Superintendent of Foreign Affairs (forerunner of Secretary of State) Jay was the face of the national government as surely as if he had been president, or king. Jay was the nation's chief executive officer, without a chief executive's power. The state legislatures had kept all the power for themselves, and they weren't about to share it with the national government.

John Jay was a graduate of King's College (now Columbia University). He married into one of New York's most prominent families, the Livingstons. As Superintendent of Foreign Affairs under the Articles of Confederation Jay hoped to strengthen the national government by increasing the power of the unicameral Confederation Congress—turning it into an Americanized House of Commons—and elevating his position to that of prime minister. It hinged on having a federal revenue stream. As Jay's friend Alexander Hamilton put it, "Power without revenue is a bubble."

Jay was tall, reserved, severe. The same could be said of George Washington, only Jay lacked the General's magnetism. Jay's rare attempts at humor generally fell flat. Jay was a man comfortable sitting at the head of the table, setting the agenda, running things, a man people looked up to for leadership. Among the Founder's he was the most openly religious. He quoted and paraphrased the Bible in his speeches and political papers. He was president of the American Bible Society and he served as leader of his parish church. With Hamilton and other like-minded New Yorkers, he formed the New York Manumission Society with the goal of freeing African-American slaves in the state of New York.

Jay had not sought the office of Superintendent of Foreign Affairs. He learned of his appointment upon returning to the United States in 1784. He'd spent the previous five years in Europe as a diplomat, first in Spain, then in France, and for a short time, in England. When he returned to America, he desired little else than to be with his family and return to his law practice. Being a good patriot, and therefore being obliged to answer his nation's call whenever it sounded, he agreed to accept the appointment on the condition that Congress moved the capital to Manhattan. Discretion being the better part of valor, perhaps Jay hoped that Congress would reconsider and rescind his appointment. What he didn't know was that the Confederation Congress was desperately in need of someone with an impeccable reputation who would take control of the national government and make things happen.

Jay had the necessary credentials. In the past he'd served in the Continental Congress, first as a delegate, then as presiding officer, or president. Called back to New York, he helped draft that state's constitution. In France, working in conjunction with John Adams and Benjamin Franklin, he negotiated the Paris Peace Treaty that ended the American Revolution.

Congress wasted little time in agreeing to Jay's terms and moved the capital to New York City.

PROXIMITY TO A KING

At some point during his tenure as Superintendent of Foreign Affairs, surely Jay looked out across the vast waters of Upper New Bay and imagined Mount Vernon somewhere far off on the horizon and realized that there, on the banks of the Potomac, lay the real capital of the United States. That's where Jay should have insisted on moving the national government; it would have made his political life so much easier. To wield the power of a prime minister he needed the power of a king behind him. In England, the prime minister worked closely with Parliament and administered the affairs of state, while the king served more as the nation's father-figure. The prime minister's role was political. The king's role was symbolic. The king was the face of the nation and the traditional source of power. For all intents and purposes, in the United States, the king presided at Mount Vernon.

George Washington could have been crowned king. The support was there. During the Revolution, some of his generals and many of the soldiers serving under him wanted him to be king, but Washington wouldn't hear of it. After the Revolution he retired to Mount Vernon content to manage his plantation and to enjoy life among tidewater society. Nonetheless, he was still perceived as something of a king, or at least royalty, and as the father of his country. His nearness to the capital would have worked miracles for Jay and the national government. Jay could have met with Washington from time to time, to seek his advice or merely to play a game of cards, it didn't matter which. Close proximity to Mount Vernon would have given Jay the very clout he needed to get a revenue bill through Congress. That's all he would have needed to be successful. With Washington in his corner, opposition from powerful state leaders like Patrick Henry of Virginia and George Clinton of New York would have gone unheeded.

In eighteenth century America, people took comfort in having a king. Prior to the Revolution, they clung to the illusion that the British king would intervene on their behalf whenever Parliament acted out of hand with some new tax. Whether true or not, the American people believed the king had their best interest at heart. When the Stamp Act was repealed in 1766, the widespread belief was that the King had responded to their petitions and taken action—sacked the prime minister, and ordered the repeal. When the Townsend Duties were enacted in 1767, there was some confusion as to why the king was slow in undoing Parliament's obvious usurpation of power. When the Duties (except for tea) were finally repealed in 1770, the king was praised for setting things right. In Massachusetts in 1774, when military rule replaced popular government as punishment for the Boston Tea Party, Parliament rather than the good king was blamed. Even as late as the Fall of 1775 when the Continental Congress petitioned the king for redress of grievances, it was still hoped that he would intervene on their behalf. Thus when news arrived from London that the king had denounced the colonists as "rebels" and personally ordered the military to use force in putting down the insurrection, Americans felt betrayed and for the first time began considering independence as a very real option.

GOVERNMENT BY COMMITTEE

The men who signed the Declaration of Independence in 1776 were justifiably distrustful of kings. They equated monarchies with abuses, corruption, excessive taxation, and tyranny. Since many of them had served in state legislatures and trusted that form of governing, they refrained from making executive appointments and prosecuted the Revolution by committee. They did so with an all-volunteer army and without a consistent source of revenue. They chose George Washington as commander-in-chief, kept a close eye on him, and went looking for ways to finance the war without taxing the public.

Almost immediately, Washington was writing from the field asking for money, money to pay soldiers, buy food, clothing, blankets, tents, medical supplies, more ammunition and more guns. Congress responded by borrowing money from wealthy Americans committed to the cause and issuing IOUs, but mostly by printing money. Between 1775 and 1780, Congress issued paper money no fewer than thirty-seven times, backed by nothing more than its solemn declaration that it was legal tender. In the end, these paper issues amounted to more than $200 million, fiat money that depreciated quickly as fiat money always does. Before the war ended, Congress was forced to revalue earlier issues to a paltry 2.5 percent of face value; virtually nothing. The government also issued interest-bearing securities as a means of payment, but without a tax from which to draw upon to make interest payments, these too dropped rapidly in value. Meanwhile, state governments requisitioned food and supplies from citizens—sometimes against their will—and paid with state securities that likewise declined in value. The only money to hold its value was silver and gold coins minted in Europe, and there were precious few of these in circulation.

By 1781, with the war ongoing and public credit in a state of near collapse, Congress appointed its first executive officer with the hope he could work a miracle. They picked a wealthy Philadelphia merchant named Robert Morris as Superintendent of the Treasury. On his own, Morris had proven very resourceful in raising money for Washington's army. He knew all the right financial people, who to see and when to see them. Born in Scotland, he migrated to the United States with only the clothes on his back, entered business and become rich, and purchased a fleet of ships to transact business.

The Morris appointment could not have come at a better time. The British Army was encamped at Yorktown where General Washington saw his chance to trap and defeat them there in one fell swoop, if he could get his army there immediately to deliver the knockout punch. His only obstacle was the lack of money. His army wouldn't move until paid with something more substantial than yet another paper issue. Soldiers wanted payment in hard currency, in specie, in silver and gold coins. On the pledge of his personal credit, Morris borrowed from friends and from the French government and, at the last possible moment, came through with a shipment of silver half-crowns packed in dozens of wooden kegs. Paid a month's salary in advance, the Continental Army marched to Yorktown and, with the help of the French Army and Navy, defeated the British in a stunning upset.

Morris now undertook a number of measures to restore financial stability to the fledgling republic, including the creation of the nation's first commercial bank, the Bank of North American. Capitalization was made possible through loans from France and Holland. The thrust of Morris's financial program, however, depended on the passage of a tariff bill. Without a revenue stream, Morris could work his magic only for so long. Passage of a bill of such consequence required amending the Articles of Confederation, which required a unanimous vote. Once debate got underway, all the old fears surfaced in a stream of accusations: Morris was making a grab for power; revenue invited abuses and corruption; where revenue flowed tyranny followed, etc. etc. Twice the measure was put to a vote, and twice the measure was defeated. After the second defeat Morris threw up his hands in frustration and resigned. A month later another savior was asked to step in—John Jay.

CAPTAIN OF THE DEBATE CLUB

At the time Jay took office in 1784, all the major players had departed from the national stage and were serving in governor's mansions and in state houses up and down the east coast. For good reason. The states had the real power—the power to tax and spend. Meanwhile, John Adams, Thomas Jefferson, and Benjamin Franklin were off in Europe serving as ministers. James Madison, after four years of frustration, was back in Virginia reading everything he could find on republics and how to make them work. Equally frustrated with the national government, Alexander Hamilton was practicing law in New York City. Having resigned as Superintendent of the Treasury, Robert Morris had returned to private business. Where once the most informed, most-educated, and most influential Americans had gathered, Congress was now a revolving door of political lightweights.

Disputes among the states were common place: over boundary lines, fishing and logging rights, and most crucially, regulating interstate commerce. States were either threatening to send in their militia to resolve a dispute with a neighboring state, or threatening to secede from the union. It seemed only a question of time before the fragile union of 13 states would dissolve and America would end up like Europe, forever at war. Patrick Henry of Virginia, George Clinton of New York, John Hancock of Massachusetts, and Samuel Chase of Maryland—all governors—spoke more like demagogues than the enlightened leaders of 1776 they once had been. Whenever there was talk of giving Congress the power to tax, the states would inevitably respond with words like "monarchy," "standing armies," and "corruption." Meanwhile, nothing was being done to address a host of national problems confronting the young republic: the Spanish blockade of the Mississippi River, British occupation of the Northwest Territory (in violation of the Paris Peace Treaty), Barbary pirates in the Mediterranean raiding American ships and making slaves of American sailors, the unpaid Revolutionary War debt, and the collapse of public credit. Topping it off, the once-robust economy was deep in recession.

Jay had the right can-do attitude, but all of his efforts were doomed from the start. Instead of reporting to a single person, he reported to an ever-changing cast of about three-dozen delegates. Congress often lacked a quorum to act on Jay's proposals, and even when it had a quorum delegates often had other priorities and shelved Jay's reports for a later date.

Under the Articles of Confederation, the only way Congress could generate revenue was by apportioning costs among the thirteen states according to the value of each state's surveyed land, and then wait for the states to issue their portion. It was an idea that looked good on paper perhaps, but in reality didn't work. Despite repeated requests, the states never offered up a farthing. What they did pay was lip service. They sent delegates that spoke well, made the right impression, but had to check back with their respective states before voting on anything of substance. Without revenue, Congress was little more than a debate club, with John Jay as captain.

In an address given at the New York Ratifying Convention in Poughkeepsie in 1788, Jay made his case for all that was wrong with the national government under the Articles of Confederation:

"(Congress) may make war, but are not empowered to raise men or money to carry it on;

"(Congress) may make peace, but without power to see the terms of it observed;

"(Congress) may form alliances, but without ability to comply with the stipulation on their part;

"(Congress) may enter into treaties of commerce, but without power to enforce them at home or abroad;

"(Congress) may borrow money, but without having the means of payment;

"(Congress) may partly regulate commerce, but without authority to execute their ordinances;

"(Congress) may appoint ministers and other officers of trust, but without power to try or punish them for misdemeanours;

"(Congress) may resolve, but cannot execute either with dispatch or with secrecy;

"In short, (Congress) may consult, and deliberate and recommend, and make requisitions, and they who please may regard them.

"From this new and wonderful system of government (Jay's rare attempt at sarcasm), it has come to pass, that almost every national object of every kind, is at this day unprovided for. . . ."

In spite of his many frustrations, Jay did a remarkable job. He prepared more than one-hundred reports for Congress and wrote more than five-hundred official letters. He helped open up trade with China; he established a system of consuls in foreign ports; he negotiated with foreign representatives living in the United States; he advised Congress on admiralty cases; he drafted a law on piracy for Congress; he corresponded with diplomats abroad, with governors at home, and with ordinary citizens. On his watch, minister John Adams negotiated a series of loans with a consortium of Dutch financiers that kept the nation financially afloat until the new government took office.

Jay's greatest contribution, however, was keeping the peace among the thirteen states, and keeping the nation itself out of foreign war.

CHAPTER 2

The Once and Future King

Outside Federal Hall, scaffolding was being taken down, while inside new plaster was still drying.

This was the state of the capitol building as congressmen arrived in New York in March 1789. By a strange quirk of fate, work on Federal Hall was not finished until both the Senate and the House of Representatives had a quorum, which wouldn't be until early April.

"The building is really elegant and well designed—for a Trap," was how Frederick Muhlenberg, a Representative from Pennsylvania, put it in a letter home. "But I still hope, however well-contrived, we shall find room to get out of it."

Despite the makeover, converting City Hall into Federal Hall, few were enamored with having New York City as the seat of government.

The last act of the Confederation Congress was the decision to keep the capital in Manhattan. Let the new Congress decide where the Capital should be, was the thinking.

The issue was decidedly political, and whatever the choice it was going to be controversial. Pennsylvania wanted the capital to return to Philadelphia. And there were those who favored a return to Annapolis, or some other more centrally-located site. George Washington suggested locating the capital somewhere west of the Appalachians. "That is where the center of the United States is going to be," he said. Southerners favored moving the capital to the banks of the Potomac, although this was a minority view that no one north of the Mason-Dixon Line took seriously.

New Yorkers, meanwhile, were sparing no expense in renovating Federal Hall in the hope of keeping the capital in Manhattan. John Jay and several wealthy merchants raised the money themselves to begin renovations. They hired architect and engineer Pierre-Charles L'Enfant, who had served as a major in the Continental Army, to convert the 85-year-old building into something befitting the new government.

L'Enfant designed an elegant Greek Revival facade of four columns to grace the front, and renovated the interior with fresh plaster and various detail changes. Midway into the project money ran out and work stopped. The state legislature stepped in and passed a law "to indemnify John Jay and the citizens who had given their notes" to fund construction. Work resumed and was nearly complete when the government start-up date of March 4 arrived. It would be another month before Congress had a quorum which, as fate would have it, was the exact amount of time needed to complete the renovation.

What was the capitol building like? From a covered walkway on Wall Street, one entered a plainly appointed hall leading to a three-story vestibule. From there, double doors opened onto the House Chamber, a large octagonal room at the back of the building. The ceiling loomed three-stories overhead. Access to the upper floors was reached by two stairways in the vestibule. One stairway was reserved for Congressmen, and the other for visitors who wished to watch the House proceedings from one of two overhead galleries. The Senate chamber and several smaller rooms occupied the second floor at the front of the building. Outside the Senate Chamber was a balcony overlooking Wall Street on which four Doric Columns stood. It was here that George Washington would be sworn in as president and deliver the inaugural address. The third floor contained the New York Society Library. Federal Hall, as renovated by L'Enfant, is credited with being the first example of Federal-style architecture in the country.

THE PALACE

James Madison, the man with the operating manual on how the new government was supposed to work, arrived in New York without fanfare on March 14. Dressed in black, he struck people as sullen and grave, until they got to know him, which took awhile. At age 42, Madison had long since given up finding a mate and getting married. It seemed no woman would have him. Eight Senators and 18 Representatives arrived ahead of him—not nearly enough for a quorum. That didn't stop them from meeting socially to discuss issues and to formulate legislation. "The old government has gently fallen asleep—and the new one is waking into activity," is how one Representative described what was happening.

In early April, Madison received a letter from George Washington, asking him to find a house for the president: "(I) take the liberty of requesting the favor of you to engage Lodging (for) me previous to my arrival . . ." Washington wrote. "I will frankly declare, I mean to go into none but hired ones. If these cannot be had tolerably convenient (I am not very nice) I would take rooms in the most decent Tavern, till a house can be provided for the more permanent reception of the President. I have already declined a very polite and pressing offer from the Governor, to lodge at his house till a place could be prepared for me. . . ."

"The Governor" was George Clinton. No, it wouldn't do for the President to be living in the house of one of the nation's leading anti-Federalists. Anti-Federalist or not, Clinton and Washington remained friends. Clinton had served with distinction in the Revolutionary War as one of Washington's trusted generals. While he wouldn't live under Clinton's roof—not as President, anyway—Washington would continue to see the Governor socially.

Congressmen arriving in New York would have to make do living in rooms above taverns and in boardinghouses, but not the President. A suitably large and well-appointed house would have to be found in a city suffering from a housing shortage. New York City in 1789 was in the midst of a post-war boom, having grown from a war-time population of 12,000 people to nearly 30,000 at the time of Washington's inauguration. Once rotting wharves were now teaming with commercial activity, and once empty streets were now clogged with ox-drawn carts and horse-drawn wagons and carriages. Small rooms were available around town, mostly in houses on muddy alleyways, but finding an entire house available for rent was nearly impossible.

Fortunately, there was one house available that was large enough to meet the needs of the president. It was the Franklin-Osgood House. Located near the East River, at 1 Cherry Street, the house was built prior to the Revolution, in 1770. Neighbors called it "The Palace." It was commissioned by a wealthy merchant named Walter Franklin, who died before the house was finished. It had been lived in by his widow and her second husband, Samuel Osgood, who later would become the nation's first Postmaster General. Previously occupied by the president of the old Confederation Congress, Cyrus Griffen, the house had been vacant since Griffen moved out the previous November.

The Palace mansion wasn't the Mount Vernon mansion, and it didn't have a river view, but this wasn't a time to be choosy. It was a three-story brick house with seven chimneys, located on the corner of Cherry and Dover Street, fully furnished, and one-third of a mile from Federal Hall on Wall Street. It had spacious rooms on the first floor suitable for offices and for receiving congressmen and foreign ministers, and on the second and third floor were plenty of bedrooms for family, staff, and servants. The streets outside were cobblestone, tree-lined, relatively free of commercial traffic and quiet. Madison booked it.

On April 8, two days after having achieved a quorum, in a joint resolution of the House and Senate, Congress directed Osgood to "put the house and the furniture thereof in proper condition for the residence and use of the President of the United States." In a little over two weeks the work was done. Total cost: $8,000. "I went the morning before the General's arrival to look at it," recalled the niece of Mrs. Osgood some years later. "The best furniture in every room, and the greatest quantity of plate and china I ever saw; the whole of the first and second stories is papered and the floors covered with the richest kinds of Turkey and Wilton carpets. There is scarcely anything talked about now but General Washington and the Palace."

The first presidential "White House" was painted yellow.

GIFTED

The political heavyweights in national politics were Alexander Hamilton and James Madison. With Benjamin Franklin and Thomas Jefferson, they were arguably the brightest group of statesmen ever to grace the halls of American government. With the exception of Franklin, who ran away from home as a youth, there seems little doubt they were each recognized early in life as gifted children. At age sixteen, Jefferson, Madison and Hamilton were each tutored by Scottish professors. At sixteen, Jefferson attended the college of William and Mary, where he was taught by William Small. At the same age, Madison was finishing his course of study with Donald Roberts. And Hamilton, in his sixteenth year, was sent to America to further his education by Hugh Knox, who recognized Hamilton's literary gifts. As writer Richard Brookhiser put it, among this exalted group, Hamilton would have scored highest on a college SAT examination while Madison would have been a close second.

Hamilton and Madison were allies since their days together as delegates in the Confederation Congress. They couldn't have been more different, however. Hamilton favored bright clothing and stood out in a crowd. He had an erect military bearing that made him appear taller than his five-feet-seven inches. He could be brash and outspoken. To him, life was a competition. That he was a brilliant thinker was sometimes overshadowed by his need to win. Madison favored dark clothing, was stoop-shouldered and unsmiling, and looked more like a care-worn school teacher than the gifted political theorist he was. It's hard to get a fix on his actual height, which may have been five-foot three or as tall as five-foot-seven. Being stoop-shouldered will do that. Madison could be easily overlooked in a crowd and therefore often surprised people with his insight, decisiveness and determination. He was quiet, subtle, cunning, and sometimes deceptive, a stealth fighter in sharp contrast to Hamilton's frontal assault. Both were charming when it called for being charming, but unlike Jefferson, neither was a flatterer. As political partners, they quite literally (as Hamilton put it) "leveled mountains of prejudice" in reshaping the nation's political landscape.

Hamilton entered Congress in November 1782, quickly realized the national government was badly handicapped by the lack of a revenue system, and departed the following July. Patience was never his strong suit. Madison, on the other hand, was the very model of patience, but even his patience had its limits. He entered Congress in March 1780 and spent the next four years trying to make the dysfunctional national government functional, before he too departed.

Hamilton and Madison joined forces at the Annapolis Convention in 1786, intent on strengthening the national government. Most states did not believe the nation was facing a crisis and failed to send delegates. As it turned out, five states were represented. The few delegates who did attend agreed that something more was needed than their original mandate of working out an interstate commercial agreement among the states. Hamilton wrote a resolution that was adopted as the official report of the convention. The report said, in effect, that the nation was in grave crisis, and that it was futile to consider commercial regulations except in the context of the larger problems that needed solving. Accordingly, the legislatures of the several states should send delegates to a general convention that would meet in Philadelphia the following May for the purpose of amending the Articles of Confederation.

Over the winter Shays's Rebellion in Massachusetts underscored the urgency of Hamilton's call for a convention. Twelve states sent delegates to Philadelphia; Rhode Island was the only holdout. In the end it, the Articles were dispensed with and Madison's "Virginia Plan" was adopted as the model for a new Constitution. Hamilton signed the document despite believing it did not go far enough in empowering the federal government.

As the new government prepared to take over in early 1789, Madison's role was clear: he would be floor leader of the House of Representatives and chief advisor to President Washington, a role not unlike England's Prime Minister, the role Jay had hoped to play as Superintendent of Foreign Affair under the Articles of Confederation. Hamilton's role, meanwhile, was yet to be determined.

On April 1, with the arrival of Thomas Scott of Western Pennsylvania, the House of Representatives had a quorum. Five days later, on April 6, with the arrival of Richard Henry Lee of Virginia, the Senate too had a quorum. That same day both Houses met in joint session and counted electoral votes. The election of president was unanimous—all sixty-nine electors voted for George Washington of Virginia. For vice president, John Adams of Massachusetts received a clear majority of thirty-five electoral votes. The next closest candidate received nine votes.

As president-elected, George Washington was the once and future king. As Commander-in-Chief of the Continental Army, Washington had been king in all but title. Now, he was about to be king again, in all but title. The Constitution didn't spell out exactly what it was the president was supposed to do, but the framers knew General Washington would act in a dignified—make that royal—manner. The job description was left purposely vague with the assumption Washington would be elected and by his example a favorable precedent would be set for future presidents to follow. In other words, George would write the job description.

On the surface, the new government did not appear that much different from the old government. The new Congress was bicameral but met in the same building at the corner of Wall and Nassau Street. John Jay and Superintendent of War Henry Knox still conducted the affairs of state from their offices on the second floor of the Fraunces Tavern at the corner of Broad and Pearl Street. And the Palace at the corner of Cherry and Dover Street would still be occupied by a president.

Yes, the buildings were the same, but there was one crucial difference—George Washington. Washington's presence would give the new government something the old government lacked—credibility. And that would make all the difference in the world.

CHAPTER 3

Washington's Coronation

The day the House of Representatives achieved a quorum, on April 1, 1789, George Washington wrote to a friend:

"(I feel) that my movement to the chair of Government will be accompanied with feelings not unlike those of a culprit who is going to the place of his execution: so unwilling am I, in the evening of a life nearly consumed in public cares, to quit a peaceful abode for an Ocean of difficulties, without that competency of political skill—abilities and inclinations which is necessary to manage the helm."'

Thirteen days later, an envoy sent from Congress named Charles Thomson arrived on horseback at Mount Vernon to make it official: George Washington was elected the first president of the United States.

Two days later, on April 16, with Thomson and Washington's aid and confidant David Humphreys as passengers, Washington boarded his coach and began the 250-mile trip north. He wrote in his journal: "I bid adieu to Mount Vernon, to private life, and to domestic felicity, and with a mind oppressed with anxious and painful sensations than I have words to express, set out for New York. . . . With the best disposition to render service to my country in obedience to its call, but with less hope of answering its expectations."

False modesty? Perhaps not. Washington knew how to guard his thoughts, but when he spoke his mind he did so candidly. He had good reason to be modest. He was coming to New York with the equivalent of an eighth-grade education and without the executive experience of having been a state governor or even a city mayor.

What he did have was eight year's experience as Commander-in-Chief of the Continental Army, and a lifetime of reading documents and reports, many of them prepared by the brightest minds of his age. Washington also had sense enough to know he didn't have all the answers, that his success as president depended on the guidance of better-educated and better-informed men. And he knew how to listen. During the hot summer of 1787, he presided over the Constitution Convention in Philadelphia for four months and rarely said a word.

Washington was not embarrassed to say he didn't have all the answers. He valued the opinions of others and, having heard everyone's opinion, had the uncanny knack of choosing the right course of action.

GRAND MARSHALL

If Washington was expecting a quiet trip he was in for a big disappointment. Expecting complete anonymity was probably asking too much, but a trip without attracting too much attention seemed reasonable. He wasn't taking his luxurious four-door coach—the stretch limo of its day—the one a grateful Congress had given him after the war. Too showy. No, he was taking his smaller, less-conspicuous two-door coach. It didn't help that every newspaper along the route had published his travel itinerary, and so at every city, town and wide spot in the road a crowd would be waiting for him. The trip was destined to be something of a parade, with Washington as grand marshal. He even brought along one his magnificent white horses (tethered to the back of the coach) to ride on various important occasions. No one looked better on horseback than George Washington.

The first stop was Alexandria, where friends and civic leaders at Wise's Tavern would not let him pass without dinner and a speech. Washington wasn't big on speaking extemporaneously. Judging by the account that was recorded, he did quite well. With words that echoed Abraham Lincoln's farewell speech to his neighbors 70 years in the future, Washington said: "Words, my fellow citizens, fail me. Unutterable sensations must then be left to more expressive silence: while, from an aching heart, I bid you all, my affectionate friends and kind neighbors, farewell."

The next stop was Spurrier's Tavern outside Baltimore, where Washington spent the first night. In the morning it was on to Baltimore proper where he was welcomed with an artillery salute and a lavish dinner at the Fountain Inn. The ceremony and speeches took the better part of the afternoon, so Washington stayed the night.

The next two days he made good time traveling through the sparsely-populated countryside between Baltimore and Wilmington, Delaware. On the morning of April 20, a crowd welcomed him to Wilmington with speeches and fanfare and then escorted him to the Pennsylvania border. Fifteen miles outside of Philadelphia, Washington left his carriage, mounted his white horse and led the Pennsylvania state militia to the Schuylkill River.

The pontoon bridge over the Schuylkill was decked in laurel and cedar bush while the arches at either end were draped with laurel rose. Riding under the first arch a young girl peered out from the brush, pulled a lever and from atop the arch a laurel wreath dropped onto Washington's head. This was too much, apparently. Washington immediately brushed off the wreath, thought better of his rashness, stopped, dismounted his horse, and gave the girl a gentle kiss.

Entering Philadelphia Washington dismounted his horse and bowed repeatedly, before cheering crowds. Cannons fired in the distance and church bells rang throughout the city. He rode down Market and Second Streets to City Tavern where yet another lavish meal awaited him. It was another long, drawn out affair with speeches and numerous toasts. Ever gracious, the General stayed to the very end.

Rain threatened throughout the morning of April 21. Sitting through yet another round of speeches, Washington sent word that he did not want the militia to accompany him to Trenton as planned, due to the weather. The militia intended to accompany him anyway. The General surprised them. He departed earlier than expected and took a different route.

Thirty-five miles on, Washington crossed the Delaware by ferry. Greeting him on the Jersey side was another welcoming committee and a band playing martial tunes. Washington mounted his white horse and led a procession through Trenton and down to the bridge over the Assunpink Creek. It was here, a focal point of the Battle of Trenton, that many had died on both sides, to the point where the bridge was covered in blood.

On this day, the bridge was covered in evergreens, and a group of women and their daughters dressed in white robes awaited him. A sign posted on the bridge displayed two dates: December 26, 1776—January 2, 1777. During those eight days the tenor of the war changed, from one of gloom to one of hope. An inscription read: "The defender of the mothers will be the protector of the daughters." Washington dismounted his horse. Thirteen ladies bearing baskets of flowers broke into song:

Virgins fair and matrons grave,
Those thy conquering arms did save,
Build for thee triumphant bowers,
Strew, ye fair, his way with flowers,
Strew your hero's way with flowers.

The ladies then flung their flowers on the bridge and the General crossed to the other side.

The following morning, Washington was off at sunrise. At Princeton, he received a formal address at the college and gave a brief acknowledgement. At Brunswick, volunteer infantry and artillery with a detachment of cavalry formed a line past which the General rode. More bands and speeches, and on to Westbrook, where he spent his last night before reaching New York.

Awakening the morning of April 23, Washington surely felt exhausted. Since leaving Mount Vernon, he had spent nearly all of his waking hours either bouncing around inside his coach or sitting through endless speeches, and making brief replies to every one of them; eating countless rich, heavy meals and drinking who-knows-how-many glasses of wine and spirits; and nearly every day being confronted by crowds of cheering and groping strangers. This was not the genteel society—the rich and well-to-do—he greeted regularly at Mount

Vernon. Oh, no. This was the hurly-burly of the masses, the common folk; this wasn't the present state of politics; this was its future. This was democracy as it would be in the Age of Jackson. Surely, for a man who liked to keep his distance, there must have been moments when the sheer tedium of it all seemed more than Washington could bear. And it wasn't over yet.

Elizabeth Town was the last stop on the long road to New York. Washington arrived a little before 9 a.m. and mounted his white horse to ride at the head of yet another procession through another town. He breakfasted at the Red Lion Inn with a number of city and state leaders, and with the two Senators and five Representatives who would accompany him across the bay to Manhattan.

It's fifteen miles from Elizabeth Town Point across Upper New York Harbor to Murray's Wharf, at the foot of Wall Street. Ferry service was an everyday fact of life for commuters to-and-from Manhattan, as it is for many commuters today. Up to this point, Washington had crossed a half-dozen or so wide rivers, using public transportation. Not today. The barge awaiting him was custom-built for the occasion, decked out in patriotic red-white-and-blue colors. Thirteen oars on either side were pulled by a seasoned staff of New York Harbor pilots. Washington stepped aboard and, with the sun shining upon him, waved his hat to the cheering crowd on the Jersey shore.

With oars rowing in unison, the barge passed purposely through the Kill Van Kull tidal straight and entered the open waters of Upper New York Bay, where a fleet of small craft awaited him. They fell in behind the presidential barge and followed it across the Bay. In the distance, a skyline of church steeples flanked by tall ships loomed in the distance—Manhattan. From the ramparts of the Battery, cannons boomed with flame and smoke, firing off a thirteen-gun salute.

The barge swung past the Battery and moved up the East River, greeted by a second thirteen-gun salute, from the Spanish galleon "Galveston" anchored in the bay. This was followed by a third thirteen-gun salute, from an American vessel anchored nearby, the "North Carolina." From the Battery up to Paulus Hook, New Yorkers stood two-and-three deep to watch the arrival of the president-elect.

Once the barge neared the wharf, longshoremen threw out ropes and leapt aboard to tie up the vessel. Washington waited as steps were set up and a red carpet rolled out. He stepped onto the wharf and was greeted by his old friend, and now governor of New York, George Clinton. Clinton spoke briefly. A carriage waited, but Washington declined; he would walk the rest of the way.

The Palace Mansion at 1 Cherry Street allowed the president-elect time for himself. A servant helped him freshen up with a cup of hot tea and a change of shirts, then the General was off again. A carriage took him to Governor Clinton's elegant townhouse on Queen Street where he was the guest of honor at dinner. Afterward, the two watched a fireworks display at the Battery.

Later that evening, Washington returned to the Palace on foot. Oil-burning street lamps shown at every corner, and in the windows of every house candles flickered in his honor. An "ocean of difficulties" lay ahead, but tonight Manhattan was celebrating his arrival.

HIS ROTUNDITY

No one had done more for the American cause than John Adams of Boston.

As a delegate to the Continental Congress, none argued longer or more effectively for American independence than did John Adams.

Indeed, his fellow delegates dubbed him "the Atlas for independence." Adams lobbied for Washington to head the Continental Army, and he personally selected young Thomas Jefferson of Virginia to draft the Declaration of Independence. In Paris in 1781, Adams helped broker the Paris Peace Treaty that ended the war with England. In Amsterdam in 1782, after a year of negotiations with Dutch financiers, he arranged a loan of 5 million guilders that literally saved the nation from financial collapse. Adams secured crucial additional loans in 1784, 1787, and 1788 netting another nine million guilders.

Having returned to America, on April 13, 1789, Adams was notified of his election as vice president. He departed Boston amidst cheering crowds and a week later arrived in New York City. The following morning he took a carriage to Federal Hall. There were no crowds, no ceremony, no oath-taking. He entered the Senate chamber and was greeted at the door by the president pro tempore, John Langdon. Langdon conducted him to his chair at the head of the chamber where Adams addressed the Senate with a short speech. After that, the problems for John Adams began.

The Senate was in the midst of a month-long debate on how to address the President. Downstairs, the House voted that the chief executive should be addressed simply as "George Washington, President of the United States." Not the Senate. How very ordinary the mere appellation of "Mr. President" sounded, observed Senator Oliver Ellsworth, and Adams agreed completely.

A committee appointed to consider the issue reported back with the suggested title: "His Highness the President of the United States of America and Protector of the Rights of the Same." Not good enough, said Adams. He said: "everything possible should be done to bring dignity and respect to the federal government and thus strengthen the

Union." Richard Henry Lee of Virginia agreed. Washington should be called "His Majesty the President," he said.

As days turned into weeks, support for grand titles waned, and Adams found himself out of step. Still, he would not be silent. He repeatedly intruded on the Senate's time to voice his views, with long lectures on what to do and how they should conduct themselves. "For forty minutes he harangued us from the chair," Senator William Maclay wrote in his journal. When Senator Ralph Izard suggested that Adams himself be bestowed with the title, "His Rotundity," the Senate roared with laughter.

On May 14, the Senate concurred with the House and voted to address Washington as simply "The President of the United States."

INAUGURATION DAY

April 30, 1789 was Inauguration Day.

Governor Clinton sent the state carriage around to pick up the president-elect. It was a regal-looking rig, drawn by six white horses, with four uniformed footmen, a driver, and a postillion riding the lead horse. Had it not been the familiar and trusted George Washington, people along the parade route might have assumed the man seated inside was a king on to his way to his coronation.

Washington was a clothes-horse who favored military attire and suits made in England, but on this day he was wearing a simple brown suit, made of fabric produced in a New England textile mill.

The carriage delivered Washington to the steps of Federal Hall. Entering the Senate Chamber on the second floor the president-elect was greeted by vice-president John Adams. Adams bowed deeply, and said: "Sir, the Senate and the House of Representatives are ready to attend you to take the oath required by the Constitution. It will be administered by the Chancellor of the State of New York." Adams then escorted the president-elect onto the balcony above Wall Street, before an estimated 10,000 citizens standing in the street below.

A Bible placed on a red cushion was used to swear in the President, the very Bible that is used to swear-in presidents to this day. Chancellor Robert Livingston addressed the General: "Do you solemnly swear that you will faithfully execute the office of President of the United States, and will, to the best of your ability, preserve, protect, and defend the Constitution of the United States?"

"I solemnly swear," Washington said, and repeated the oath.

Chancellor Livingston turned to the crowd, with much gravity, said: "It is done. Long live George Washington, President of the United States."

The crowd cheered. A signal was somehow relayed to the Spanish Galleon anchored in the bay which responded with a booming thirteen gun salute. When all was quiet again, Washington, visibly nervous, removed some papers and began reading his speech. "The great man was agitated and embarrassed more than even by the leveled cannon or pointed musket," one Senator reported later. "He trembled, and several times could scarce make out to read."

The address, which James Madison had written for him, was short. For the most part, the speech consisted of generalities and emphasized the public good. Unlike an earlier, longer draft that Washington had written that was more a to-do list for Congress than a speech, Madison's revised version made only one request of Congress: that it draft a bill of rights.

Afterward, the President joined Congressmen and local politicians at Saint Paul's Chapel on Broadway for prayer and a short sermon by Bishop Provoost. That afternoon, the President attended two receptions held in his honor, followed by another fireworks display at the Battery.

Washington told friends that day the new government was an experiment. They had no way of knowing the success or failure of that experiment very soon would depend on the state of Washington's health.

CHAPTER 4

UNTRODDEN GROUND

It seemed too good to be true.

Alexander Hamilton's two great passions in life—politics and economics—were headquartered on the same street where he lived—Wall Street. There was Federal Hall where Congress met daily, and one block down was the commercial bank Hamilton founded, New York Bank. It was a one-minute walk from his townhouse to the front door of either building.

George Washington did not have a place for Hamilton in the new government, but he would. James Madison was having discussions with the President about the creation of the executive departments of state and treasury, and who Washington should appoint to fill them. Both of Madison's recommended appointees were his friends: Thomas Jefferson and Alexander Hamilton.

While Madison and Jefferson were born into the Virginia aristocracy, Hamilton was born on the island of Nevis in the Caribbean, in near poverty. His was a tale right out of Horatio Alger, the poor boy who works hard and rises to middle-class respectability, or in Hamilton's case, upper-class respectability.

Adding further resistance to Hamilton's climb was that he was born out of wedlock. His father and mother never married. His father disappeared when he was nine and his mother died when he was eleven. His mother taught him to read, and the books she owned—some 30 in all—constituted his sole inheritance. Not yet a teen, Hamilton went to work clerking for a wealthy merchant on the nearby island of St. Croix. The merchant thought so highly of him that when he became ill and went to New York to recuperate, he put Hamilton in charge of his business. Hamilton was 14 and kept the business running smoothly the four months the merchant was away. At 16, Hamilton was sent to America by his Scottish tutor Hugh Knox, a Princeton graduate who was the first to acknowledge his genius.

Hamilton arrived in New York not exactly a penniless immigrant. He had papers of introduction and what amounted to a college scholarship, thanks to Knox and his deep-pockets friends. There was a problem, however. Before entering college Hamilton would need three years of preparatory school which, when completed, would leave him with just enough money for one year of college. As it turned out, it was more than enough. Hamilton was not only gifted, he was highly motivated. He completed his prep-school studies and passed his exams in one year, and completed his four-years of college in two years. He would have graduated had it not been for the Revolution.

Hamilton sided with the patriot's cause and quit school a month shy of graduation. He took a crash course in trigonometry, learned the art of artillery, and before his twentieth birthday caught the attention of General George Washington. He served on Washington's staff as aid-de-camp for four years. In October 1781, at Yorktown, he led a charge that captured a key redoubt that helped turn the tide on a day that ended in victory for the Continental Army. Horatio Alger never wrote a story quite so bold, and it was only the beginning.

In 1780, while in the army, Hamilton married Elizabeth Schuyler, daughter of General Philip Schuyler. The Schuylers were among New York State's most prominent families. If Hamilton was seeking a life of ease, he'd found it. He wasn't. He wanted to pay his own his way. After three months of intensive study of the law in Albany, he was admitted to the bar in July 1783. When the British army evacuated New York city later that fall, he opened his law office at 57 Wall Street.

With John Jay, he formed the New York Manumission Society, dedicated to the gradual emancipation of slavery in New York state. In 1784, he founded the Bank of New York. Today it is the oldest ongoing banking organization in the United States. Working with Jay and others, he helped revive his alma mater King's College (today's Columbia College), which had been suspended since the Battle of Long Island in 1776.

Politics was never far from his mind, however. He served as delegate from New York in the Confederation Congress in 1782 and 1783, and resumed his public career by attending the Annapolis Convention as a delegate in 1786. He wrote the call letter for the Constitutional Convention. In Philadelphia he made an impassioned speech for an "energetic" chief executive. He suggested making the presidency a lifetime appointment, as with Supreme Court appointments, subject to removal by impeachment. He was not alone in this line of thinking. However, Madison's Virginia Plan of a cleverly balanced government had by then held sway and carried the day.

Hamilton was not satisfied with the new Constitution, convinced it did not give the Federal Government nearly enough power to succeed. He signed the document anyway and urged others to sign it too. Afterward he co-authored "The Federalist Papers," eighty-five essays written to rally support in New York State the proposed Constitution. In Poughkeepsie, working in concert with John Jay, he beat overwhelming odds and made New York the eleventh state to ratify the Constitution. Lastly, in a series of letters, he helped convince George Washington to run for president.

On April 30, 1789, from the balcony of his house on Wall Street, Hamilton watched George Washington be sworn in as president. All that remained now was to wait for his appointment as Secretary of the Treasury. Funding the war debt and creating a national bank to use the funded debt as investment capital would, in Hamilton's mind, further strengthen the federal government and thus insure the success of the young Republic.

New York was Hamilton's kind of town: fast-paced and money-minded. (Both Madison and Jefferson loathed New York.) In 1789, New York had a population of 33,000 souls, with twenty-two churches, one synagogue, six markets, 4000 houses (many of them boardinghouses), 300 taverns, five newspapers, one college, one public library, one theater, one post office, one bank (Hamilton's), a debtors' prison, no hotels, and no hospitals (doctors made house calls and treated patients in their parlors).

As with most eighteenth-century cities, New York was a city of foul smells, especially in the heat of summer. Most streets were dusty in summer and muddy in winter. The streets where the wealthy lived, such as Broadway, White Hall, Barclay, Vesey, Broad, and Wall Street, were paved in brick or cobblestone, and were tree-lined. New York City was decidedly commercial. People walked fast and talked faster. It was a city of immigrants and the most racially diverse city in America, with four prominent ethnic groups: Dutch, French, German, and English. While a number of wealthy households utilized slaves, the peculiar institution was on the decline and many African-American New Yorkers were free.

WASHINGTON'S MODUS OPERANDI

George Washington did not trust the spoken word. He asked his aids to put their ideas in writing. If Washington had learned anything in his 57 years, it was that he didn't know everything. He needed the advice of learned men. He needed opinions that conflicted with his own. Don't tell me what I want to hear; tell me what you think in your gut. That's how Washington conducted a war; that's how Washington would conduct a presidency: give me your gut opinion, and put it in writing. He'd been in New York only a few days and already he needed advice. The problem: how to get some privacy.

From the moment Washington took possession of the Palace Mansion at 1 Cherry Street, it was overrun with well-wishers, job-seekers, ex-soldiers, and a few people who actually had a reason to see the President. On the first morning Washington was in the house—as he was climbing out of bed—people began to come, and kept coming until he went to bed that night. It was like that every day.

Washington didn't know what to do. Everything was new. The government was new. The office of president was new. How was the president supposed to act? It was not his house; it belonged to the people. He wanted to be hospitable, but this was too much. Could he ask them to leave?

After several days, when it was obvious the stream of people would not let up, and he could get nothing done, he called in John Adams, James Madison, John Jay and Alexander Hamilton and asked for their advice. This was what was decided: dinners would be held every Thursday afternoon at four, for government officials and their families, by invitation only, in an orderly system of rotation to avoid charges of favoritism. The general public would be invited twice weekly, at a levee for men, on Tuesday afternoons, between three and four, and at a tea for men and women, on Friday evenings. Anyone dressed respectably could attend without invitation. The rest of the time the Executive Mansion would be closed to the public.

Washington felt awkward at these social functions. He was never one of the boys, never a back-slapper, never one with an easy quip, an amusing story to tell, or a tired joke to recycle. His special genius was to operate above the fray, and thus be able to find order in chaos. Being above the political fray would make him one of the nation's most effective presidents. In social situations, however, such an approach didn't work. Washington came off as aloof, distant, even arrogant, which he wasn't.

Washington had another problem: he wasn't sure how the president ought to act. Somehow, he had to embody the new government's dignity and authority while at the same time not appear to be kingly. Pennsylvania Senator William Maclay, watching the president at one of these functions, observed: "General George Washington stood on as difficult Ground, as he ever had done in his life." The tea parties, hosted by Martha, and attended mostly by women, were more to his liking. He enjoyed circulating among the ladies, who tended to swoon over him. Wrote Abigail Adams: "(The President) moved with a grace, and ease that leaves Royal George far behind."

George Washington did not want to rush into things. This presidency thing was all new. The Constitution didn't provide a lot of information. The heart of it was Article II, Section 2 and 3, amounting to about 300 words and purposely vague. It would be a matter of learning on the job and, as Washington acknowledged in letters he wrote at the time, setting a precedent for future presidents. He wanted to get it right.

"I walk on untrodden ground," Washington wrote in a letter to family friend Catherine Macaulay Graham. "There is scarcely any action, whose motives may not be subject to a double interpretation. There is scarcely any part of my conduct which may not hereafter be drawn into precedent. Under such a view of the duties inherent to my arduous office, I could not but feel a diffidence in myself on the one hand; and an anxiety for the Community that every arrangement should be made in the best possible manner on the other."

Satisfied with the house at 1 Cherry Street, Washington sent for his wife, Martha. At some point, perhaps in the first month, Washington decided to keep his residence and his administrative offices under one roof. The Palace Mansion was large enough to accommodate both. The first floor had rooms suitable for receiving state officials and foreign dignitaries, as well as rooms for his office and those of his personal secretaries and staff. The second floor had plenty of bedrooms for his family and his two personal secretaries, Tobias Lear and Col. David Humphreys. The third floor served as sleeping quarters for live-in servants. Until Congress created the executive departments, Washington would continue with two holdovers from the old government: John Jay, as Superintendent of Foreign Affairs, and General Hugh Knox, as Superintendent of War. These two and their staffs would continue their work in offices above the Fraunces Tavern.

Washington spent much of his first month in office involved with social activities. He attended the Inaugural Ball, held at the Delancey House on Broadway, on May 7. It was a chance for George Washington to show New York society that their president was a first-class performer on the dance floor. Women waited in line for a turn with the elegant gentleman from Virginia. Abigail Adams "gushed like a school girl" at seeing him for the first time.

From May 10 to May 23, Washington made a personal call on every member of Congress. Who were these men who comprised the First Congress of the United States? They were lawyers, merchants, and wealthy land owners. More than half fought in the Revolution. Nearly all had served as state legislators, delegates in Congress, or delegates to the Constitutional Convention. They were men of impressive bearing and fine oratory skills, accustomed to being at the controls of power. Some were hotheads; most were steady, practical men of reason. Many wore wigs. All knew how to dress. Some brought a valet. Washington's call on these men was mostly symbolic—and brief. Senator Maclay observed in his journal that the President arrived at his boardinghouse on horseback, dismounted, said good-day, made two "complaisant Bows," mounted his horse and rode off.

George Washington was a man of few words.

THE SENATE CALLS ON THE PRESIDENT

In keeping with British, colonial and state practice of the legislature issuing a reply to executive speeches, on May 18th the Senate called on the Palace Mansion to issue a formal reply to the President's Inaugural Address.

Charlie Chaplin could not have made it more amusing.

After knocking on the door, John Adams and eighteen Senators filed into the levee room and were greeted by Washington and two aids, presumably Lear and Humphreys. After nervous bows and clearing of throats, Adams removed a written speech from his pocket but could not read it because he could not keep his hands from shaking. What to do? He placed the manuscript in his hat and, holding the hat with both hands, read the speech, occasionally pausing to turn the page.

It doesn't stop there.

Washington then removed his written reply from his pocket with his right hand but could not read it without his glasses. He couldn't remove his glasses from the case because in his left hand he was holding his hat. For an awkward moment he looked at the paper in his right, his hat in his left hand, and his glasses case on the counter, wondering what to do. After shifting some items, he put his hat under his left arm and the paper in his left hand, and with his right hand removed the glasses from the case. He put his glasses on his nose only to be still holding the glasses case. After another awkward moment looking around the room, he placed the glasses case on the chimney mantle. That done, he adjusted his spectacles and read the reply without emotion. The President then invited everyone to sit down. Adams, however, was wearing a sword and having difficulty. Thus, he remained standing and, not knowing what to do, bowed and departed. The Senators rose and one-by-one bowed and followed him out. The meeting, presumably, was then over.

THE FOURTEEN-MILES ROUND

The Palace Mansion was not the Mount Vernon mansion house, and Manhattan was not the Mount Vernon plantation, but there were similarities. At Mount Vernon, partly as an escape from the always-present visitors, but mostly to oversee management of five farms, Washington rode circuit most days, except on Sundays, a journey of about 20 miles. The Mount Vernon plantation ran parallel to the Potomac River for about ten miles and at its widest point penetrated inland about four miles. In New York, Washington continued riding circuit—around Manhattan.

Manhattan was roughly similar in size, being twelve miles long and at its widest about two-miles across. With the exception of New York city, which occupied the southern tip, Manhattan was mostly farmland and therefore was familiar territory to George Washington. There were two crucial differences however: in whatever direction Washington rode, if he rode far enough, he encountered water, as Manhattan was an island. Also unlike Mount Vernon, he didn't own it. The farms he passed were not his and the farmers and their families were free and white. The President would occasionally stop and "talk shop" with farmers along the way. He enjoyed himself. He needed to get away from time to time and "The Fourteen Miles Round," as the locals called it, met that need.

As president, Washington would find a much larger circuit to ride—around the entire nation. Beginning with New England in 1789 he would travel as far north as Portsmouth, Maine. Two years later, he would travel as far south as Savannah, Georgia. What was the United States in its early years but a larger version of Mount Vernon? It stretched along the East Coast for a distance of about 1200 miles, and inland about 400 miles. In place of the five farms were five regions. There was (1) the rice producing low country of South Carolina and Georgia, (2) the tobacco belt extending from middle South Carolina through North Carolina, Virginia and much of Maryland, (3) west of the tobacco belt and extending northwest to central Pennsylvania was the frontier country where corn was the cash crop, (4) in the east, north of the tobacco belt, was the wheat belt, extending from Mount

Vernon to the middle reaches of the Hudson Valley, and (5) was all of New England, where lumber and fishing were the principle industries.

As with Mount Vernon in 1789, the nation was operating in the red. Before Washington would leave office eight years later, both would be in the black.

CHAPTER 5

Master of the House

Who was the man dressed in black speaking from the floor of the House of Representatives in a voice not much louder than a whisper? People in the overhead gallery had trouble hearing him. Expecting to be entertained with heated arguments and shouting matches—which on occasion they were—they threw nuts at him and cried, "Hey, you down there, speak up. We can't hear you."

Some men enter a room and make it feel small; such is their magnetism. Frail, stoop-shouldered James Madison entered the cavernous House Chamber and made it feel larger. What mattered was Madison was in control. House speaker Frederick Muhlenberg presided, but as anyone in the gallery soon realized, the gentleman with the low-wattage delivery was Master of the House.

Next to George Washington, James Madison was the most influential man in the country. How could that be? The Virginian was not a signer of the Declaration of Independence, nor was he a war hero. Outside of Virginia he was little known. But in the elite world of eighteenth-century American politics, where everyone knew everyone else, James Madison was the ultimate insider.

When Madison spoke—however softly—people paid attention. Madison's mastery of the facts was peerless, due in no small part to his willingness to continue working late into the night while others had gone home to bed. He would never think of entering upon a question of policy or law without first making a thorough investigation of the issues, which meant he would know twice as much as anyone else. As a result, Madison commanded the meeting, whether it was the Virginia legislature, the Constitutional Convention, or the House of Representatives.

Alexander Hamilton was as formidable—with economics. Both men were ambitious in the extreme. With Hamilton, brimming with self confidence, his ambition was obvious. With Madison, shy and self-effacing, his ambition was subtle and not at first obvious. Hamilton looked like what he was—a New York attorney. Madison looked like a care-worn school teacher. Both were bookish, and could quote from the writings of David Hume and Adam Smith, among others. Hamilton leavened his ideology with the pragmatism of a businessman. Madison, never having held down a job, did not possess the experience of the work-a-day world that otherwise might have tempered his idealism. This was the extent of difference between Hamilton and Madison and eventually it would drive them apart.

For three years the Hamilton-Madison juggernaut worked its magic, elevating the national government into the supreme law of the land while relegating the states to a subordinate role. Now, in the second month of the new federal government, a crack appeared in the Hamilton-Madison collaboration. It began April 8, two days after Washington's election. James Madison stood up in the House of Representatives and proposed that the 1783 Tariff Bill be enacted immediately. Had Madison stopped there, the Bill would have passed the House before word reached Washington that he was elected president. What held up the Bill was Madison's addendum, a discriminatory tax against British imports designed to hurt England in the pocketbook. The problem was it would hurt American business in the pocketbook much more.

CREATING A FEDERAL REVENUE STREAM

If the new national government was going to succeed, a federal revenue system was needed to pay the bills. A tariff bill would serve that purpose. The principle failure of Congress under the Articles of Confederation was its inability to pass the 1783 Tariff Bill. Under the old government, passage required a unanimous vote. Under the new Constitution, that was not the case; a two-thirds vote of approval in both houses was all that was required. Madison dusted off the 1783 Tariff Bill and attached an addendum for tonnage duties that went beyond revenue into the thorny realm of ideology. Congressmen from Georgia and South Carolina fearing it would hurt the business of their states objected so strongly that it was decided to shelve debate until after the president's inauguration.

Madison's Tariff Bill was in three parts: Parts One and Two were holdovers from the 1783 Tariff Bill; Part Three was Madison's addendum. Part One was an *ad valorem* tax of five percent on all imports. Part Two contained a short list of enumerated articles (rum, wine, tea, molasses, and the like), to be taxed by duties of a specified amount. This would make the tariff mildly protective, in that business interests with a reasonable claim to protection would receive at least a token of protection, consistent with the government's claim to revenue. Part Three was Madison's addendum that all goods entering the country be taxed according to tonnage, and that such taxes be levied on three types of vessels:

First type, American-owned vessels, that would pay the lowest duties.

Second type, foreign vessels of which the United States had commercial treaties, that would pay a somewhat higher duty.

Third type, foreign vessels of which the United States did NOT have commercial treaties, that would pay the highest duties of all. Therein lay the problem: the United States did not have a commercial treaty with its biggest trading partner, Great Britain. It did, however, have a commercial treaty with its war-time ally France. In effect, Madison was proposing a tax that favored France and discriminated against England. This was somewhat understandable. France had been an American ally during the Revolutionary War and Great Britain had been the enemy. Madison's reasoning, however, ignored an indisputable business fact: Great Britain needed American goods (and vice-versa) and France did not.

Nearly all government income from customs duties was from English imports, and eighty percent of all American exports went to England. What Madison's tariff amounted to was wishful thinking. His discriminatory tax would limit trade with America's most lucrative trading partner and attempt to replace it with a nation that had no need and no desire for American goods. England was a trading nation that valued American goods. France was not a trading nation; what trade it did have was with continental nations—with Italy, Spain, and Germany. England could take its business elsewhere, but what of America? Who was going to buy American goods in the quantity England bought them? To Alexander Hamilton—and to anyone with a head for business—Madison's Tariff Bill was a textbook example of cutting off the head of the goose that laid the golden egg.

The question is why? Why would Madison turn a blind eye to American business interests and propose a bill that discriminated against Great Britain?

VIRGINIA WRIT LARGE

James Madison and Thomas Jefferson shared an image of what America should be, and it looked like Virginia. It was a land without the filth and corruption of cities, without stock brokers and bankers or immigrant labor, a land of vast plantations and plentiful forests, of stately homes and Sunday socials, with the Blue Ridge Mountains as a backdrop and the James River running through it. It was where both the wealthy plantation owner and the small farmer lived in harmony. Such a place, however, was more illusion than reality. However grand and well-ordered they appeared to be, plantations were prison-houses for slave labor, and the small farmer barely eked out a living.

Despite employing slave labor, Virginia planters were up to their ears in debt. To whom did they owe so much money? To British merchants who purchased their tobacco. Thomas Jefferson was an example. His fortune literally rose and fell on the balance sheet of a London counting house. As with most Virginia planters, Jefferson never quite understood why tobacco prices at the commodities exchange would be up one day and down the next, or why his annual yield would net one amount one year, and quite a different amount the next. His very livelihood depended on the numbers entered in the ledger of the British agent with whom he met annually.

Under such a system, wealth was locked up in land. Jefferson, like so many Virginia planters, was land rich and cash poor. He wasn't paid for his tobacco in specie. He was issued credit by which he could purchase English goods from a catalogue—clothes, furniture, fine china, silverware, even the French wines he relished. With his expensive tastes, Jefferson often spent more than he took in. Watching his plantation slip further and further into the red, he at first suspected—and then became convinced—that he was being duped by unscrupulous money men. So did most Virginia planters, including George Washington. However, Washington diversified—switched from tobacco to growing wheat and barley—and broke free. Jefferson merely fell deeper in debt.

It seemed to a majority of Virginia's planting class that America had won political freedom from Great Britain only to find it was an economic captive.

Madison offered several reasons for discriminating against British trade that revealed his ignorance of America's business climate: (1) trade with Great Britain was "artificial" and gave that country "a much greater proportion of our trade than she is naturally entitled to" (2) Britain needed American trade more than America needed hers; (3) most of the manufactured goods being imported from England would soon be produced in the United States, and (4) American commerce was highly favored by the French, and with some encouragement (i.e. lower tonnage rates) France would become the United States' most valued trading partner.

Meanwhile, across an ocean, Thomas Jefferson was doing his best to make France see the light and become the United States' number-one trading partner.

JEFFERSON SPEAKS FRENCH AND BUYS ENGLISH

Sent to Europe in 1784, Thomas Jefferson hoped to create a series of commercial treaties with various European nations that would lead to a true free-trade community and, he hoped, would bring an end to England's trade monopoly with the United States. However noble an idea, it had absolutely no basis in reality. Most countries were either indifferent or did not have colonial possessions. None was willing to grant special privileges beyond that of "most favored nation" status, which in eighteenth-century Europe was worth little more than the paper on which it was written.

Having replaced Benjamin Franklin as Minister to France in 1785, Jefferson opened talks along similar lines with various French Ministers. For the most part, they were quite agreeable to Jefferson's proposal, but woefully out of touch with the business needs of their own country. French merchants had little interest in American goods, other than tobacco. In turn, American merchants had little interest in French goods, other than French wine. Whatever American merchants needed was readily available in England. Thanks to the most advanced manufacturing techniques in all of Europe, English products were better made, in greater supply, and cheaper to buy.

Whether he would admit it or not, Jefferson knew this to be true. Having searched all over Paris for a new high-efficiency oil lamp, he found exactly what he was looking for in London. On another occasion, he had to apologize to a French friend for buying an English harness. Said Jefferson sheepishly:

"The reason for my importing (a harness) from England is a very obvious one. They are plated, and plated harness is not made at all in France. . . . It is not from a love of the English but a love of myself that I sometimes find myself obliged to buy their manufacture." It would seem Jefferson wanted Americans to buy expensive and inferior French goods, while he himself was free to purchase cheaper and better-made English goods.

The British economy was dependent on overseas trade, while the French were at best reluctant traders. French merchants were more content with protecting and stabilizing what limited trade they had than in reaching out for new markets to exploit. Despite Jefferson's best efforts, between 1784 and 1790, French imports amounted to no more than one-twentieth of British imports.

The underlying issue was not trade but resentment against England. In the immediate post-war years resentment was understandably high. It grew worse when England reimposed the Navigation Act, which prohibited American trade with the British West Indies. Alexander Hamilton and John Adams spoke of retaliation. The correspondence of Jefferson and Madison during this time reek with hatred of all things English.

As years passed and the American economy picked up, resentment lessened. Given London's easy credit it was highly beneficial to be doing business with England. At the same time, American merchants were finding new markets for their goods, in Russian ports on the Baltic, even in far away China. As important, the British West Indies, closed as it was to American trade, was in fact remarkably accessible to enterprising American shippers. By 1789, hatred of England was still given voice, but with less conviction. Among American merchants from Boston all the way to Savannah, Britain was no longer viewed as the enemy, but as a business partner. Finally, there was no escaping the fact that nearly all government income was generated from taxes on English goods entering the country. Madison chose to ignore these facts, and under his influence, so did the House of Representatives.

MADISON'S MASTERY DOES NOT EXTEND TO THE SENATE

Since April 8, when Madison introduced the tariff bill, opposition to the tonnage discrimination clause gradually faded. In May, after two days of debate, the House passed the bill and sent it upstairs to the Senate for confirmation.

Occupied with business of its own, the Senate did not act on Madison's Tariff Bill immediately, thus allowing opposition time to its make its case. Senate record keeping in 1789 was dismal at best so there is no record of what actually transpired when the Senate debated Madison's discriminatory clause. From letters and journal entries, however, it seems clear that city merchants did a fair amount of lobbying, probably at Alexander Hamilton's directing. Whether or not James Madison knew that Hamilton was in fact working against him is not known. They continued to be on good speaking terms. That summer, a woman remembered seeing them together "turn and laugh and play with a monkey that was climbing in a neighbor's yard."

When the Senate voted the decision was nearly unanimous—in opposition to the bill. Such a policy as Madison's, argued the Senate, would only lead to needless and ruinous commercial warfare, and Great Britain had far greater capacity to injure America economically than America to injure her. It sent the tariff bill back to the House minus the discrimination clause. Twice the House returned the bill to the Senate with Madison's clause reinserted, and twice more the Senate rejected it.

At some point, the Tariff Bill was divided into two bills—a tariff bill (basically the 1783 Tariff Bill), and a tonnage bill, to be debated and voted on as separate issues. Thus separated, the Tariff Bill was approved by both houses without further debate. Washington signed the Tariff Act into law on July 4. The House eventually relented and passed the Tonnage Bill minus Madison's discriminatory clause. The Tonnage Act was signed into law on September 17, 1789.

THE TARIFF ACT AND ITS AFTERMATH

Madison, normally the conciliator, took the result in stubborn bad grace, characterizing the opposition as "chiefly abetted by the spirit of this City, which is steeped in Anglicism." Massachusetts Senator Fisher Ames wrote in his journal: "The Senate . . . as if designated by Providence to keep rash and frolicsome brats out of the fire, have demolished the absurd, impolite, mad discrimination of foreigners in alliance from other foreigners."

The Tariff Act and the Tonnage Act raised the necessary revenue to fund the federal government, but who was going to collect it? That was determined by two additional bills—The Collection Act, and the Coast Act, passed in Congress and signed into law in 1789.

The Collection Act established a number of collection districts, each with a port of entry at which resided a number of federal officials, including a collector, a naval officer, and a surveyor. Other ports in the district were designated as ports of delivery only, and all ships bound from them had to stop first at the port of entry to declare its cargo and pay the federal duties. Revenue officers had powers of search and seizure and to enact penalties for violations. A revision in 1790 established the United States Coast Guard, that included the construction of 100 cutter ships used as enforcement.

The Coast Act of 1789 established federal forms for registering and clearing all vessels plying American coastal waters and regulated the domestic, undutied trade among the states up and down the Atlantic Coast.

With the Lighthouses Act of 1789 the federal government assumed control of all lighthouses, beacons, and buoys which previously had been the domain of the states.

These newly created federal departments would employee 500 people who in turn would report directly to the newly created Treasury Department.

Hamilton remained Madison's choice for Secretary of the Treasury, but the day was not distant when the Virginian would turn on his friend.

CHAPTER 6

Rumors

New York City was a hotbed of rumors in the spring and summer of 1789.

The most persistent rumor was that a second constitutional convention was going to be held, when and where to be determined. Ostensibly, it would be to amend the Constitution with a bill of rights, but no one actually believed that to be the real reason. The anti-Federalists were behind the rumor, and their intent was to dismember the new federal government and restore the confederation.

The House of Representatives was prepared to draft a bill of rights—when it was ready. In April, it had more pressing issues to deal with, such as creating a federal revenue system. In the meantime, something had to be done to prevent or at least to delay a second convention from being called. But what? James Madison had the answer: improvise.

The Monday following Washington's inauguration, on May 4, 1789, Madison rose from his seat in the House and made an announcement: in three weeks he would open debate on a bill of rights. Yes, James Madison, who opposed a bill of rights at the Constitutional Convention in Philadelphia, now was in favor of a bill of rights. In fact, he said he would write them, and have them approved by Congress and ready for the President's signature before the first session adjourned in September.

Having made the announcement, it was now a matter of public record and therefore news on the streets of New York. Within a week or two it would be printed in newspapers throughout the country. If Congress was going to amend the Constitution with a bill of rights, there was no need for a second convention. In less than five minutes, Madison had trumped the anti-Federalists.

Or had he? The following day, Theodorick Bland—an ally of the nation's most vocal anti-Federalist, Patrick Henry—presented a petition calling for a second constitutional convention. Madison knew exactly what Bland would say next, that such a convention would meet only to consider "the defects of this Constitution that have been suggested by the state (ratifying) Conventions, and report such amendments thereto, as they shall find best suited to promote our common interests, and secure to ourselves and our latest posterity, the great unalienable rights of mankind" and blah, blah, blah.

Alas, Bland was one day too late. The issue was already settled in the minds of Congressmen: the matter would be dealt with in three weeks. The House entered Bland's petition into the journal and kept the original on file in the clerk's office, where it was immediately forgotten.

WASHINGTON TAKES CONTROL

Washington, meanwhile, was taking control of the affairs of state. He asked two officers of the old government, John Jay (Superintendent of Foreign Affairs) and Henry Knox (Superintendent of War) to stay on until such time as Congress created new executive departments and new officers were appointed. They both agreed.

Washington requested the nation's financial records from the outgoing Board of Treasury and to his disgust and horror discovered that he had inherited an accountant's worst nightmare. The records were filled with floating bond rates, complicated currency conversion tables, and guesswork revenue projections. Worst of all, the Board had no idea how much money the government actually owed. The combined total of state, domestic and foreign debt was anybody's guess. For a while Washington (with help from Tobias Lear) tried to make sense of the numbers but gave up in despair. Only a financial genius could make sense of such a mess.

The financial genius would be Alexander Hamilton. For now, he was practicing law while awaiting creation of the Treasury Department. Hamilton wouldn't be appointed and begin to unravel the accounting nightmare until late in the year.

In mid-May Martha Washington departed Mount Vernon to join her husband in New York. She brought her two grandchildren in the four-door coach and a wagon following loaded with clothes chests and furnishings, and seven slaves.

Some Historians have portrayed Washington's marriage as loving but passionless. Perhaps. What they had was a partnership.

The two were quite different. Martha enjoyed people and made friends easily. George was reserved and difficult to know well. She was barely five-feet tall and plump (or "healthy" as she referred to herself). He was six-foot-two, angular and well-muscled. She had wonderfully straight white teeth that shown whenever she smiled, which was often. What teeth Washington had were bad, and were seldom seen because he seldom smiled. In his later years, he wore ill-fitting dentures.

Washington was a 27-year-old Colonel in the Virginia militia when they first met. It was at a social gathering where the young colonel was a surprise guest. Martha Custis Dandridge had been a widow for nearly a year, and had two small children. She was the richest and most sought-after unmarried woman in Virginia. What began as an exchange of pleasantries turned into a marathon conversation. He did most of the talking; she was an attentive listener. They talked from early afternoon until late into the evening. They resumed their conversation the following morning and spoke on through the afternoon dinner. It was obvious to everyone there that these two were made for each other. They were what today would be called soul-mates. Within days of their meeting a wedding date was set.

Martha Dandridge needed a man with the strength and experience to manage her large plantation, and who would be a loving father to her two small children. She had many suitors but none who would allow her to raise her children as she saw fit, without interference, as Washington would.

Martha may not have been as dowdy as she has been portrayed down through the years. According to a recent biographer, Patricia Brady, as a young woman Martha was slim and attractive. "Martha pretty much had everything," writes Brady. "She married to please herself and she wanted George. I think she decided, 'I'm young, I'm rich, I need to have the man I want and a man I can trust to look after me and my children.' George Washington was a sharp dresser, and thought a lot about what he wore. He never would have wanted his wife to be dowdy. And she wasn't."

They were married January 6, 1759 and honeymooned for three months at White House, Martha's large plantation near Williamsburg, Virginia. They moved to Washington's then-modest Mount Vernon estate that he inherited from his late step-brother, Lawrence. Washington enlarged the mansion house, sold or leased much of Martha's property, and extended the Mount Vernon landholdings. By 1775, the year he was appointed Commander-in-Chief of the Continental Army, Mount Vernon comprised five farms and stretched ten miles along the Potomac River. The mansion house, dependency buildings, stables, orchards, gardens and lawns looked much as the English estates Washington had long admired in books he imported from England. Martha's wealth allowed him to fulfill his childhood dream of becoming a wealthy Virginia squire and respected member of Tidewater society.

Martha supported her husband in everything he did, including fighting a war. She was with him at Valley Forge during the terrible winter of 1777, and at Morristown during the even-more terrible winter of 1779. She nursed wounded solders, darned their shirts and socks, and after the war campaigned for veteran benefits.

The last thing Martha wanted for her husband was to be president. He had done his duty, she said. He had lived a life of public service. He had served in the French and Indian Wars. He had served in the Virginia House of Burgesses. And for eight years he had served as Commander-in-Chief on the Continental Army. Let him live out his last years at his beloved Mount Vernon. However, when he decided to answer his nation's call and accept the presidency, she supported him completely. A month after Washington departed for New York, Martha followed.

Why the Washingtons brought seven slaves north to New York when Congress was providing them with fourteen hired servants seemed extravagant. Much of it had to do with the way the Washingtons were accustomed to living. Two of the slaves were handmaidens: one was Martha's body servant, the other was her personal maid. Of the other five, four were stablehands, and one was Washington's valet.

Valets and personal servants of great people, whether slaves or not, seldom receive mention in the biographies of famous people and certainly not with early Americans. They are history's invisible personages. A number of Congressmen who traveled to New York, especially those south of the Mason-Dixon Line, were accompanied by a valet . Travel was not easy in eighteenth-century America, and for a man of means someone was required to handle the clothes chest, to see that daily he had a clean change of shirts, to brush the dust from his coat and hat, wash his undergarments, polish his boots, tend to his wig, and in the morning help him dress. Sometimes the relationship between master and servant was close, as with George Washington and Billy Lee.

By all accounts, Billy Lee was an incredible athlete: short, powerful, built like an NFL running back. He was the only horseman in Virginia who could keep pace with Washington in a fox hunt, racing through thickets and leaping over fallen trees. Like Washington, Lee was fearless. He was at the General's side all eight years of the Revolution. Lee not only served as Washington's valet but rode with him into battle. When Washington rode to the front to have a closer look at the fighting, Will was at his side, as much a target as the general.

After the war, Lee fell from his horse and broke a kneecap. Two years later, he fell again and broke the other kneecap. By 1789, Billy Lee was a cripple, but insisted on traveling to New York to continue as Washington's valet. On the way there he stopped in Philadelphia to see a medical specialist. Nothing could be done about his knees, and he travelled on to New York. Lee tried but could no longer assist the General. His brother Frank replaced him as Washington's valet, and at some point Lee returned to Mount Vernon. He was freed at Washington's death, and lived another thirty years on a pension the General had provided for him.

Once Martha arrived in New York with the slaves, a decision was made to keep them out of the public's sight. It wouldn't do having slaves be seen working in the President's mansion, what with New Englanders, Quakers, and New York's manumission society looking on with disapproval. Therein lay a problem. Southern congressmen were offended. What was wrong with slavery? Like Washington, they too had brought slaves north. Should they hide them too? Slavery was an economic necessity and an accepted part of life south of the Mason-Dixon line, something northerners didn't understand. Question slavery and you question the honor of southern gentlemen everywhere. What right did northerners have to judge them? New York was hardly a garden of eden, with its ragged poor and exploited workforce. How were northern unskilled workers better off than southern slaves?

WASHINGTON'S BRUSH WITH DEATH

It wasn't long after Martha arrived that the New York rumor mill was at it again, this time with news of the President's failing health. Word on the street was George Washington had fallen ill and was near death.

Was it merely a baseless rumor or was it true? By all appearances, Washington had been in the peak of health. People were always commenting on how well he looked. Besides, he was never sick. He was vigorous, strong, athletic. He was seen almost daily on horseback or taking brisk walks to the Battery and back. For much of May he called on Congressmen at their respective lodgings. Three times a week he hosted levees and teas at the Executive Mansion. On May 28, he took a boat across the bay to meet his wife on her arrival from Mount Vernon.

Washington began feeling ill on June 4. Within a few days he was bedridden with a fever that would not yield to normal treatment. Straw was put down on the street outside the Palace Mansion, to quiet the sound of passing carriages. Later, the street was cordoned off all together. A protuberance developed on the president's left thigh. Doctors were called to the mansion to have a look. Dr. Samuel Bard, a leading practitioner, and several consultants examined Washington and were unable to make a diagnosis. This was on June 17. Despite efforts to keep the president's illness a secret, word leaked out that Washington might die.

Panic set in, especially among Congressmen. What if the president died? What would become of the federal government? For several days Congress did nothing and for a time it seemed the game was up. The Republic was doomed. No one could replace George Washington as president. Certainly not John Adams. Oh, he was next in the line of succession, but he woefully lacked the General's prestige and charisma. He was fussy and hyper-sensitive, and a polarizing force—a divider, not a uniter. It seemed all too clear: without George Washington, the anti-Federalists would stage a second constitutional convention and that would be the end of "the experiment." If Washington died, the Republic died with him.

The tumor grew fast and took on a fiery hue. Around June 20 the fever abated and the tumor showed itself as an abscess. Surgery was then considered necessary. This was before anesthesia. The young doctor performing the surgery was fearful of hurting the president, of cutting too deep or too far. "Cut away," the older surgeon urged him. "Deep—deeper—deeper still. Don't be afraid. You see how well he bears it."

The General survived the ordeal but afterward needed plenty of rest. He was in a lot of pain and recovery was slow. As soon as he could bear the discomfort, he took carriage rides—laid full length across the seat. Seeing the presidential carriage on the streets of New York again gave people hope all might yet be well. No longer distracted, Congress resumed business but with more urgency.

It would be forty days before Washington returned to his desk. In the meantime, working from his bed, he did what he could. On July 4, he signed the Tariff Bill into law. Indeed, on a day celebrating the nation's political independence, Washington signed into law a bill guaranteeing the federal government's fiscal independence.

With Washington on the mend, the Senate could begin creating a federal judicial system, and the House could focus attention on drafting a bill of rights.

CHAPTER 7

Drafting a Bill of Rights

A peculiar thing happened at the Constitutional Convention in 1787: the framers left out the Bill of Rights.

What would become the cornerstone of Constitutional Law wasn't even mentioned until the final week of the convention. George Mason, one of the wealthiest men in Virginia (and George Washington's neighbor), raised the issue almost as an afterthought. Mason said he wished the Constitution "had been prefaced with a bill of rights" and he added, "It would give great quiet to the people."

A bill of rights could be composed in a few hours, Mason said, if the committee simply referred to the various state declarations and used them as a model. Eight of the thirteen state constitutions had a bill of rights, so the idea wasn't new. Mason, in fact, had written the Virginia bill of rights. A motion was made and seconded. After a short discussion, a vote was taken and the motion was defeated by a unanimous vote. Mason was crushed. When it was time to sign the Constitution, he couldn't bring himself to sign the document he'd worked so hard to help create.

A week later the Constitution went to the states for ratification. A number of states grumbled that there wasn't a bill of rights, but in the end eleven states ratified the Constitution, two more than was needed. The holdouts were North Carolina and Rhode Island.

Why were the delegates opposed to a bill of rights? The short answer: they didn't think it was necessary. As they saw it, the Constitution itself was a bill of rights. Alexander Hamilton declared that a bill of rights was not only unnecessary, it was dangerous. "Why declare that things shall not be done which there is no power to do?" In the past, a bill of rights was a stipulation between kings and their subjects, Hamilton pointed out, like Magna Carta, putting legal restraints on kings from stepping on the rights of citizens. In America, there was no king. In America, Congress protected the rights of the people. With no king there was no one to trample on the people's rights.

Writing to Thomas Jefferson in France, James Madison gave four reasons why he was against a bill of rights: (1) rights not given up were reserved for the people, (2) a list of rights could be either too broad or too narrow and not offer sufficient protection of those rights, (3) state governments would be "jealous" of the powers granted to the new federal government and thus would provide a check on its powers "which has not existed" before, and (4) a bill of rights might not be as effective as people think. "Repeated violations of these parchment barriers have been committed by overbearing majorities in every State," wrote Madison. If most Virginians were of one religious sect, Madison said he did not expect a few sentences in Virginia's Declaration of Rights would deter the majority from imposing its will on a religious minority. In such a case, the government would not be the source of oppression; the source of oppression would be the majority in the community.

The Virginia state ratifying convention helped change Madison's mind. In order to get Virginia's delegates to ratify the Constitution, Madison had no choice but to agree that, yes, a bill of rights was necessary after all, and to promise to amend the Constitution once the new government was in place. Even so, he remained luke-warm at best. Later, in order to get elected to the House of Representatives, he reiterated the need for a national bill of rights. If he still had any misgivings, once he arrived in New York and got wind of the anti-Federalist call for a second constitutional convention, he changed his mind at once. Madison realized that if a bill of rights was not passed by Congress before the Fall adjournment, the anti-Federalists would make good their threat to hold a convention and everything he had worked for during the past three years would be in jeopardy. The problem now was convincing Congress, which had yet to see the light.

THE MAN IN THE MIDDLE

"Best House for Company and Entertainment in the City," was the word on the street. That was the boardinghouse at 19 Maiden Lane run by Dorothy Ellsworth. James Madison roomed there with three fellow Virginians and two Pennsylvanians, all members of the House of Representatives. The Ellsworth Boarding House was central to everything in Madison's life. From there it was a five-minute walk to Federal Hall on Wall Street, and a 10-minute walk to the President's Palace Mansion at 1 Cherry Street. That and attending Sunday service at St. Paul's on Broadway pretty much comprised Congressman Madison's world in the spring and summer of 1789.

Prematurely gray and stoop-shouldered, seeing James Madison treading the lonely byways of New York City was to see a man carrying the weight of the world on his shoulders, or, more accurately, the weight of the federal government. It wasn't easy being James Madison. He didn't make friends easily and didn't have a wife. It seemed no woman would have him (until he met the lovely, widowed Dorothea "Dolley" Payne Todd, whom he would marry in 1794). To his constant annoyance, newspapers were forever misquoting his speeches in Congress. Little wonder: reporters had trouble hearing the the exact words of the soft-spoken Virginian.

Madison was feeling particularly burdened during the first few months of the new government: he was the man in the middle of two opposing political forces. On one side was Congress, dominated by the Federalists who opposed amending the Constitution with a bill of rights. On the other side were the anti-Federalists who were threatening to call a second constitutional convention if something wasn't done about it and quickly.

Madison had one thing in his favor: the support of a hugely-popular president. Getting Washington's support was always the smart move, whether starting a revolution, framing a constitution, or ordering up a new government. Madison courted Washington the previous winter by making three separate visits to Mount Vernon, first to talk Washington into running for president, and second to convince him of the need to amend the new Constitution with a bill of rights.

At first Washington was cool to the idea. Like most Federalists, he saw no reason to amend the Constitution without first giving the new government "a fair trial." He also feared that one amendment would lead to another and to another, and that over time the Constitution would be diluted and thus federal power would be diluted, and the nation would revert back to the bad-old days of the confederation. Madison shared

Washington's fear but said not to amend the constitution would be playing into the anti-Federalists' hands. The risk was there either way. Washington reluctantly agreed, and officially announced his support in the inaugural address. He urged legislators to be careful with what alterations they proposed making to the Constitution. He said: "For I assure myself that whilst you carefully avoid every alteration which might endanger the benefits of an United and effective Government, or which ought to await the future lessons of experience; a reverence for the characteristic rights of freemen, and a regard for public harmony, will sufficiently influence your deliberations on the question."

In case there was any doubt that the president's intentions hadn't been made clear, a month after the inaugural Madison presented the President with 19 bills of rights—a first draft of what would become the United States Bill of Rights. Washington read them carefully and gave his blessing—in a letter to Madison. That summer, whenever the need for a bill of rights was questioned in Congress, Madison only had to produce Washington's letter and to say (presumably), "See this? I have the President's backing."

WHIPPED SYLLABUB

Whipped Syllabub. That's how Aedanus Burke of South Carolina described James Madison's first draft of a bill of rights. It was not meant as a compliment. Madison's list of rights, said Burke, was "not those solid and substantial amendments which the people expect." Burke characterized them as "little better than whip(ped) syllabub, frothy and full of wind, formed only to please the palate. . . ."

The dictionary defines syllabub as a dessert made by beating to a froth sweetened milk or cream, sometimes adding egg whites, and flavoring with wine or liquor. Pour over cake or fruit and you have—that's right—a palate pleaser.

Never mind that Madison's draft was based on the Virginia Declaration of Rights written by scholarly George Mason, or that Mason had borrowed liberally from England's venerable 1669 Bill of Rights. In Burke's mind, Madison hadn't gone far enough. On the other hand, most members of the House saw no need for a bill of rights in the first place, and believed the matter was purely political. Hadn't Madison changed his mind in order to get elected? Besides, a bill of rights had no place in a document that simply described the mechanics of government and granted it limited power. In Federalist No. 84 Hamilton wrote: "Why, for instance, should it be said, that the liberty of the press shall not be restrained, when no power is given by which restrictions may be imposed?"

The road to amending the Constitution with a bill of rights was uphill every step of the way. Madison not only had to convince Congress, but he had to keep reminding himself that it was necessary. As late as June 8, when he addressed Congress in detail about the bill of rights, he made this notation on the outline he had prepared: "Bill of Rights—useful—not essential—." However, believing as he did that the greatest likelihood of tyranny and the true danger to liberty lay in abuses by the majority rather than by the government, Madison put his heart into it by reasoning that a bill of rights would function not so much as a specific set of rules but as a kind of public standard. In time, the values that it embodied would gradually be internalized by society as a whole. "The political truths declared in that solemn manner acquire by degrees the character of fundamental maxims of free government, and as they become incorporated with the national sentiment, counteract the impulses of interest and passion." And, should liberty be endangered by the government, such a standard would be "a good ground for an appeal to the sense of the community."

As we have seen, Madison planted the idea four days after Washington's inaugural address, on Monday, May 4. There was so much other legislation that needed addressing first, however, it seemed Congress would never get around to it. Madison's pledge that debate would begin in three weeks seemed plausible, until reality set in. On May 11, the Senate began debate on the judiciary act. On May 19, the House began debate on the creation of the executive departments of state, treasury and war. On May 25—the fourth Monday of the month—Madison moved to begin debate on the bill of rights amendments. The House had more pressing business and postponed debate. On June 8, Madison raised the issue again, faced the same excuse, but this time he was insistent. If the House continued to postpone debate, Madison said, "it may occasion suspicions, which, though not well-founded, may tend to inflame or prejudice the public mind, against our decisions." Indeed, the public—and most assuredly the anti-Federalists—may very well decide that "we are not sincere in our desire to incorporate such amendments in the constitution as will secure those rights, which they consider as not sufficiently guarded."

Whether or not the House was swayed by his speech, or merely acting out of respect for Madison—or both—a vote was taken and debate began the following morning.

NOWHERE TO HIDE

The atmosphere inside the two chambers of Congress could not have been more different. With only 22 members, the Senate was like a club—exclusive, secretive, cut off from the workaday world. Early on the Senate voted to keep press and public out, and in so doing unwittingly enforced a feeling of exclusivity. Not so inside the House chamber: no clubby atmosphere here and nothing secretive. The House voted to let the press and public in. Suspended above the House floor were two galleries for this purpose—literary "peanut galleries"—where public and press could sit, eat nuts (which they did) while watching the proceedings going on below. It was great theater, as we shall see in later chapters. However annoying the sound of cracking nuts may have been—the acoustic inside the House chamber was reportedly quite good—inviting the outside world in paid unexpected dividends. The press recorded what was taking place on the House floor, and their reports were published in newspapers throughout the thirteen states. This worked to Madison's advantage.

Within eight days of Madison's May 4 announcement that a bill of rights amendment was due up for debate, Madison received a letter from a friend in Virginia telling him that the news of his announcement had been well received among Virginia's anti-Federalists. Madison received another letter from a friend in North Carolina saying now that a bill of rights proposal was in the works, plans were underway in North Carolina for a ratifying convention in November, so it was "extremely important that the amendments, if any, should be proposed before that time."

After the House spent June 8 debating Madison's proposal, it voted to delay further debate for another six weeks, due to the Congressional workload. While Madison was disappointed with yet another setback, this too worked in his favor. His 19 bills of rights that he presented to the House on June 8 were published in the newspapers and therefore were a matter of public record. Six weeks was plenty of time for citizens to read and digest the proposed amendments and to decide their merit. Were they worthwhile or were they, as Burke so colorfully put it, "frothy and full of wind." The people had time to decide for themselves.

With the press reporting House proceedings, it must have seemed to Congressmen that the entire nation was watching. Newspapers would report events and a week or two later House members would receive letters from constituents and friends on how well their actions were being received back home. There was nowhere to hide. Whatever position taken by a Congressman—be it pro or con—became a matter of public record. This too worked in Madison's favor. Congressmen couldn't ignore his proposed amendments—not with North Carolina and Rhode Island awaiting the outcome. Action had to be taken before Congress adjourned at the end of September.

On July 21, Congress took up the issue again. Instead of focusing on the amendments themselves, House members spent most of the day arguing whether or not Madison's amendments should be considered by the House as a whole or by special committee. Late in the day a vote was taken and the matter was sent to special committee. A week later the committee reported back to the House. It accepted most of Madison's recommendations, but made several significant changes, replacing some of his words with phrases that would eventually be incorporated into the Bill of Rights as we know them today. The report was then tabled.

On August 13, and continuing for the next eleven days, the House met as a whole and went over the amendments line-by-line, making more changes. When they were finished, Madison's 19 amendments had become 17 amendments and, in fact, were no longer Madison's amendments: they were the House of Representative's amendments. A vote was taken and at least two-thirds of the 65 House members voted in the affirmative. The amendments now went upstairs to the Senate.

Because the Senate met in private (until 1794), little is known about the Senate debate. What is known is that by the time the Senate completed its work on September 14, it made twenty-six changes to the House amendments. It tightened the language, rearranged some amendments, combined others, and reduced the total number from 17 to 12.

The House agreed with some of the Senate's changes, but rejected others. On September 21, the House appointed a conference committee to meet with their Senate counterparts to iron out the differences. Three days later, having reached agreement, the conference committee issued a report. That same day the House approved the committee's report 37 to 14. The following day, September 25, the Senate approved the report as well. With that, the Bill of Rights passed Congress. A week later, George Washington submitted the 12 amendments to the states for ratification.

An immediate benefit was realized in November when North Carolina joined the Union. Rhode Island would join the following spring. In the end, ten of twelve amendments were ratified by the states for inclusion in the United States Constitution. Madison's home state of Virginia was the tenth and deciding state to vote approval, on December 15, 1791. Three of the original thirteen states that did not ratify the Bill of Rights—Massachusetts, Connecticut, and Georgia—finally did so in 1939, in preparation for the Bill of Rights' sesquicentennial celebration, in 1941.

CHAPTER 8

A Question of Balance

Oliver Ellsworth: now there's a Founding Father you rarely hear about.

Ellsworth was not a pamphleteer like Thomas Paine, nor a mesmerizing orator like Patrick Henry, nor a war hero like George Washington, nor a student of government like John Adams.

Ellsworth was a Connecticut Yankee lawyer whose effectiveness was in smoke-filled rooms where the real business of politics takes place. He was one of the few Founders who actually worked for a living. He was among the four or five most influential delegates at the Constitutional Convention in Philadelphia, although you will not find his name on the document. Once the Constitution was finished and before delegates signed it, Ellsworth was on his way back to Connecticut to resume his law practice.

If Thomas Jefferson is the father of the Declaration of Independence and James Madison is the father of the United States Constitution, Oliver Ellsworth is the father of the United States judicial system. Under his watch the third branch of government—the Supreme Court and the federal appellate court system—was fleshed out.

Curiously, there was no legal precedent for the U.S. Supreme Court. Having three separate-but-equal branches of government—legislative, executive, and judicial—each one acting as a check on the other—was the idea of a French philosopher named Charles Montesquieu (1689-1755). Whether or not Montesquieu's idea would actually work was anybody's guess. The Founding Fathers, however, were determined to give it a try. It was a question of achieving balance among the three branches of government. If they could do that, individual rights and freedoms would not be trampled upon and the experiment that was the United States republic might actually have a chance of surviving.

Most of the debate at the Constitutional Convention was devoted to the creation of the legislative and executive branches. By the time the delegates got around to creating the judicial branch, they were exhausted and ready to go home. The only thing about the federal judiciary on which they all could agree was to say as little as possible and to let the first Congress figure it out later.

In 1789, the time had come for Congress to figure it out. Enter Oliver Ellsworth. Ellsworth was Madison's counterpart in the Senate. Madison was floor leader in the House. Ellsworth was what today would be called the Senate Majority Leader.

On April 7—the day after Congress counted ballots and announced that George Washington was President—the Senate appointed a Special Judiciary Committee with Ellsworth as chairman. The committee consisted of 10 members, one from each state (New York, North

Carolina and Rhode Island were not yet represented). This many people on one committee, each one looking out for the interests of his own state while working on what was a potentially divisive issue, proved unworkable. After one month it was decided the task would be better addressed by a subcommittee of three, chaired by Ellsworth. The Senate subcommittee was comprised of Ellsworth, William Paterson of New Jersey, and Caleb Strong of Massachusetts.

Ellsworth's committee was confronted by two very big problems. One was legal, the other was political.

The legal problem: each of the thirteen states had derived its laws and legal procedures from Anglo-Saxon jurisprudence, which in itself was a veritable legal maze, involving common law, equity, chancery, and statutory law. On top of that, over the previous hundred years, the laws of each state had evolved along somewhat different lines. Each state originated as a colony with its own charter and its own way of dealing with legal issues. With time, each state added new laws and interpreted English law to meet the needs unique to its particular region. By 1789, American law was, as historian Forrest McDonald put it, Anglo-Saxon law compounded by a factor of thirteen.

Ellsworth's job was to create the Supreme Court and a network of inferior federal courts that would insure uniform law throughout the land. The federal court system would have power over the state courts, of course, but how much power? The answer posed a sensitive political problem. The states had been asked to give up a fair amount of executive and legislative power when they ratified the Constitution, and they did so; but when it came to the judiciary they weren't quite as amenable.

Up to this point the anti-Federalists had been playing a losing game. With the federal judicial system being debated in Congress—and opinion about equally divided pro and con—the anti-Federalists saw an opportunity to make converts—should Ellsworth go too far, which seemed likely. Ellsworth was among the staunchest Federalists.

The most eloquent anti-Federalist in the land—Patrick Henry of Virginia—had been predicting all along that the national government would swallow up the states, and that the agent of the devouring would be—what else?—the federal judiciary. Up to now, few had listened to him. His spokesmen in the Senate—Richard Henry Lee and William Grayson—were aping Henry's words and a number of Senators were beginning to listen. In May, when Ellsworth's committee began to meet, it seemed likely that whatever they drew up, if it didn't make broad concessions to the states, would be defeated.

ELLSWORTH'S SLEIGHT OF HAND

The Constitution does not specify the number of Supreme Court justices that are to sit on the bench, but in Article III it authorizes Congress to decide the exact number. Ellsworth and the Special Judiciary Committee fixed the number at six (today the number is nine). That was the easy part. The hard part was creating a system of inferior federal courts that somehow would overcome the objections of both the Federalists and the anti-Federalists.

Ellsworth and his committee drew up a mixture of jurisdictions—a compromise if you will, of federal courts manned by local judges—thereby granting a degree of concurrent jurisdiction to both state and federal courts.

How it worked: the committee proposed one district court for each state. The district courts would be federal, but the judges would be residents of the state to which they were appointed. This would insure that traditional local procedures would be followed, except when different procedures were carefully specified by national law, and thus imposed little that was alien to local lawyers. Moreover, Ellsworth and his committee proposed creation of circuit courts, to consist of two traveling members of the Supreme Court and the district-court judge in the state in which trials were held, the primary function of the district-court judge being to make sure that trials were conducted according to local rules. Finally, Ellsworth proposed to arrange jurisdiction so that in many cases state courts would have concurrent jurisdiction with federal courts, the sanctity of the Constitution being preserved by provision for direct appeal to the United States Supreme Court whenever the constitutionality of state law was in question.

Ellsworth's subcommittee turned the bill over to the Senate at large on June 30. The Senate debated the bill at length, exploring all its aspects: common law, chancery, the number of justices on the Supreme Court, jurisdiction, and jury trials, while at the same time seeking outside advice from constituents, especially attorneys and judges. After 18 days of debate, the Federal Judicial Bill passed the Senate by a vote of 14 to 6. The bill was then sent to the House.

The House sat on the bill for a month while it completed the federal revenue system and began work on the Bill of Rights. Taken up in late August, the bill was delayed yet again when debate began on relocating the capital. When at last the bill was debated in the House, Senator Robert Morris noted that the representatives who were lawyers kept "snarling at it" but could find nothing objectionable. The House passed the bill 29 to 22. On September 24, the president signed the Judiciary Act of 1789 into law.

The Judiciary Act also created the office of Attorney General, and for each judicial district provided for the appointment of a district attorney, a marshal, and one or more deputy marshals.

Years later, James Madison wrote: "It may be taken for certain that the bill organizing the judicial department originated in his (Ellsworth's) draft, and that it was not materially changed in its passage into law." It's likely Ellsworth wrote Section 25, the most important component of the Judiciary Act. This gave the Supreme Court the power to veto state supreme court decisions whenever the state supreme court upheld state laws that conflicted with the U.S. Constitution. At the time, this gave the federal government its only effective authority over state governments.

So it was done. In five months Ellsworth and his committee of two had managed to get the Judiciary Act written, passed by Congress, and signed into law. However, more was needed if the Supreme Court was to be the equal of the executive and legislative branches.

JUDICIAL REVIEW

The Founding Fathers considered the Supreme Court to be the "least dangerous" of the three branches of the federal government. After all, Congress held the purse strings and the President commanded the army. What commensurate power did the Supreme Court have? The possibility that the the Court could, under the principle of judicial review, overturn duly approved legislative acts made it "dangerous" in the eyes of those who saw Congress as enactors of "the will of the people."

Enter James Wilson. Wilson is another Founder you rarely hear about it.

Born in Carskerdy, Scotland, Wilson attended a number of universities in his native country without actually receiving a graduate degree, prior to emigrating to the United States. Once he arrived in American, he took up law and developed a thriving practice in Reading, Pennsylvania that made him rich. He was a signer of the Declaration of Independence, and at the Constitutional Convention he spoke 168 times, more than anyone with the exception of James Madison.

At the Convention, everyone agreed the Supreme Court embodied a basic principle, that self-government could only function under the rule of law, with an independent judiciary interpreting its key provisions. Judicial Review—the court's ability to strike down laws that conflicted with the Constitution—would seem to fall under that provision, but most delegates did not not agree. Judicial Review would give the Supreme Court too much power, they said, and render it "dangerous."

Wilson argued otherwise. The purpose of a Supreme Court was not to undermine legislative authority or to "confer upon the judicial department a power superior, in its general nature," Wilson said. Judicial Review would give the federal government something it would dearly need if the framers were serious about protecting individual liberty against government encroachment, and that was the power of reflection, the power to decide whether a particular law fit within the framework of the Constitution. Judicial Review would act not in defiance of the will of the people, Wilson said, but in addition to it, since judges would sit not as a body of legal experts but as a body of citizens.

As Wilson saw it, the Supreme Court would be one of the United States' most democratic institutions, and would become "the jury of the country." Congress might be enactors of "the will of the people" but the Supreme Court would be protecters of people's individual rights. Despite Wilson's eloquence, a majority of delegates did not agree. After considerable debate Judicial Review was voted down.

As a result, in the first decade (1790-1800), the Supreme Court was hardly the equal of the executive and legislative branches. The first chief justice, John Jay, quit the Court because he thought it had no future.

THE SUPREME AUTHORITY

Enter John Marshall. Unless you're a student of Constitutional Law, Marshall is yet another Founder you rarely hear about. He was not a delegate at either the Continental Convention or the Constitutional Convention. Born in a log cabin in a Virginia frontier settlement, he never left home until he joined Washington's army.

Marshall never went to college. He was instructed at home by his father. Later, he spent a few months listening to legal lectures at the College of William and Mary. That was the extent of his education. He married, settled permanently in Richmond, and by character and brilliance rose to prominence as one of the nation's leading attorneys.

In 1788, at the Virginia Ratifying Convention in Richmond, Marshall spoke in favor of Judicial Review. He told delegates that an independent federal judiciary was a necessary bulwark against an overreaching Congress. If Congress were to exceed its powers, argued Marshall, it would be the duty of the judiciary to declare such action void.

Marshall caught the attention of Washington and Adams who both had an eye for talent. In 1797, President Washington appointed Marshall to a three-man diplomatic team to France to negotiate the infamous XYZ affair. Marshall then served briefly as secretary of state under Adams prior to being appointed chief justice of the Supreme Court in 1800.

Marshall's appointment to the bench was partly Adams' way of getting back at his political nemesis, Thomas Jefferson, for having defeated him in the politically messy 1800 presidential election.

Jefferson was determined to destroy everything the Federalist party had done to strengthen the national government. Well, Adams would see about that. With the appointment of John Marshall, Adams appointed the staunchest Federalist in the land to the one governmental department Jefferson could not control—the Supreme Court. Jefferson was furious with Adams, but there was nothing he could do about it. The lame duck Congress quickly approved the appointment and that was that.

Incredibly, Marshall would put his stamp on nearly every important decision issued from the bench for the next 35 years and in so doing foil every attempt by Jefferson's party to restore power to the states.

"My gift of John Marshall to the people of the United States was the proudest act of my life," Adams said later.

With Jefferson in office, and his party firmly in control of the House and Senate, Marshall feared for the republic's life. He bided his time, however, waiting for a case that would address the balance of power among the three branches of government. He picked a case so trivial and ruled so cleverly that it seemed to give Jefferson the victory.

The case was Marbury v. Madison. The facts were these: President Adams made last-minute, lame-duck appointments of 42 justices of the peace in the District of Columbia, including one William Marbury. Led by Secretary of State James Madison, Jefferson's party withheld a number of these commissions, and Marbury sued. It was a small but implicitly fundamental challenge to the judiciary. Marbury's brief commission had actually expired when the decision was made.

Marshall criticized Madison but ruled Marbury out on a technicality: He didn't have standing.

Jefferson won. Or had he? In a unanimous decision, the court said Marbury didn't have standing because he had brought his case under an earlier congressional act that was unconstitutional. The court ruled in Jefferson's favor by asserting the court's own right to overthrow acts of Congress.

Jefferson was nobody's fool. He knew what Marshall had done, and suspected that the chief justice was hoping to set a precedent that with time would harden into irrevocable law. The only way he could counteract Marshall was to appoint judges who were members of his own party, which Jefferson and his like-minded successors did. It didn't work. Marshall was charismatic as well as smart and made converts of them all. Despite a number Jeffersonian appointments over the years, under Marshall's watch, decisions invariably went against Jefferson's party and were usually unanimous.

From the Marshall court emanated a subtle offensive of Federalist ideas: the rule of law, the sanctity of property, the corporation clothed like an individual, the rights of expanding capitalism, the supremacy of the national government. At the same time, Marshall elevated the Supreme Court to a status equal with that of the executive and legislative branches. The result was what the framers hoped to achieve all along: a government of checks and balances.

Marshall rarely cited cases. He launched his opinions as though they were inevitable deductions from self-evident propositions. When a precedent was called for, he asked Justice Joseph Story—a renowned legal scholar—to find the necessary precedent, saying, "There, Story; that is the law of this case; now go and find the authorities."

While Marshall was not present at the Philadelphia Convention in 1787, according to Richard L. Strout, he was the last great founder of the American Republic. The Continental Congress, the Articles of Confederation, the Declaration of Independence, the Constitution—he put them together and found their essence.

From Marshall's time down to ours, it has not been the legislature nor the presidency, but the Supreme Court that has been the nation's protector of individual rights and freedoms.

CHAPTER 9

AN ENERGETIC EXECUTIVE

You had to be there.

It was Saturday, August 22, 1789. The Senate was in session and who should appear at the door dressed in full military regalia but President George Washington, with the Secretary of War Henry Knox at his side.

The Constitution states that the president shall make treaties "with advice and consent of the Senate." President Washington and Secretary Knox were negotiating a treaty with a southern Indian tribe and were calling on the Senate to seek advice.

The Senate doorman announced Washington's presence. Silence engulfed the chamber as the President entered, dignified, erect, the best-dressed man in the room.

Here's what precipitated the meeting. On August 7, Washington asked Congress to approve his effort to reach an accord with the Creek Indians through "a temporary commission . . . to consist of three persons, whose authority should expire with the occasion." Both Houses agreed and appropriated the necessary funds to carry out the negotiations. Washington selected Gen. Benjamin Lincoln to head up the commission and asked Secretary Knox to draw up instructions. As an afterthought, Washington decided this was the appropriate time to seek the "advice and consent of the Senate."

By prearrangement, Washington wrote out a series of questions. As he entered the chamber he handed his questions to the president of the Senate, Vice President John Adams. What with the street noise coming through the windows, and confusion on the Senate floor, Adams had to read the document twice before submitting the matter to the floor for debate. Senator William Maclay of Pennsylvania protested against taking immediate action and sought to have the questions sent to committee or to have action deferred. Therein a prolonged debate ensued over questions of procedure that became increasingly heated and turned into a shouting match.

How long Washington stood still for this is unknown. At some point, probably when the shouting subsided, Washington declared, "This defeats every purpose of my coming here." He then turned and abruptly walked out. He did so as one witness reported, "with a discontented Air . . . of sullen dignity." And with this parting shot: "I'll be damned if I ever come here again."

In fact, Washington did return, two days later. Cooler heads prevailed, and Washington received the Senate's approval for all that he asked, though he found the debate to be deadly dull. It was the last time Washington would visit the Senate.

As with nearly every action he took as president, Washington had set a precedent. Ever since, presidents have not called in person on the Senate for advice. What, if anything, was lost?

Here's what three of Washington's biographers have written:

Joseph J. Ellis: "From that time onward, the phrase "advise and consent" meant something less than direct executive solicitation of senatorial opinion, and the role of the Senate as an equal partner in the crafting of treaties came to be regarded as a violation of the separation of powers principle."

James Thomas Flexner: "Thus was forever ended the possibility that the American executive might, like the British, present and defend its acts at legislative sessions."

Richard Norton Smith: "(the Senate) had asserted (its) independence, undone the executive's plan to treat them as a kind of privy council, and laid the groundwork for a very different set of presidential advisers, the Cabinet."

WASHINGTON'S CABINET

More than George Washington, it was James Madison who directed the ship of state during the first year of the federal government. Madison was the president's chief advisor. As floor leader of the House of Representatives, he steered all major legislation through Congress. While he didn't always get precisely what he wanted—the 1789 Tariff Act being a prime example—what he did get served the federal government's purpose.

The final piece of important legislation passed in the first session of the First Congress was the creation of the executive departments, and here again Madison was the major player.

On May 19 Elias Boudinot of New Jersey opened the debate, but Madison soon took charge. It was generally agreed that three departments were necessary and that they should have the same responsibilities as the earlier administrative arms of the Confederation: foreign affairs, war, and finance.

As with the Confederation, the primarily concern was with the enormous power vested in the treasury department. The Confederation Congress had addressed the matter in 1874 by replacing Robert Morris—who was thought to have had too much power—with a three-man Board of Treasury.

Debate caused more than one temper to flare in what was a renewal of an old controversy, between those who had supported Morris as superintendent of finance in 1781-1783 and those who had opposed him. Those who had supported Morris believed his financial wizardry saved the nation from certain defeat by the British, while those who had opposed him were convinced he mismanaged public funds, fattened his own purse and those of his friends, and by his actions actually prolonged the war.

Madison favored a single treasury secretary, and steered the thinking in that direction. When the matter was put to vote, advocates of a single treasury secretary prevailed by a narrow margin. However, the uneasiness aroused by the debate led to another decision—to tie the Treasury Department's power to Congress. The Treasury Secretary would be equally accountable to the President and to Congress. Unwittingly, the effect was to pave the way for the first Treasury

Secretary—Alexander Hamilton—to become for all practical purposes prime minister, similar to the chancellor of the exchequer who served in that capacity in England.

The bills establishing the three executive departments were enacted in late summer. The Department of Foreign Affairs (re-designated as the State Department on September 15), was enacted on July 27; the War Department on August 7; and the Treasury Department on September 2. In addition, Congress also provided for the two federal agencies that had less than departmental status: the office of Attorney General, wherein a lawyer was to be placed on retainer to advise the president on matters of constitutionality and law; and the office of Postmaster General, to oversee the execution of the Constitutional mandate for Congress to establish post offices and post roads.

As the summer of 1789 progressed and as Congressional Acts were signed into law, Washington found himself with nearly a thousand appointments to make for a variety of government positions. In making appointments, Washington consulted a number of people, but for the highest offices he consulted with Madison.

For Secretary of State, he wanted John Jay, but Jay had served in that capacity for nearly five years and wanted out. Instead, Washington appointed him as Chief Justice of the Supreme Court. Washington went with Madison's choice to head up the State Department—Thomas Jefferson. Washington's friend Henry Knox was retained as head of the War Department. For Secretary of the Treasury, Washington named his former aide-de-camp Alexander Hamilton. Rounding out the major appointments, Edmund Randolph of Virginia was named Attorney General, and Samuel Osgood of Massachusetts (the same Samuel Osgood who owned the Palace Mansion) was named Postmaster General.

THE VITAL CENTER

Washington supervised the activities of his department heads closely. One didn't drop in on the president "to talk things over." Washington wanted everything in writing—questions, ideas, opinions, policy issues. The President was good at delegating. He had his department secretaries writing reports on matters he referred to their attention: proposed plans of action, opinions, drafting of public papers, and so on. Usually, after an exchange of letters, Washington would invite a respective department head to breakfast where an issue would be discussed until the president was satisfied he understood the matter fully, and had agreement as to the best course of action.

Washington's administration was not about friendship; cabinet members were not cronies. He expected cabinet members to keep him informed, to work hard, and to get results. George Washington would never be mistaken for an "old boy."

Thomas Jefferson, who didn't join Washington's administration as Secretary of State until March 1790, gave the following description of how the executive departments functioned under the first President:

"Letters of business came addressed sometimes to the President, but most frequently to the heads of departments. If addressed to himself, he referred them to the proper department to be acted on; if to none of the secretaries, the letter, if it required no answer, was communicated to the President, simply for his information. If an answer was requisite, the secretary of the department communicated to the letter & his proposed answer to the President. Generally, they were simply sent back after perusal, which signified his approbation. Sometimes he returned them with an informal note, suggesting an alteration or a query. If a doubt of any importance arose, he reserved it for conference. By this means, he was always in accurate possession of all facts and proceedings in every part of the Union, and to whatsoever department they related; he formed a central point for the different branches; preserved an unity of object and action among them; exercised that participation in the suggestion of affairs made incumbent on him; and met himself the duo responsibility for whatever was done. . . . (Washington's system) gave, indeed, to the heads of departments the trouble of making up, once a day, a packet of all their communications for the perusal of the President; it commonly also retarded one day their dispatches by mail. But in pressing cases, this injury was prevented by presenting that case singly for immediate attention; and it produced us in return the benefit of his sanction for every act we did."

Washington proceeded cautiously in 1789 and relied heavily on the advice of others, particularly James Madison. Once he got his bearing, however, he became what Alexander Hamilton described as an "Energetic Executive."

"Energy in the executive," Hamilton wrote in Federalist Essay No. 70, "is a leading character in the definition of good government." He described this quality as "decision, activity, secrecy, and dispatch" and as "vigor and expedition."

"The man at the vital center" was how John Kennedy described an energetic executive. That was George Washington: the man at the vital center, with everything revolving around him. In the affairs of the State Department, Washington believed himself an expert; and in the affairs of the War Department he unquestionably was an expert. In practice he was his own secretary of state and his own secretary of war, which often reduced the roles of Jefferson and Knox to that of mere clerical workers. Jefferson, who was not fond of clerical work, was not always as diligent an administrator as he might have been. Given a free hand on a subject that interested him, he worked promptly and thoroughly, but if he was given only a passive role or (as increasingly happened as time went by) Washington adopted policies with which he disagreed, Jefferson tended to be an obstruction by doing as little as possible. Knox was diligent and relished his position, never initiated or questioned anything, and executed orders with promptness. Hamilton, on the other hand, was an expert in finance and commerce, matters clearly outside of Washington's interest and expertise. As a result, Hamilton enjoyed a much freer hand. Nonetheless, Washington questioned everything he did.

NEWS FROM VIRGINIA

On the first of September, a letter arrived at the Palace Mansion. It came while dinner was being served. The company was good, the mood was light, and the food and drink were plentiful. The President was in high spirits. His health, which was as much a topic of conversation in New York as the latest debate in Congress, was good although Washington was still weak from his June illness. Rumors of a second constitutional convention had mostly ceased. With the 1789 Tariff Act in force, the national government at last had a revenue stream: money to pay salaries and to cover expenses.

Baron Friedrich von Steuben, drillmaster of the Continental Army, and Washington's chief of staff during the final years of the war, was among the dinner guests. The Baron had everyone in stitches, until a mail courier arrived. He had a letter from Fredericksburg, Virginia which was handed directly to the President.

The color in Washington's face drained immediately. He had been dreading this letter since arriving in New York in April. He knew what it said before he opened it. It was word from home that his mother had died. Washington excused himself to read it. Dinner was effectively over and guests departed.

For most of his adult life, Washington's mother had been an embarrassment to him. During the Revolution, she encouraged a motion in the Virginia legislature to grant her a pension, which prompted the General to dash off a letter of protest to the Speaker of the House: "Before I left Virginia, I answered all her calls for money, and since that period, have directed my steward to do the same. Whence her distresses can arise, therefore, I know not . . . she has not a child that would not divide the last sixpence to relieve her. . . ." Mary Ball Washington never acknowledged her son's many accomplishments and his wide-spread fame. As one Washington biographer put it, she was stingy with praise and lavish with demands.

Washington ordered black cockages (a type of flower), sword knots and arm-ribbons to be worn by the men of the Palace household, but he did not "go into deep mourning." The regular levees were suspended for a week; after that social activity resumed as before.

On September 13 Washington wrote his sister Betty Washington Lewis, revealing something of how he felt:

"My dear Sister, Colonel Ball's letter gave me the first account of my Mother's death—since that I have received Mrs. Carter's letter written at your request—and previous to both I was prepared for the event by some advices of her illness communicated to your Son Robert.

"Awful, and affecting as the death of a Parent is, there is consolation in knowing that Heaven has spared ours to an age, beyond which few attain, and favored her with the full enjoyment of her mental faculties, and as much bodily strength as usually falls to the lot of four score. Under these considerations and a hope that she is translated to a happier place, it is the duty of her relatives to yield due submission to the decrees of the Creator—When I was last at Fredericksburg, I took a final leave of my Mother, never expecting to see her more."

SIX HOUSES FOR THE PRESIDENT

On another occasion at the Palace Mansion, during a public dinner, something both comic and nearly tragic occurred. A woman attended wearing a tall headdress made of ostrich feathers. The ceiling was low and she brushed her headdress against the candles on the overhead chandelier and the feathers caught fire. The fire was put out quickly and no one was hurt, but for George Washington it was yet another reason why he wanted to move.

The Palace Mansion at 1 Cherry Street had proved too small to meet the President's needs. There were not enough rooms to meet the growing needs of the nation's chief executive. And there was that low ceiling. It was fine if you were, say, five-foot-seven, as most men were then, but not if you were six-foot-two, as Washington was. There were other problems as well. When the house was built in 1770, the neighborhood was among the finest in the city; since the war, however, the neighborhood had deteriorated. Two blocks over from the mansion, the wharves along the East River had extended farther north and now crowded the waterfront, bringing with them the noise and smells of commercial activity. Since moving to New York, Washington missed the view of the Potomac, and the East River was no Potomac. The East River was the business-side of Manhattan, where longshoremen were forever transferring cargo on and off ships.

Washington wanted a house on the west side of Manhattan, one with a view of the Hudson. There were two such houses that met the President's needs. One was Richmond Hill, situated a mile north of town on a high promontory overlooking the Hudson. It had two problems. One, it was occupied by vice president John Adams, and, two, it was too far out of the way. The second house was located on Broadway. Currently, it was rented by the French minister, the Comte de Moutiers, who, as luck would have it, would be returning to France after the first of the year. This was the Macomb House, at 39 Broadway. Built in 1786, the Macomb House was the largest residence in the city: four-stories tall and occupying most of a city block. Washington planned to take possession in February.

There was a third house to consider, but it had yet to be built. It was called The Government House and was designed expressly to be the permanent residence of the President of the United States. It was yet another attempt by New York politicians to convince Congress to keep the nation's capital in Manhattan. Government House was to be built at the foot of Broadway and to face Bowling Green Park. The windows facing south would have an unobstructed view of Upper New York Bay. The state legislature passed an act to build the house on March 16, 1790. Commissioners announced "they are desirous of receiving plans for a house to contain, a room for the reception of the Legislature on public business, and drawing and dinning room for special occasions; a drawing and dining room for private use, a room for a library with other requisite apartments and accommodations."

The state also planned to widen Broadway and to build a larger Capitol Building, on Broadway or possibly across the East River in Brooklyn.

By April 20, 1790 the commissioners agreed on a plan and authorized the construction of The Government House to begin. The cornerstone was laid on May 21, and the building was completed the following year, in the spring of 1791. By that time, the federal government had moved to Philadelphia. Government House became the home of state governors until 1799, when the state capital moved to Albany. After that, it was used as a customs house until 1815, when it was unceremoniously torn down.

There were three other executive mansions, bringing the total to six. One was the Masters-Penn-Morris House at 190 High Street in

Philadelphia, which served as the Presidential Mansion for the ten-year period the capital was in Philadelphia; another was The President's House, on Ninth Street, in Philadelphia. The President's House, like New York's Government House, was built expressly for the President in what was Philadelphia's attempt to keep the capital in that city. Also like Government House, no president ever lived there. The sixth Presidential house is in Washington, D.C. Today it is known as the White House. With the exception of George Washington, every president of the United States has lived there. For 100 years it was known as the Executive Mansion. It was Theodor Roosevelt who, in 1901, first referred to the Executive Mansion as "The White House." He had the name printed on presidential stationary and it caught on with the press. Thereafter the Executive Mansion has been known as "The White House."

CHAPTER 10

The People's Champion

"A Complete Revolution In France."

That was the headline of the New York Daily Gazette of September 19, 1789. By the time news of the French Revolution reached American it was two-months old.

On July 14, 1789, after five days of rioting, an angry mob stormed the Bastille, released seven prisoners, killed the commanding officer and, brandishing his decapitated head on a pike, paraded through the streets of Paris. In the days that followed, the rampaging mob took control of the city. France, friend and ally of America in her time of revolution, was herself now embroiled in revolution.

Two Americans were in Paris at the time: Thomas Jefferson, U.S. minister to France; and Gouverneur Morris, signer of the U.S.

Constitution, who was there on personal business. Neither saw the crisis coming. No one had.

The revolution was mainly the result of French foreign policy, particularly (and ironically) as the result of France's support of the American Revolution, which had bled the state treasury dry. The problem worsened considerably by a bread shortage and became intolerable when Louis XVI fired the one government minister in whom the common people of France had faith, a Swiss financier named Jacques Necker. Necker was the people's hope, a government official of high political standing who championed their cause.

Born in Geneva, Necker moved to Paris in 1750 where he made his fortune in banking and in grain speculation. In 1776, on the recommendation of Paris bankers, the king appointed him director of the state treasury; a year later he was promoted to director-general of finance. Necker knew how to make money multiply, and he pushed for social reform. While reform measures endeared him to the downtrodden (which included nearly everyone outside the clergy and nobility) it made him an enemy of the nobility.

Necker refused salary, and lent the cash-strapped treasury two million livres out of his own pocket. Rather than raise taxes ("the people have been taxed enough," he said), he was able to float loans that within a year brought to the treasury another 148 million livres. He established better order, accountability, and economy within the treasury department, and abolished over 500 government jobs, most of which paid a salary but required little or no work. He reduced inequities in taxation, improved hospitals, and organized pawnshops to lend money to the poor at low interest. He prevailed upon Louis XVI to allow the establishment of provincial assemblies in Berry, Grenoble, and Montauban, and he set an important precedent by arranging that in these gatherings, the representatives of the Third

Estate (the middle and lower classes) should equal those of the nobility and the clergy combined.

The king, however, who chose the members of these assemblies, would not grant them any legislative authority. Undeterred, Necker won a substantial victory by inducing the King to free all remaining serfs on the royal domain, and invited all feudal lords to follow the king's example by freeing their serfs. They declined. In 1780, again on Necker's prompting, the king ordered an end to judicial torture, the disuse of subterranean prisons, the separation of prisoners duly convicted of crimes from those not yet tried, and the separation of both of these groups from those arrested for debt.

Across the Atlantic, meanwhile, Americans were fighting a war for independence. The American Revolution was popular with nearly everyone in France—king, clergy, the rich and the poor. It was Necker's job to raise the necessary sums that France lent to America: one million livres in 1776, three million in 1778, another million in 1779, four million in 1780, four million in 1781, and six million in 1782. In addition, he raised money to finance the French government, army, navy, and court. He did so without raising taxes.

To foster confidence in the financial community, and with the King's blessing, Necker published in 1781, "A Compte rendu au Roi," a report that said the French government was once again financially sound. Necker was acclaimed as a financial genius who had saved the government from bankruptcy. With that, the attacks began, mostly from within the French court which resented his increasing influence with the king. Necker was accused of cooking the books and of being a revolutionist who planned to undermine the monarchy by establishing more provincial assemblies. Necker did not help his cause by demanding more and greater reform powers. Government ministers joined together and threatened to tender their resignations if the king didn't fire Necker at once. The King saw no choice but to acquiesce. Necker was out, and all Paris mourned.

Without Necker, the French government slipped into bankruptcy. Necker, meanwhile, retired to his Swiss estate and wrote his memoirs: "A Treatise on the Administration of the Finance of France." It was published in 1784. Alexander Hamilton who by now had read Adam Smith's "Wealth of Nations," got his hands on the English edition and devoured all three volumes.

NECKER'S RETURN

In 1788, with the French monarchy teetering on the brink of financial collapse, Louis XVI asked Jacques Necker to return to his position in the French government, with the promise of more power than before, the new title of secretary of state, and a seat on the Royal Council. Necker accepted.

A huge crowd gathered in the courtyard of the Versailles Palace to welcome him back. "Yes, my children," he said, tearing up. "I remain; be comforted."

As a gesture to restore confidence, Necker put two million francs of his own into the treasury and pledged his personal fortune as partial guarantee of the state's financial commitments. He revoked an earlier order requiring bondholders to accept paper instead of money and as a result government bonds rose thirty percent on the market. The bankers, happy that Necker was back, advanced the treasury sufficient funds to tide over the financial crises for one year.

Superficially, France was in a situation similar to that of America in 1787; it was saddled with a crushing war debt, a political system that blocked any revenue stream, and a government in need of reform. Change was needed and fast. Where to begin? Tax reform. France's wealthy elite—the clergy and the nobility—paid little or no taxes while the commoners shouldered the bulk of the nation's tax burden—on very little income. While Necker was out of office the Assembly of Notables had met for the purpose of changing the tax structure, and failed. On Necker's advice, the king called for an assembly of the Estates General, which was comprised of representatives of all three Estates: the First Estate (clergy), the Second Estate (nobility), and the Third Estate (commoners). It was an historic occasion: the first meeting of the Estates-General in over 150 years, but did it mean anything? Could they do what the Assembly of Notables had failed to do? No one realized it at the time, but the fate of France hung in the balance.

Many people were hopeful, including Thomas Jefferson. He was appalled at the grinding poverty he saw daily in the streets of Paris, and on occasion he had seen angry crowds roaming the streets "rehearsing revolution" as one historian put it. His letters home, however, brimmed with confidence that reforms were under way and that all would be well in the end. Gouverneur Morris saw no reason not to be optimistic either. Necker had averted a famine by putting a stop to the export of grain and by importing seventy million livres' worth of additional grain into the country. A number of the wealthy had even opened their doors to feed and warm the poor, and one monastery had fed twelve hundred people daily for six weeks.

Once the Estates-General convened in June, however, any chance of the three Estates working together vanished quickly. The Third Estate, which had as many numbers as the First Estate and Second Estate combined, demanded that voting be by head, rather than by Estate. This would have boosted its relative strength and given it the power necessary to bring equity to the tax laws. When this was denied by the First and Second Estates, which weren't about to give up their advantage over the commoners, the Third Estate walked out, changed its name to the National Assembly, and began meeting separately.

Louis XVI, who was willing to inaugurate a reform movement that he could control, reacted badly. Over Necker's objection, on July 1 he summoned ten regiments to threaten the National Assembly and make it disperse. Instead, the Assembly began drawing up plans for a new government—a constitutional monarchy similar to that of England. On July 8, the Assembly asked the King to remove his troops. Louis XVI refused, saying something to the effect that the troops were there not to harm them but to protect them from outside danger. Three days later, on July 11, the King dismissed Necker and ordered him to leave Paris at once.

With the sudden fall of Necker—the only man in government in whom the people had faith—the streets of Paris erupted. On July 14 the Bastille was taken. The French Revolution and the horror it would unleash had began.

HAMILTON DREAMS BIG

It was one of the defining moments in Alexander Hamilton's political career, perhaps the defining moment. He began reading Jacques Necker's memoirs and in the introduction was a passage that seemed to be addressed directly to him. It read:

"There are men whose zeal ought not to be cooled. Such are those who being conscious that they are qualified for great things, have a noble thirst for glory; who being impelled by the force of their genius, feel themselves too confined within the narrow limits of common occupations; and those, more especially, who being struck with the idea of the public good, meditate on it, and make it the most important business of their lives. Proceed, you, who after silencing self-love find your resemblance in this picture."

Alexander Hamilton was the type who liked to throw caution to the wind, who leaped before he looked, and always made a big splash. When the American Revolution begun, he quit school to join the Continental Army and missed college graduation by a single month. It wasn't enough for him to rise up through the ranks and become General Washington's chief-of-staff. Against the General's wishes, he demanded—and got—his own battalion, and at Yorktown led a bayonet charge into enemy fire to take a key redoubt that led ultimately to General Cornwallis' surrender.

Having helped initiate the federal government, Hamilton's next goal was to replace land with money as the source of wealth, because money rewarded merit and was oblivious to class, color, and social standing. He hoped to achieve this goal as Secretary of the Treasury, first by funding the war debt with a new issue of United States securities, and second by creating a national bank. Without a gold reserve, he hoped to make public securities—mere paper—as good as gold.

As with Necker, Hamilton saw his role as two-fold: as the nation's accountant, and as a social reformer.

Exactly when Washington decided to make Hamilton Treasury Secretary is not known, but it must have been early on. Hamilton had been preparing himself to be the nation's treasurer, and acted as if he were confident that the appointment would be forthcoming. In 1788 he was active politically but avoided running for office. In 1789, a few days after Washington's inaugural, he told fellow lawyer Robert Troup that the president had asked him to accept the secretaryship, and he asked Troup to be prepared to take over his law practice. Four weeks after the inauguration, in a letter dated May 27, Madison wrote

Jefferson that Hamilton would likely be appointed once the Treasury Department was created.

If Hamilton's grand schemes were to succeed, he knew three conditions had to be met. First, he would need the support of James Madison, the ablest and most influential man in government. Second, the Treasury Department would have to be under the control of one man, not three as had been the case with the impotent three-man Board of Treasury under the Articles of Confederation. Third, and most important, he would need a measure of independence from the president and be permitted to deal directly with Congress. With regard to the third point, what he really wanted was to have a role similar to that of the British Prime Minister, be appointed and replaced with consent of Congress, and be unencumbered by term limits.

What Congress created was not too far removed from what Hamilton wanted. The Treasury Department would operate under the direction of one man, with an auditor and comptroller to settle and keep track of public accounts, a register to record them, a treasurer to hold the money, and so forth. The idea was to keep the Treasury Secretary free of mundane tasks, and not to place him in a position where he could be easily accused of improprieties. The only government money that actually would touch his hands would be his own salary. The president would appoint him to office, with advice and consent of the Senate, and he would report directly to the House on matters concerning revenue and public credit.

The Treasury Secretary was given a wide range of duties and a goodly measure of latitude in carrying them out. He was empowered to appoint his assistant, superintend the collection of the revenues, decide upon the forms of keeping accounts, and prepare and report budgetary estimates. He would make reports, "and to give information to either branch of the Legislature, in person or in writing (as he may be required), respecting all matters referred to him or which shall pertain to his office."

Among his immediate tasks was to prepare a special report, due to be given in Congress the following January, that would "digest and prepare plans for the improvement and management of the revenue, and for the support of public credit." This would include determining the extent of foreign and domestic debt, and recommending a systematic means of payment.

Nine days after signing the Treasury Department Act, Washington sent Hamilton's nomination to the Senate for confirmation. It was confirmed on the same day. Two days later, on Sunday, September 13, Hamilton went to work.

CHAPTER 11

Pleasing No One

Of all the issues addressed by Congress in the first session, it was by far the most divisive. In April, mere days after achieving a quorum, the issue threatened to destroy the fragile government before it had a chance to prove itself. The issue? Deciding where to relocate the nation's capital.

An observer wrote: "Special interest, always more active than public interest, was at the point yesterday of inciting a great tumult in Congress at its very debut. The Pennsylvanians . . . want this sovereign Assembly to reside in their State at all costs. . . . It was only with difficulty that they decided to defer this distinct measure." This was on April 17, 1789, before Washington even arrived in New York.

As he would do many times that first year, James Madison restored order. He told the Pennsylvanian Congressmen to be patient. The residency question would be addressed before the end of the first session, and everyone would have a say in the decision. On August 28, with the end of the first session in sight, the question of where to move the capital was addressed once again.

Congress was clearly divided and emotions ran high. The Pennsylvanians wanted the capital moved back to their beloved Philadelphia, the city that had given birth to the Declaration of Independence and to the U.S. Constitution. Other northern states preferred to keep the capital in New York City. Southern states, not at all happy with the north's growing abolition movement, were intent on moving the capital to a southern location where slavery wasn't questioned, such as Maryland or Virginia.

As debate got underway it was clear Philadelphia had the most support in both houses. It was a large, cultured city, and centrally located. Philadelphia was ruled out, however, when it was decided that the capital should not be within the confines of an existing city. What was being called for was the creation of a new city, within a 100-square mile federal district, over which Congress would have exclusive jurisdiction.

Where to put such a city? The Pennsylvania delegation made a strong case for locating the new capital on an open tract of land on the Susquehanna River, between Lancaster and York. James Madison, the leader of the Potomac faction, argued long and vehemently for locating the capital near Georgetown, Maryland, on the banks of the Potomac. At times the debate turned ugly. Richard Bland Lee of Virginia intimated darkly that the fate of the Union rested on the House decision, saying, "should Congress dare to keep the capital in Pennsylvania, it would devastate Southerner's faith in the union." The Potomac faction, however, could not muster the necessary votes.

When the question was put to a vote, the House passed the bill designating the Susquehanna River as the site of the new capital. The fate of the Residency Bill was now in the hands of the Senate.

Had the Pennsylvania delegation been united, the bill likely would have passed the Senate and today the Capital of the United States would be on the banks of Susquehanna River and not on the Potomac, in the state of Pennsylvania instead of Maryland. But the Pennsylvania delegation was split.

The leading advocate for the Susquehanna location was William Maclay, of Harrisburg, Pennsylvania. He knew the Susquehanna well, having surveyed the land along its banks. The debate pitted Maclay against fellow Pennsylvanian Robert Morris. Morris, it will be remembered, was the Philadelphia merchant who pledged his personal fortune as collateral to pay Washington's army at Yorktown. As the archetypal money man, he had a reputation for being someone who could get things done. Morris favored a location either at Germantown, just outside Philadelphia, or on the Delaware River near Trenton, New Jersey where he had been acquiring land. To sweeten the deal, Morris promised to throw in $100,000 of his own money.

Behind the scenes, Morris lobbied Senators from several Northern states to switch their support from the Susquehanna to the Delaware. He promised the two New York senators that if they voted for Germantown, he and his allies would agree to block removal of the government from NewYork City before 1793, even if the new capital was ready sooner. When Maclay found out what Morris was up to, he became enraged. "Mr. Morris (was) running backwards and forwards like a boy, taking out one senator after another to them," he wrote in his journal. "No business was ever treated with more barefaced partiality."

On September 24 Morris moved to delete the Susquehanna from the bill, and to leave a blank in its place, confident that the space would be filled with Germantown. For much of the day, conflicting motions clouded the debate, among them a motion to reconsider the Potomac for the seat of government. Finally, as Morris had hoped, his back-room lobbying paid off. When at last the votes were counted, the Susquehanna was struck out. Morris immediately proposed inserting Germantown in its place. Maclay was so furious that he voted against the motion, leaving the Senate evenly divided, nine to nine. Who would break the tie? Vice President John Adams.

What say you, Mr. Vice President? The Susquehanna or the Delaware?

According to Maclay, who left the only record of Adam's response, the vice president at first tried to please everyone. He praised the Potomac location. He praised New York. He praised Philadelphia. He said if it were up to him, the capital would alternate between these two cities, spending four years at a time in each. Finally, he tipped his hand by saying a few disparaging remarks about the Susquehanna location, and then cast his vote for Germantown. Maclay was devastated, certain it was Morris's $100,000 that clinched the deal. On September 28, the bill went back to the House for approval.

At that point, Morris surely assumed the House would pass the Residency Bill and the future capital of the United States would be located on the banks of the Delaware near Germantown, Pennsylvania. What he hadn't counted on was James Madison's tenacity and resourcefulness.

Madison knew the stakes. Unless he found a way to cripple the bill, his dream of seeing the capital located on the Potomac would be dashed forever. But how? When attempts by fellow Southerners failed to postpone the vote, Madison turned to several influential New Yorkers for assistance. He persuaded them to pressure their senators to help postpone the bill until the next session. Postponement would give New York a chance, however slight, of keeping the capital in New York City. They agreed.

Madison next proposed a minor amendment to the Bill which the House approved. The Bill went back to the Senate for a vote on the amendment. As Madison hoped, the Senate decided to postpone their vote until the next session, beginning in January 1790.

According to one historian, Morris had over-played a winning hand. On September 30, Congress adjourned.

JOHN ADAMS—OUT OF STEP

Trying to please everyone and pleasing no one. That was John Adams in 1789.

Perhaps he'd stayed in Europe too long, become too accustomed with the ways of monarchical government, and grown out out-of-touch with America. One thing was certain: he was out of step with George Washington.

Upon his return to America in 1788, Adams was viewed as a great statesman with a number of impressive accomplishments to his credit, including the Paris Peace Treaty that ended the Revolution, and several Dutch loans that kept the nation's ailing economy on life support. It was no surprise when he was elected second in command to George Washing as vice president.

In the early months of Washington's administration, Adams was guilty perhaps of trying too hard. He was too nice, too guarded, and perhaps too eager to please the president. He made himself a laughing stock in the Senate when he insisted the president be addressed as "His Excellency" or "His Majesty." Yes, in the early days of the new government, Adams clearly was out of touch.

Twelve years earlier, at the Continental Congress in Philadelphia, it was a different story. Adams was at the center of the whirlwind, the agitator, the firebrand, the unstoppable force who convinced the delegates to go against their better judgement and declare independence from England. Adams was a king-maker: he picked George Washington to lead the Continental Army. He recognized talent: he picked Thomas Jefferson to draft the Declaration of Independence. While he was away in Europe, a new generation of national leaders had risen—James Madison, Alexander Hamilton, and John Jay. In Adams' absence, the Constitution was drafted, "The Federalist Papers" were written, and the new government was ratified by the states. And the status of General George Washington was elevated to that of king.

John Adams biggest problem was himself. He was honest, forthright, and brilliant. And fussy, hypersensitive, and opinionated. He said what he felt, which often got him in trouble. Somehow, he managed to offend nearly everyone he met.

Ben Franklin characterized Adams as "always an honest man, often a great one, and sometimes absolutely mad."

Said Thomas Jefferson: "He hates Jay, he hates the French, he hates the English."

As James McHenry, who would later serve as Adams' secretary of war, explained, whether Adams was "sportful, playful, witty, kind, cold, drunk, sober, angry, easy, stiff, jealous, careless, cautious, confident, close, open, it is almost always in the wrong place or to the wrong person."

While Adams was second in command, he didn't feel like he was second in command. He felt far down on the list of important people. Adams' feelings at the time can be summed up best in his owns words, spoken after he was sworn is as vice president. "Gentlemen, I feel a great difficulty how to act. I am vice president. In this I am nothing, but I may be everything. But I am President also of the Senate." He then asked, "When the President comes into the Senate, what shall I be?"

What Adams would not be was Washington's leader in Congress. That role belonged to James Madison, the floor leader in the House of Representatives, and in 1791 it would pass to Alexander Hamilton. Nor would Adams be among Washington's inner circle of Madison, Hamilton, Jay, and Knox. He would not be among the select group of decision-makers who would shape the nation during Washington's crucial eight years as president. Washington would have nothing to do with a man who could not control his mouth or his emotions. Adams was invited to the Executive Mansion on social occasions, of course, but when Washington's cabinet began meeting in 1790, Adams was left out.

Adams did enjoy one small consolation. No one else in the federal government lived in as nice a house. "Never did I live in so delightful a spot," Adams said. Located one mile north of town, on a promontory overlooking the Hudson River, the Richmond Hill manor was a royal retreat but too far off the beaten path. The house, like Adams himself, was outside the sphere of activity.

John Adams would be the first but certainly not the last vice president to complain about the office. "(It is) the most insignificant office that ever the invention of man contrived or his imagination conceived," Adams said. Thomas R. Marshall, the 28th Vice President said: "Once there were two brothers. One ran away to the sea; the other was elected vice president of the United States. And nothing was heard of either of them again." John Nance Garner, who served as vice president from 1933 to 1941 under FDR, perhaps said it best. "The vice presidency isn't worth a pitcher of warm piss."

It all might have turned out differently had someone else been elected as the first vice president of the United States. In an era of precedent-setting, it seems the Adams' vice presidency set the precedent for all future vice presidents.

CHAPTER 12

THOMAS JEFFERSON, AESTHETE

Thomas Jefferson was not good at goodbyes.

When he left Paris on September 28, 1789, he avoided bidding adieu to all but a few kindred spirits (Lafayette, La Rochefoucauld, and Condorcet) and slipped out of town quietly.

The political storms that overtook Paris in July had given way to relative calm in August and September, as the nation waited for the National Assembly to create a constitutional government. Having seen his personal guard wiped out, King Louis XVI was relegated to the role of interested observer. Outside Paris, the king remained popular with the common people. But for how long? Bread shortages continued to be an everyday fact of life.

On August 4, the National Assembly abolished feudalism in what was known as the August Decrees, sweeping away both the signeurial rights of the Second Estate (nobility) and the tithes gathered by the First Estate (church). Using the United States Declaration of Independence as a model, on August 26 the Assembly published the Declarations of the Rights of Man and the Citizens. At the same time, next to nothing was being done about the financials crisis, which was the reason for calling a meeting of the National Assembly in the first place.

Jefferson watched these events with an approving eye, convinced that something wonderful was happening. He planned to spend Christmas at Monticello, pay his debts, and return to Paris in the spring. At the port of La Harve he was confronted with a storm out on the Atlantic that delayed his voyage for two weeks. On the day of departure, a fellow traveler observed the tall Virginian standing out in the weather with his daughters Patsy and Polly gathered around him, reading out loud to their father while he helped Polly pronounce the difficult words. The Jefferson party included two slaves: Jim Hennings, who had been taught the fine art of French cooking while in Paris, and his sister Sally Hennings. Among the items being shipped to Monticello were 288 bottles of French wine, a coach, and a harpsichord.

While on a short layover in England, Jefferson read in the London newspapers that back in France 5000 angry women had marched to Versailles demanding that more be done about the bread shortages, and that as a sign of good faith the king and his administration return to Paris. Despite Jefferson's letters to America stating that the worst of the crisis was over, the French Revolution was in fact just beginning, and would last until 1799 and be far bloodier than anyone dared imagine.

The crew on board Jefferson's ship *The Clermont* predicted a nine-week voyage. Crossing the Atlantic was always a dicey business. Pirates could attack; a sudden storm could rise up and dash the ship to pieces. Even on the calmest of days passengers were confined to their tiny wooden cubbies below deck, with little to do and little to eat but hard biscuits, salt port, and fish. All the while waves toyed with the ship, tossing, turning, and dropping it fiercely, so that it pitched and rolled and for the first couples of weeks made passengers sick.

With storms having subsided, Jefferson's ship encountered favorable winds and made the journey in a remarkably short 26 days (just shy of three weeks). *The Clermont* made port at Norfolk on November 23.

Jefferson so admired the lines of a table on board the ship that he left word with the captain that he wanted a duplicate made in London, of the finest mahogany, and be shipped to his hotel in France. As it turned out, he received the table one year later, not in France, but in Virginia, as Jefferson's plans changed. While crossing the Atlantic, President George Washington had appointed him Secretary of State. Jefferson received word of his appointment when he arrived in Norfolk.

THE AMERICAN ATHENS

Thomas Jefferson liked to speak of Republican simplicity and virtue. He said, "The government that governs least, governs best." When it came to public buildings, however, these sentiments flew out the window. For the capitol building of Virginia, he wanted something with, as he put it, "the ring of eternity." In the heart of rural Virginia, in a town of about 1,800 people, he wanted to replicate a Roman Temple. In the great hall inside, in place of a Roman god, he wanted a statue of George Washington.

As minister to France, Thomas Jefferson fell passionately in love with a number of grand buildings. According to his biographer Dumas

Malone, he "was so violently smitten with the *Hotel de Salm* that he used to go to the Tuileries almost every day to see it, generally sitting on a parapet and twisting his head around until his neck got stiff." He so loved the building that he used it as his model for the redesign of Monticello he planned to undertake once he returned home.

While governor of Virginia, Jefferson ordered the state capital be moved from Williamsburg to a small town on the upper James. At the time, Richmond was a mere shadow of the cultural, intellectual and economic center that was Williamsburg. The move would presage by fifteen years the relocation of the nation's capital from New York to a cow pasture on the Potomac, also instigated by Jefferson. Jefferson relished the idea of creating a city from scratch, one that would be unmarred by commerce, industry, and moneymen, with buildings of white marble and grand columns that recalled classic Athens.

The design of the Virginia capitol had yet to be determined when Jefferson was appointed minister to France. No matter. After finding a suitable model in France, he would draft a blueprint and forward it home. In the south of France he found the perfect building—the *Maison Carree.* A Roman temple no less, with Corinthian columns, a deep portico, pilasters on the sides, and no windows. Now this, Jefferson thought, was a building with "the ring of eternity."

Back in Richmond, meanwhile, work began on a building that, to Jefferson's taste, simply would not do. From France, he ordered all work to cease, the building be torn down, and work to begin anew on his design, the plans of which would be forthcoming. He wrote: "(My plans) are simple and sublime. More cannot be said. They are not the brat of whimsical conception never before brought to light, but copied from the most precious, the most perfect model of ancient architecture on earth." Who was the Virginia Assembly to question Thomas Jefferson? They agreed.

The *Maison Carree* may have been (in Jefferson's words) "the most perfect model of ancient architecture on earth," but it was not designed to function as a public building. Several changes were needed in order to make it habitable for government use. The design was enlarged to house the executive, legislative and judicial branches of state government; Ionic columns were substituted for Corinthian (too impractical to replicate); the pilasters were removed from the sides (also impractical); the depth of the portico was reduced from three columns to two; and windows were cut in the walls to let in light (marring the building's unbroken lines).

Construction was not finished at the time Jefferson returned from France, but what he saw he didn't like. They had ruined his perfect building. Jefferson, who avoided confrontation like the plague, travelled on without comment. He arrived home in Monticello two days before Christmas, and wasn't happy with the building he saw there, either. His time in France had heightened his aesthetic sense.

MR. JEFFERSON BUILDS HIS DREAM HOUSE

It was not the Monticello we know today. The house Jefferson returned to on December 23, 1789 was similar to most southern plantation homes in Virginia. It was impressively large and consisted of a central two-story block of rooms with wings on each side. What set the house apart were the double porticoes—one order of columns on top of another—on the east and west sides of the house. The lower level consisted of four Doric columns that were topped on the upper level by four Ionic columns. Jefferson copied this double portico motif from Andrea Palladio's architectural treatise, *The Four Books of Architecture.*

Before unpacking his bags, Jefferson walked around the exterior of his house and noted signs of neglect during his long absence: flaking paint, warped panels, the still-unfinished porticos. A few repairs here and there, the completion of the porticos, and a fresh coat of paint and the house would be good as new. He then would have a house that, well, bored him.

Jefferson decided much of the existing house would have to come down. He had a new design in mind. His European experience had given him an opportunity to see for himself several of the most stylish examples of French Palladianism. The Palladian design that captured his heart was the aforementioned *Hotel de Salm* in Paris. It was a wide rectangular building with a central, semicircular columned bay, capped with a dome. Because the structure sat low on the foundation, it appeared smaller and more compact than it actually was. When Jefferson redesigned Monticello, the image of this intriguing rectangular building with the unique dome was foremost in his mind.

Those who knew Jefferson well believed Monticello would never be finished. It would always be a work in progress and therefore subject to change, depending on Jefferson's latest architectural whim. Work originally began in 1768 with the clearing of a mountaintop near the Jefferson family home. The decision to build his dream house atop an 867-foot mountain rather than beside a broad river set Jefferson apart from other Virginia planters and added significantly to building difficulties.

Rivers were the lifeblood of Virginia. Rivers joined the interior regions to the Tidewater, and to the world. The Potomac, Rappahannock, York, and James Rivers allowed Virginia's chief commercial product, tobacco, to be transported with relative ease from the inland counties to the shipping ports of the Chesapeake. It was along these rivers that the great plantation manor houses were built. Rivers made it easy to transport the needed building materials, furniture, and supplies. Deciding to build his house atop a mountain meant that lumber, bricks, doors, windows, furniture, Jefferson's voluminous library, as well as drinking water, would have to be hauled to the mountaintop. Why go to all the trouble? To enjoy the panoramic view from the top, of course. It was a case of putting aesthetics ahead of practicality.

Most substantial plantation homes were built by skilled craftsmen. Usually, a master bricklayer or carpenter assumed the role of what today would be a general contractor; he would hire and supervise other carpenters, sawyers, joiners, bricklayers, plasterers and painters. Slaves did the digging, the hauling, the heavy lifting. Architectural designs were either copied from existing houses or selected from pattern books and modified to meet the owner's requirements. Jefferson, however, not only designed his own house, he acted as his own general contractor. He insisted on paying as he went in order to keep from going deeper in debt. Money often ran out and Jefferson was away a lot. As a result, work proceeded at irregular intervals. Sixteen years passed when he departed for France in 1784, and still his Monticello dream house was not finished.

Upon his return in 1789, he decided to tear down much that was finished and start over again. It must have seemed like madness to his neighbors, but to Jefferson it made perfect sense. He wasn't building a house; he was creating art. Nowhere was this more evident than with the dome. Other than providing an elegant cap for a stylish Palladian residence, the dome had no real purpose. Building it would stretch the capabilities of his skilled craftsmen to the absolute limit. No doubt they learned as they built, tearing down and rebuilding until they got it right. When it was finished, the dome room, or "sky room" as it was sometimes called, was used as a children's playroom, a spare bedroom, and finally as a storeroom. Other than that, Jefferson had no real purpose for the space beneath the dome.

Jefferson was unique among the Founding Fathers in his interest in the arts. None of them could match his knowledge or interest in music, literature, or architecture. Great as his political writings were, Jefferson was, as one scholar put it, "first of all an artist." Work on Monticello would continue for the rest of his life. Indeed, the final touches would not be completed until 1823, three years before his death.

A WEDDING

It happened by chance, as they were returning home. Somewhere on the road between Norfolk and Monticello, the Jefferson party encountered Thomas Mann Randolph, Jr. For Jefferson's daughter Martha and for young Randolph, it was love at first sight They were second cousins who had known each other since childhood, but apparently met for the first time as adults while the Jeffersons were in transit. It wasn't long afterward and the couple announced their engagement.

Jefferson, meanwhile, was undecided about his appointment as Secretary of State. His heart was set on returning to Paris, and he worried that domestic duties—supervising territorial governments, issuing commissions, handling patents, and doing loads of paperwork—might not suit him. James Madison, who was home for Christmas, rode over from Orange County to assure him that State Department assistants would handle the more mundane tasks and that he would be free to concentrate on foreign issues. Madison also tried to convince him that he would be more effective as a policy maker at home than as a minister in France. Jefferson was neither convinced nor ready to make a decision.

Madison wrote Washington that Jefferson was cool toward the appointment but thought his friend would accept with some encouragement from the President. Put another way, if Washington really wanted Jefferson as Secretary of State he would have to convince him himself. Either way, Jefferson wouldn't be leaving Monticello anytime soon. His daughter's wedding was planned for February 23 and Jefferson planned to be there to give her away. Then and only then would he come to New York, if he was coming at all.

CHAPTER 13

George Washington Slept Here

If you're staying at a bed-and-breakfast in New England and the sign over the door reads, "George Washington Slept Here," chances are it's true.

In the fall of 1789, President George Washington slept in 18 inns between New York and Maine, most of them country houses. Many are still standing today.

When Congress adjourned in late September, legislators packed their bags and headed home. Not the President. As much as he longed to return to Mount Vernon, Washington decided to stay in New York for the three months Congress was in recess. He intended to spend one of those months touring New England. He discussed the idea with his closest advisors: Hamilton, Jay, Knox, and Madison. His diary entries for October 5 - 7, when the decision was made, reads in part:

"Monday 5th. Exercised on horse back between the Hours of 9 and 11 in the forenoon and between 5 and 6 in the Afternoon. on foot. Had conversation with Colo. Hamilton on the propriety of my making a tour of the Eastern states during the recess of Congress to acquire knowledge of the face of the Country the growth and Agriculture there of and the temper and disposition of the Inhabitants toward the new government . . . .

"Tuesday 6th. Exercised in a Carriage with Mrs. Washington in the forenoon. Conversed with (Secretary of War) Genl Knox on the above tour who also recommend it accordingly. . . .

"Wednesday 7th. Exercised on horseback; & called on the Vice President (Washington fails to mention if he consulted with Adams about the trip). In the afternoon walked an hour. Upon consulting Mr. Jay on the propriety of my intended tour into the Eastern States, he highly approved it. . . ."

Washington had another reason for taking the trip. He wanted to see firsthand New England's growing textile industry. Like Hamilton, he believed America's future economic prosperity lay not with agriculture but with industry.

TRAVELING FIRST CLASS

Accompanying Washington on his trip were two personal secretaries (Tobias Lear and Major William Jackson), and six servants: two coachmen, two footman, an outrider, and a valet. The servants maintained the coach, tended to the horses (eight in all), and handled the luggage. The valet cleaned and pressed Washington's clothing, polished his boots, and each morning combed his hair and helped him dress. The outrider scouted the network of roads ahead and arranged dining and sleeping accommodations in advance. The daily routine was to depart at dawn, log in 10 to 15 miles before stopping for breakfast, travel another 20 miles, stop for dinner between two and three in the afternoon, proceed for another ten miles and stop for the night.

Washington began his journey on Thursday, October 15. Day one was uneventful. Day two, approaching Stratford, Washington was met on the road by a military retinue that escorted him into town. It was a pattern that would be repeated in town after town: the local townspeople would send a welcoming party out to meet him, entertain him at the local assembly hall with speeches and dinner, and afterward escort him out of town.

The next stop was New Haven. Washington attended Sunday church service and toured his first textile mill. At Wallingford and Mansfield, where the cultivation of silkworms was a cottage industry, he visited a mill that specialized in silken fabric. He spent a full day in Hartford, toured a textile plant that specialized in wool, and ordered a new suit of clothes.

On the 21st, Washington entered Massachusetts, and stopped for the night in Springfield. He wrote in his journal: "There is a great equality in the People of this State—Few or no opulent Men and no poor. . . .." He saw none of the large land holdings that comprised much of his native Virginia. "The farms . . . are small not averaging more than 100 acres."

The next morning he received a letter from John Hancock: the governor of Massachusetts was inviting him to lodge at the governor's mansion. Washington sent a reply by outrider declining the governor's invitation. The reply read in part: "From a wish to avoid giving trouble to private families, I determined, on leaving New York, to decline the honor of any invitation to quarters which I might receive while on my journey—and with a view to observe the rule, I had requested a Gentleman to engage lodgings for me during my stay in Boston."

Entering Worcester on the twenty-third, he was greeted by a 13-gun salute. The same day he received another letter from Hancock: an invitation to dine with the governor the following evening. Washington accepted. That night he lodged in Weston.

Arriving in Cambridge the next morning, Washington was greeted by town dignitaries and the local militia who escorted him to Boston. In Boston, Washington was met with "parade and ceremony." Hancock, however, was nowhere to be seen. Vice president John Adams, having traveled to Boston himself, welcomed him. Later, Washington received word that Hancock was too ill to meet him but that the invitation for dinner was still on. Following protocol, Washington assumed the governor—ill or not—would call on him first, prior to dinner. Hancock never showed and Washington dined alone. Why hadn't Hancock followed protocol? Was he too ill or merely being a prima donna? The next day Hancock finally showed and assured the President he had indeed been ill, and that, yes, ill or not, it was improper of him to expect the president to call on him first. Word of the incident leaked out and to the governor's embarrassment was reported in the local newspaper.

The following day, Monday, October 26th, a rainstorm swept through Boston. Washington, who was fighting a cold, spent the day in his room. On Tuesday, the President was feeing better and met with local clergy, the town council, and the president of Harvard College. That afternoon, Washington dined at historic Fanuiel Hall, the Boston marketplace where revolutionary speakers Sam Adams and James Otis once called for American independence.

On Wednesday, Washington toured two textile mills: the Card Manufactory, which employed 900 workers; and the Boston Sailcloth Manufactory, one of the first mills to harness water to power the looms. Most of the workers were women. An observer reported that the President "made himself merry on this Occasion, telling the overseer he believed he collected the prettiest girls in Boston."

On Thursday, Washington met up again with John Adams and the two toured Harvard College together. In the afternoon, Washington traveled on to Marblehead, where the local industry was fishing, and spent the night in Salem. Attending a reception at the Salem Town Courthouse, an observer noted: "(Washington) looked oppressed by the attention that was paid him, and as he cast his eye around, I thought it seemed to sink him at the notice he attracted. When he had got to the Court House, and had patiently listened to the ditty they sung at him, and heard the shouts of the multitudes he bowed very low, and as if he could bear no more turned hastily around and went into the house."

On Friday, Washington toured another textile mill, the Beverly Cotton Manufactory, and in his journal wrote: "In this manufactory they have the New Invented Carding and Spinning Machines—one of the first supplies the work; and four of the latter; one of which spins 84 threads at a time by one person." That afternoon, approaching Newburyport, he was met by town leaders and another military regiment. He liked what he saw in Newburyport and wrote: "This place is pleasantly situated on the Merrimack River, and appears to have carried on (here & about) the Ship-building business to a grt extent."

The next day was Saturday, October 31. Town leaders and businessmen escorted him to the New Hampshire border where he was met by the president and vice president of New Hampshire, both Senators, and the state militia. They accompanied him to Portsmouth, near the mouth of the Piscataqua River, where he was "received with every token of respect and appearance of Cordiality under a discharge of Artillery."

On Sunday, November 1, Washington attended two church services: one at a Episcopal church, the second at a Presbyterian church. He spent the afternoon in his room writing letters.

Monday morning, Washington was taken aboard a ship and spent the day deep sea fishing off the coast of New Hampshire.

Tuesday, November 3, the President attended another reception, this one at the Portsmouth town assembly hall. Noted Washington: "The Assembly Room . . . is one of the best I have seen any where in the United States." The same day he changed his travel itinerary. Winter was approaching. Due to recent snow, he decided not to travel through Vermont to Albany and then follow the Hudson back to New York City as planned. Instead, he would take the shortest route possible, by making a southwesterly diagonal cut across Massachusetts and Connecticut.

RETURN TRIP

Washington's journal entry for Wednesday, November 4 reads: "I left Portsmouth, quietly & without any attendance, having earnestly entreated that all parade & ceremony might be avoided on my return." He reached Haverhill, Massachusetts, in mid-afternoon, and spent the night.

Thursday, the fifth, having stopped in Lexington, he "viewed the Spot on which the first blood was spilt in the dispute with great Britain on the 19th of April 1775." That night he lodged in Watertown.

On Friday, November 6, despite rain mixed with snow, Washington logged in 36 miles prior to nightfall and spent the night in Uxbridge. His journal entries, which until now had been upbeat, began to show the strain of the journey. He was now critical of nearly everything he saw. "The Roads in every part of this State are amazingly crooked, to suit the convenience of every Man's fields; & the directions you receive from the People equally blind & ignorant; for instead of going to Waltham we should in 13 Miles have saved at least six. . . ." As for the Uxbridge tavern, the owner and staff "were obliging, (but their) entertainment was not very inviting."

Saturday the 7th, Washington logged in 35 miles, crossed into Connecticut, and roomed in Ashford. Due to a local ordinance which prohibited Sunday travel, the President was forced to spend the day there. The inn, Washington concluded, "is not a good one," while the sermon delivered at the local church was "very lame."

The following day, Monday, November 9, Washington "set out about 7 O'clock and for the first 24 Miles had hilly rocky and disagreeable Roads. Arrived in Hartford a little before four."

Tuesday the 10th. Washington departed at dawn, logged 26 miles and arrived in New Haven "about half an hour before Sun-down."

Wednesday the 11th was another day spent on the road. That night he slept at an inn somewhere between Fairfield and Stamford, and it was "Not a good one."

Thursday the 12th, Washington departed before dawn intending to reach New York by nightfall but was delayed at Rye "by lame horses." His last night on the road was spent where he slept the first night of his trip, at Mrs. Haviland's Tavern, which was "agreeable."

The following day, Washington arrived back at the Palace Mansion on 1 Cherry Street, where he "found Mrs. Washington and the rest of the family all well."

"HAMILTONIAN PARADISE"

While Washington was away, Hamilton had been busy. Treasury Secretary was a job he had been preparing for all of his adult life. While in the army, amid his regular duties at headquarters he found time not only to read extensively but to compose a series of what can only be called state papers. In this category were a seven-thousand-word letter to James Duane in 1780 with a plan for the creation of a national bank, a longer letter to Robert Morris in 1781 outlining a complete system of national finance, and a series of six essays entitled "The Continentalist," published in the New York Packet in 1781 and 1782, giving a whole set of political and economic prescriptions for imparting strength and energy to the national government.

As newly appointed Secretary of the Treasury, Hamilton now had the opportunity to put his ideas into action. "I'm sure he couldn't get there fast enough, sit down and begin," says Yale historian Joanne B. Freeman. "What's confronting him is lack of order. There's chaos, there's not good records, nobody quite knows what's going on. So actually, for most people, I think, it would have been a remarkably terrifying thing to walk into. I think for him it was like a little Hamiltonian paradise—you know, 'omigod, it's disordered, and I'm going to order it!'"

The first executive mansion, at 1 Cherry Street in New York City. Also known as "The Palace," the house proved too small for Washington's needs. (Illustrated by Dea Lenihan HYPERLINK "http://www.dealenihan.com")

The First Congress met throughout the Spring and Summer of 1789/90 in Federal Hall on Wall Street, and where on April 30,1789, George Washington was sworn in as the nation's First President. (Illustrated by Dea Lenihan HYPERLINK "http://www.dealenihan.com")

The second executive mansion, at 39 Broadway in New York City. Also known as the Macomb Mansion, the house featured a panoramic view of the wide Hudson River. (Illustrated by Dea Lenihan HYPERLINK "http://www.dealenihan.com")

The Royal Exchange Building at the intersection of Broad and Water Streets in New York City, where the Supreme Court met for the first time. (Illustrated by Dea Lenihan HYPERLINK "http://www.dealenihan.com")

CHAPTER 14

A Matter of Perception

Wall Street, 1789: at one end was Murray's Wharf with its tall ships, at the other end was Trinity Church with its majestic 200-foot steeple.

In between were Federal Hall, New York Bank, an insurance company, police headquarters, the post office, a grocery store, a tavern, Merchant's Coffee House (where much of the city's investment business was transacted), a goldsmith's shop, and the townhouses of two of New York's leading attorneys: Alexander Hamilton and Aaron Burr. In 1789, Wall Street was New York's marketplace.

Within three years 24 stockbrokers would meet under a buttonwood tree on Wall Street, join forces and create what today is the New York Stock Exchange. The Buttonwood Agreement as it was known would transform New York's marketplace into the nation's marketplace, and eventually into the world's marketplace.

The person responsible for this remarkable transformation was Alexander Hamilton. As Daniel Webster put it, "He touched the dead corpse of the public credit, and it sprung to its feet. The fabled birth of Minerva from the brain of Jove was hardly more sudden or more perfect than the financial system of the United States as it burst forth, from the conception of Alexander Hamilton."

From near-worthless paper, Hamilton turned public securities into something akin to gold. Everyone wanted to own them. The Buttonwood Agreement was a direct result of the demand. In England—America's erstwhile enemy—demand for U.S. Securities was so great they were trading at ten-percent over par. In three years, the credit of the United States went from the world's worst to the world's best.

At the root of what Hamilton did was to change public perception. Money and what it involved—finance, investment, banking—was a matter of what people believed. At worst, it was an illusion, a con game. Banks, however grand their outside appearance—their marble columns and imposing bulk—kept very little hard currency inside. They did business with paper. Was a mere IOU money, with nothing behind it but a promise to pay? It was if people believed it was. In English the root of "credit" is credo, the Latin for "I believe." Where most Americans saw the Revolutionary War debt as a liability, a curse, something to be paid off quickly or to be repudiated, Hamilton saw opportunity. If "funded" properly, the debt was a vast resource of liquid capital that could be used for business investment to spur economic growth.

With someone in charge who possessed the genius to create the necessary financial system to manage it, the public debt was, in Hamilton's words, a national blessing. Coupled with a national bank, funding would legitimize mere paper promises, and U.S. bonds would trade hands almost as easily as gold and silver coins. Just such a financial system had made the Netherlands the world's banker and Great Britain the world's most powerful nation. Hamilton believed it would do as much and more for the United States.

Hamilton began studying economics as early as 1777, as aide-de-camp to General George Washington. At that early stage of the Revolutionarily War, the nation's financial underpinnings already were becoming unraveled. Again and again Washington pleaded to Congress for more ammunition, more clothes, blankets, medical supplies, and especially for more money to pay his army. Without a revenue stream, Congress printed money, or Continentals, as they were called, which quickly depreciated. The expression, "Not worth a continental," is from this time. Next, Congress issued bonds. Without taxation, interest payments could not be made and these bonds depreciated quickly, too.

When Robert Morris stepped in as Superintendent of Finance, he was forced to use his personal fortune as collateral to borrow money. Had Morris not arranged for payment in specie—in silver Half Crowns—Washington's army would not have fought the British at Yorktown and the war likely would have dragged on for several more years and ultimately been lost. It was a lesson not lost on Hamilton. If the new nation was to succeed and become a world power, it would need a sound financial system to support it. Words like "liberty" and "democracy" sounded nice, but they didn't pay the bills. Money, fluid and plentiful, was the stuff that made liberty and democracy possible.

The new nation did not have gold and silver reserves. What it did have was something more valuable, a people willing to work hard to get ahead. What Hamilton hoped to foster was an economy that would reward initiative. The young republic was well on the road to becoming an aristocracy, with wealth concentrated in the hands of a few; Hamilton wanted to make the nation a meritocracy.

What economic treatises did Hamilton study? Primarily the books of three Enlightenment philosophers, all Scots: "Inquiry into the Principles of Political Economy" by James Denham-Steuart; "Political Discourses" by David Hume; and "The Wealth of Nations" by Adam Smith. Hamilton also studied the financial doings of Robert Walpole, England's First Lord of the Treasury, of Jacques Necker, France's Director-General of Finance.

The study of economics was a creation of the Enlightenment. It started more-or-less with a book of doggerel poetry entitled, "The Fable of the Bees."

LIFE, LIBERTY, AND THE PURSUIT OF PROPERTY

It was not the first treatise on economics, but it was the first to have *attitude*. It was a poem written by a Dutch moralist named Bernard Mandeville, published in 1705. It was an allegory of a beehive in which everyone was motivated by unquenchable desires and yet, because of the mysterious workings of the social structure, the result was prosperity for all:

Millions endeavoring to supply
Each other's Lust and Vanity . . .
Thus every Part was full of Vice,
Yet the whole Mass a Paradise.

All was well until the bees prayed to be made virtuous. Their prayers were answered. Avarice, luxury, competition, waste, intemperance, suddenly disappeared; and as suddenly, millions were unemployed. Prosperity, Mandeville was saying, depended not on the designs of the state nor upon the benevolence of individuals, but upon individuals acting freely in their own self-interest.

Mandeville's poem was attacked at the time as cynical, degrading and false. Nevertheless it proved to be influential. One of those influenced was Adam Smith as the following passage attests, from "The Wealth of Nations": "It is not from the benevolence of the butcher, the brewer, or the baker that we expect our dinner, but from their regard to their own interest. We address ourselves, not to their humanity but to their self-love, and never talk to them of our own necessities but of their advantages."

By some strange coincidence, "The Wealth of Nations" was published the same year as America's independence—1776. The publisher told Smith it was unlikely his book would be widely read. He could not have been more wrong. Smith's book was an instant best-seller. Within six months, a second printing was ordered to meet demand. "The Wealth of Nations" sold well in the United States. Nearly every one of the 55 delegates at the Constitutional Convention had read it or were familiar with it.

Alexander Hamilton probably read "The Wealth of Nations" during the war. Hamilton displayed a remarkable grasp of advanced economic principles as early as 1781, in a letter addressed to financier Robert Morris: "No paper credit can be substantial, or durable, which has no funds, and which does not unite, immediately, the interest and influence of the moneyed men, in its establishment and preservation," wrote Hamilton. "A credit begun on this basis, will, in process of time, greatly exceed its funds: but this requires time and a well-settled opinion in its favor." Time and opinion, as Hamilton uses these words, are intangibles, and a vital part of money management that increases wealth. The letter contains one of Hamilton's oft-quoted lines: "A national debt, if it is not excessive, will be to us a national blessing."

The full title of Smith's book is: "An inquiry into the Nature and Causes of the Wealth of Nations." Smith makes the case that a nation's wealth resides not with precious metals nor with natural resources, but with individual self-interest. All people want to live better than they do. Smith finds a "desire of bettering our condition, a desire which, though generally calm and dispassionate, comes with us from the womb, and never leaves us till the grave." Smith argues that society should exploit these natural drives, not repress them. Self-interest is itself a rich natural resource, and the true source of a nation's wealth. As proof, Smith need point no farther than to the Netherlands. With little usable land and no natural resources, the Netherlands grew to become one of the richest countries in the world. In Smith's time, the Netherlands was banker to the world. It was no coincidence that the Netherlands also was one of the freest countries in Europe, and the most tolerant. The Dutch were free to pursue their self-interests, without government restriction or centralized market planning to hinder them, and the nation benefitted as a whole. As a counter-example, Smith could point to Spain which had glutted itself on the silver it had mined in South America, and destroyed its economy in the process.

With everyone pursuing their own self-interests, why doesn't anarchy result? Because an "invisible hand" guides the whole. Smith had studied astronomy and embraced the idea of a natural harmony in the planets, even if each planet moved in its own orbit. People, he believed, could move in different paths yet harmonize and help each other, though not intentionally. "He . . . neither intends to promote the public interest, nor knows how much he is promoting it . . . he intends only his own gain, and he is in this, as in many other cases, led by an invisible hand to promote an end which was no part of his intention.

"Free market competition leads a self-interested person to produce not what he wants, but what others want; not in the quantities he prefers, but in the quantities his neighbors prefer; not at the price he dreams of charging, but at a price reflecting how much his neighbors value what he has done."

Hamilton was not content with merely restoring the nation's credit; he wanted to change the rules of the game so that it rewarded work and ingenuity, and promoted manufacturing over farming. Other ideas of Smith's that Hamilton found useful:

— Slavery had to go. Not only was it morally wrong, it was costly. Wrote Smith: "The experience of all ages and nations, I believe, demonstrates that the work done by slaves, though it appears to cost only their maintenance, is in the end the dearest of any. A person who can acquire no property, can have no other interest but to eat as much, and to labour as little as possible."

— Military power depends on economic success. "Fleets and armies are maintained, not with gold and silver, but with consumable goods."

— Economic success depends on freedom. "No regulation of commerce can increase the quantity of industry in any society . . . It can only divert a part of it into a direction into which it might not otherwise have gone." Indeed, democracy only flourishes where there is a free-market economy.

— Money is imaginary. "Money is neither a material to work upon, nor a tool to work with . . . money, by means of which the whole revenue of the society is regularly distributed among all its different members, makes itself no part of that revenue." Being imaginary, it can't. "The great wheel of circulation is altogether different from the goods which are circulated by means of it."

— Liberty and property rights go hand-in-hand. "The property which every man has in his own labour, as it is the original foundation of all other property, so it is the most sacred and inviolable." Writer P.J. O'Rourke, in his commentary on "The Wealth of Nations," puts it this way. "Any definition of liberty, that is not based on a right to property and a right to the same rights as all other people have is meaningless. What we have is ours, and nobody can push us around. This is practically all we mean when we say we are free. Other rights derive from these, when we even bother with those other rights . . . Property rights are the deed we have to ownership of ourselves."

MONETIZING THE DEBT

As advanced as Adam Smith's economic theories were, they fell short on public finance. Smith thought capital could be accumulated only by frugality, and he failed to recognize the most potent source of capital formation was the public debt. To Smith, the United States' public debt was an economic liability, to be dispensed with as quickly as possible. To Smith's fellow Scottish economist James Steuart, the public debt was no less than an economic gold mine. Steuart was, it turns out, a thorn in Adam Smith's side. Smith wrote "The Wealth of Nations" partly to refute Steuart's 1767 economic treatise, "Inquiry into the Principles of Political Economy." Among their differences, Steuart advocated mercantilism as a means of protecting and nourishing domestic economic markets, while Smith, a laissez-faire economist, favored free trade.

Hamilton read Steuart's book to learn about monetizing the public debt. A monetized public debt, if managed properly, would create a large pool of liquid capital that would foster economic growth and create wealth. It had been done before, in England. Like the United States, England had run up a huge war debt, in the late seventeenth century. The war exhausted traditional sources of deficit financing and forced the government to find new sources of financing. As a result, Parliament authorized a group of London businessmen to set up the Bank of England and granted the bank special privileges. With a capitalization of 1.2 million pounds, the bank bought up state debts and issued them as interest-bearing annuities. These annuities were guaranteed by the government and backed by income from various taxes. Growing doubt among investors that the debt would in fact never be paid off, coupled with increasing speculation, however, put the scheme in grave danger.

To stabilize the system, in 1717 Sir Robert Walpole, the Chancellor of the Exchequer (alias secretary of the treasury), devised a "sinking fund" or cash reserve drawn from fixed taxes from which annuities would be repaid. Or so it would appear to investors. In fact, Walpole had no intention of paying down the debt. The sinking fund was created only to convince the public that the debt would be repaid. Investors bought it—literally. Sales of annuities began to climb again and interest rates stabilized. To enhance the illusion, the Bank of England began buying and selling annuities like any other large business interest. Investor confidence increased and the result was a permanent and functioning securities market. The outcome was that business investors—whether in London, Amsterdam, Geneva, or Paris—were now convinced that state bonds could be exchanged at any time at face value, and paid in specie (gold and silver). As a result, the Bank of England could issue notes which, like hard currency, could be spent or invested as if they were hard currency. Government bonds—the annuities in the portfolio of the Bank of England—thus joined gold as acceptable security for large-scale business transactions. As a result, annuities and bank notes, as business investment instruments, functioned interchangeably. Thus the national debt was monetized. As the national debt grew larger, which it did by leaps and bounds, the money supply grew with it. The result was no less than a financial revolution. Where landholding had once been the source of wealth and of political power, money in its many forms was the new source of wealth and power. Not even the forthcoming industrial revolution would create as much wealth.

SYMBOLIC MONEY

If you were planning to buy a new car, Adam Smith would have you save up until you had enough money to pay for it; James Steuart would have you buying the car on credit and making monthly payments. Which is better for you? Which is better for automobile sales, for auto makers, for the creation of new jobs, for the economy, alas, for increasing national wealth? Adam Smith's "The Wealth of Nations" is among the 100 most influential books ever written, but when it came to debt Smith was a scrooge. His advice: pay it off as quickly as possible. Good advice for individuals perhaps, but not good advice for nations. As advanced as Smith's ideas were, he lacked Steuart's grasp of the principles of public finance. The "Father of Capitalism" as Smith has been called, stated "the practice of funding (public debts) has gradually enfeebled every state which has adopted it." Not England; funding made England filthy rich.

It was, therefore, James Steuart that Alexander Hamilton turned to for advice on monetizing the public debt. Steuart's 1767 economic treatise "Inquiry into the Principles of Political Economy" makes two points that Hamilton would embrace:

One: Mere coins are not only awkward to handle but ultimately inadequate as a viable money supply. Therefore, provision must be made for paper money in all its forms. This is done by developing institutionalized forms of credit, whereby "solid property" is monetized, made liquid in the form of bonds, notes, mortgages, accounts, and other instruments. Steuart calls such financial instruments "symbolic money." The result has a leveling effect on society, between haves and have-nots, of spreading wealth around and benefitting the many, as opposed to hoarding and benefiting the few. One example: people with money deposit it in a bank, and the bank in turn lends it to those who need it. Writes Steuart: "(symbolic money) enables those who have effects, which by their nature cannot circulate (and which, by-the-bye, are the principle cause of inequality), to give, to the full extent of all their worth, an adequate circulating equivalent for the services they demand. In other words, it is a method of melting down, as it were, the very causes of inequality, and of rendering fortunes equal." Another example is gold. Gold that is molded into religious icons or secular objects represents wealth taken out of circulation. It benefits the few. Melted down and minted into coins, it increases the money supply: loans are easier to get, interest rates are lower, and therefore more people can partake of the benefits.

Two: The most efficacious means of creating symbolic money is to monetize the public debt, which will create a vast fund of symbolic money that can supply the means with which banks and other financial institutions can "melt down" the rest. Steuart illustrates his observation with a detailed account of how the British system evolved and turned England into one of the world's wealthiest and most powerful nations on earth.

There was one final piece of the financial scheme that Hamilton was planning, and that would be supplied by David Hume, the same David Hume who had fueled the ideas behind James Madison's Virginia Plan at the Constitutional Convention.

CHAPTER 15

The Better Life

While Congress was in recess, Alexander Hamilton did something the previous three-man Board of Treasury had failed to do—determine the amount of the public debt. It was $76 million. At the time, the nation's entire amount of money in circulation was less than $6 million.

Hamilton opposed paying off the debt as soon as feasible, as some were advocating. To do so would result in oppressive taxation, deplete the nation's money supply, and further burden the nation's already-ailing economy. Still others were advocating repudiation of the debt in order to start over with a clean slate. Hamilton opposed that too, knowing such rashness would destroy the nation's ability to borrow money on favorable terms for a generation at the very least.

In funding the debt, as Hamilton proposed, the nation's money supply of gold and silver coins would remain in circulation. If funded properly, the debt would stabilize and public securities could be used in business transactions much like bank notes. Coupled with a national bank, the funded debt would be available as investment capital to grow the economy. As the economy grew the money supply would grow with it, and in time the $76 million public debt would shrink in proportion to the money supply and be less costly to pay off. Hamilton's plan called for retiring the debt in 20 years.

In 1789 America, few actually dealt in hard currency. Most business was transacted by means of barter, or with the use of IOUs, or with a line of credit at, say, the local dry goods store. In the southern states, warehouse receipts for tobacco often circulated as money. There was another form of money and that was the Bills of Exchange used in ports where international trade held sway. More a form of credit than money, it was the means by which importers and exporters conducted business with overseas traders around the world.

There were but three banks in America in 1789—all commercial banks—one in Philadelphia, one in New York, and one in Boston. It was in these northern port cities where commerce was king and coins were in greater circulation. Every spring, as ships arrived from Europe, the supply of coins in circulation greatly increased. Most were of British and Spanish mintage. The most widely-circulated coin was the Spanish milled silver dollar, which, in order to make change, was cut into eight pieces, or bits, as they were called. One bit would get you a glass of ale and something to eat at the corner grog house. The terminology is still used today: a Quarter Dollar is still known as "two-bits."

Hamilton did not want to merely increase the nation's money supply. He wanted everyone to know the feel of having coins jingling in their pockets. Hamilton's goal was to transform the nation's economy from one of land and agriculture, which benefited the few, to one of money and industry, that benefited the many. He wanted the United States to be a place where everyone had the desire for a better life and had the opportunity of attaining it. To accomplish this, Hamilton drew upon the writings of yet another Scottish economist, David Hume.

HUME'S ECONOMIC PHILOSOPHY

A taste for the better life. Once indulged, people will work harder, arts and learning will flourish, the nation will grow richer, and liberty and equality will abound. In a nutshell that is the economic philosophy of David Hume. Hume did not write a weighty tome to express his economic views, as with so many economists then and now. He did not produce a lengthy treatise, but a series of short essays. Published in 1752, his seven essays on economics run to 97 pages. The most quoted is Essay II , "Of Refinement in the Arts," all of 13 pages.

While many eighteenth-century thinkers romanticized the notion of "the noble savage" Hume would have none of it. Life in hunting-and-gathering societies was crude, violent, and short. "I believe every man would think his life or fortune much less secure in the hands of a Moor or Tartar, than in those of a French or English gentleman." As a youth, Hume had seen his share of the sloth and poverty in Scotland at a time when it subsisted off the land, and he didn't like it. The philosophers who espoused such notions had never known what it meant to forage and hunt from dawn to dusk, twenty-four-seven. In his lifetime, Scotland had been transformed into a vital and thriving nation by a rising class of merchants, manufacturers, and artisans. As he grew older, he saw his life become easier, less precarious, and more comfortable, with better and more plentiful food, more plentiful and affordable goods, and an increase in learning and in the arts. Eke out a living tilling the soil? Forget it. The good society was one in which commerce was king.

If Alexander Hamilton was looking for justification for transforming the American economy from one of agriculture in to one of commerce, David Hume supplied it. In his first essay, "Of Commerce," Hume made a strong case for commerce over agriculture. A society that is predominantly agricultural tends to produce at a level little beyond than to sustain itself. With few consumer goods available, the incentive to work harder to raise a surplus is limited. In a time of crisis the very act of raising an army would mean the removal of essential labor and thus force the economy below the level of subsistence.

On the other hand, a society that enjoys a prosperous commerce and industry could create the same measure of military strength without making comparable demands on society. With the promise of luxuries and amenities, people are motivated to work harder to get ahead, resulting in higher productivity in both commerce and in agriculture. Eventually a substantial portion of the population would be engaged in the production of goods and services that fulfill wants beyond mere subsistence. Similarly motivated, farmers and artisans would seek ways to increase their efforts until the basic needs of society were provided by a fraction of the labor force. In time of war those devoted to the production of luxuries represents a surplus that can be tapped. They can be re-employed in the production of armaments without affecting the basic needs of society.

In his essay "Of Refinement in the Arts" Hume states that commerce and industry not only make a nation stronger militarily, but also better socially and intellectually. It's the prosperous commercial state rather than the pinched rustic one that produces humane, sociable, and virtuous people. "The same age, which produces great philosophers and politicians, renowned generals and poets, usually abounds with skillful weavers, and ship carpenters." As commerce increases, refinement in the arts advances, and people become more sociable. "They flock into cities; love to receive and communicate knowledge; to show their wit or their breeding; their taste in conversation or living, in clothes or furniture. Curiosity allures the wise; vanity the foolish; and pleasure both." Thus "industry, knowledge and humanity are linked together by an indissoluble chain. . . ."

Hume goes one step further. "If we consider the matter in a proper light, we shall find, that progress in the arts is rather favorable to liberty, and has a natural tendency to preserve, if not produce a free government." However, where commerce is neglected, "all labour is bestowed on the cultivation of the ground." Society becomes divided into two classes: landowners and tenants. Land owners have all the power and run the affairs of state, while those working the land have no power and are fit subjects for slavery.

Where "luxury nourishes commerce and industry, the peasants, by a proper cultivation of the land, become rich and independent; while the tradesmen and merchants acquire a share of property, and draw authority and consideration of the middling rank of men, who are the best and firmest basis of public liberty." This "middling rank" is, of course, the middle class. And who should comprise the membership of the House Commons? Why, the English middle class, the very safeguard of British liberty and equality.

Hamilton studied the works of Adam Smith, James Steuart, Jacques Necker, and the like, but he absorbed the ideas of David Hume and made them his own.

Hamilton saw his economic principles as having a great leveling effect on society. He did not want money hoarded by the wealthy few, but free-flowing and ever-changing hands, rewarding the initiative of anyone willing to work hard to get ahead. Hamilton was among the nation's first abolitionists. He may have spoken like an elitist, but his economic policies were color-blind and class free, and therefore democratic.

HAMILTON GOES TO WORK

Hamilton's first job as Treasury Secretary was to secure a short-term loan. The government was in need of $100,000 to meet operating expenses. Hamilton arranged two loans, one with the Bank of New York for $50,000, and the second with the Bank of North America, in Philadelphia, for $50,000. The loan with the New York bank Hamilton arranged personally on his first day in office, on Sunday, September 13th; the loan with the Philadelphia bank he arranged by letter, sent overnight by special courier to be in the hands of the bank president when the bank opened for business on Monday morning. (Both loans would be paid in full by the following March.) Hamilton then instructed all state tax collectors that they were to accept the bank notes of the two banks for tax payments in place of gold or silver because of the limited supply of hard currency.

In the following days Hamilton met with the French minister, the Comte de Mousier, about servicing the American debt to France. From one of the commissioners who had been appointed to settle the public accounts during the Revolution, he asked for information on the current state of those accounts. He sought additional information from the state governors on their states' indebtedness. He also prepared a special letter to help gather vital information concerning import and export activity. The letter, dated October 15, 1789, concerned shipping and consisted of seven broad questions, each of which invited an essay-answer as well as hard facts and figures. The letter was sent to customs collectors and to everyone else Hamilton had reason to believe had useful information. The replies provided him with a wealth of data and practical wisdom, much of which was contrary to common assumptions. When all the returns were in and Hamilton had digested them, he knew more about the ordinary business of his fellow citizens than anyone else in the country.

"I hazard much," Hamilton said of his new job in a letter to his friend Lafayette in Paris, "but I thought it an occasion that called upon me to hazard. I have no doubt that the reasonable expectation of the public may be satisfied, if I am properly supported by the Legislature, and in this respect, I stand at present on the most encouraging ground." Hamilton was counting on the support of his friend James Madison. However, even at this early date, there were signs that Madison was having second thoughts concerning Hamilton's approach to resolving the public debt.

While the two remained friends, Hamilton knew of Madison's discrimination scheme against British shipping, and Madison surely suspected Hamilton's role in the Senate's revision of the tariff bill. To his surprise and disappointment, Hamilton learned the Virginian had remained in town a full week after Congress adjourned without telling him. Later, in an exchange of letters, Hamilton suggested that a meeting between the two would have been advantageous and certainly appropriate prior to Madison's departure.

In his letter, Hamilton asked the Virginian for his opinions on ways of increasing government revenue and in making provision for the public debt. Writing from his home in Orange County, Virginia, Madison recommended an excise tax on home distilleries, a higher duty on imported liquor, and a tax on land. Regarding the debt, Madison suggested in vague terms that it be extinguished as quickly as feasible, rather than be perpetuated. His reasoning? "The public expected as much," and because he feared that if the public debt were funded it might fall into the hands of foreigners and somehow be used against American interests.

Hamilton was perplexed at Madison's recent behavior, and admitted as much to British agent George Beckwith, who was in New York at the time. Beckwith replied by saying he too was surprised that Madison, a man "of good sense" should be "so decidedly hostile to us" by wanting to discriminate against British shipping. It was bad for business on both sides of the Atlantic and certainly didn't help the healing process that was taking place between the two nations.

While "a clever man, he is very little Acquainted with the (business) world," Hamilton said. Despite their recent differences, he told Beckwith not to worry. Ever the optimist, Hamilton said he and the Virginian had a good working relationship and he expected that to continue. "That (Madison) is Uncorrupted and Incorruptible I have not a doubt," Hamilton said. "He has the same End in view that I have, And so have those gentlemen, who Act with him, but their mode of attaining it is very different."

Hamilton was mistaken, as he would soon discover. Due to political pressure at home, Madison was evolving into an anti-Federalist and in fact no longer shared Hamilton's political and economic views.

CHAPTER 16

State of the Union

Early to bed, early to rise: that was the farmer in George Washington.

Each day, the President rose before dawn, shaved by candlelight, dressed with the help of his valet, and while the house was quiet he read several newspapers and did correspondence work. After two hours, he stopped for a breakfast of hoe cakes smothered in butter and honey and chased with several cups of tea taken with milk.

After breakfast, he studied state papers, signed documents, met with staff and, as necessary, met with advisors, cabinet members, congressmen, and foreign ministers. At two in the afternoon, he stopped for dinner. Dinner consisted of various meat dishes: fish, fowl, ham, beef steak, accompanied with a variety of fruits and vegetables and rounded off with lavish deserts. Washington usually dined on a single entree and afterward drank champagne or Madeira wine while conversing with guests and friends. Later, he went for a walk, usually to the Battery and back, or rode on horseback, or took a carriage ride with Mrs. Washington. When he could get away for an extended period—such as on the weekends—he rode "The Fourteen Miles Round" Manhattan island.

In the evenings, as often as he could, he attended the theater. There was one theater in New York City, the John Street Theater, where the President was often seen in the company of dignitaries, cabinet members, Congressmen, family and friends. After the theater, and on most nights, Washington would eat a light supper and go to bed. Most nights he was in bed by nine.

George Washington loved the theater. He appreciated its power, not merely to entertain, but to communicate ideas. He enjoyed Shakespeare's plays, particularly "Julius Caesar." During the bleak winter at Valley Forge, he staged a play for his soldiers, one with an unmistakable message, entitled "Cato." Cato was a Roman patriot and staunch supporter of the Roman Republic who opposed Caesar. Rather than capitulate to a tyrant and give up his freedom, he commits suicide in the end. The message: freedom was more precious than life itself.

Washington's journal entry for Tuesday, November 24, 1789 reads: "A good deal of Company at the Levee to day. Went to the Play in the Evening." What did he see? A comedy entitled, "The Toy; or A Trip to Hampton Court." A newspaper reported: "On the appearance of The President, the audience rose, and received him with the warmest acclamations." The play must have been very funny because this was said to have been the only pubic occasion at which George Washington was seen to laugh.

It was around this time Washington received word that North Caroline had ratified the Constitution thus becoming the twelfth state to join the Union. The only hold-out now was Rhode Island. The first of the original 13 colonies to declare independence from British rule, Rhode Island would be the last of the original 13 to join the union.

Thanksgiving was celebrated that year, on November 26. In his journal Washington wrote: "Being the day appointed for a Thanksgiving I went to St. Paul's Chapel though it was most inclement and stormy—but few people at the church." In honor of the day, he contributed seven pounds, ten shillings out of his own pocket to purchase "provision & beer" for inmates at the City's debtor prison. Before adjourning in September, Congress had resolved that the president should proclaim a national day of thanksgiving. Thus, on October 3, Washington issued a proclamation assigning November 26 as Thanksgiving Day. This was the first national day of thanksgiving to be celebrated in the United States.

Going forward, Thanksgiving would be celebrated irregularly. For example, the next thanksgiving day was not proclaimed until 1795. Washington's successor, John Adams, would proclaim but two Thanksgiving Days; Thomas Jefferson none at all. Thanksgiving would not become an annual national holiday until 1863 when President Abraham Lincoln instituted Thanksgiving as a yearly event.

On Christmas day, 1789, Washington wrote in his journal: "Went to St. Paul's in the forenoon. The visitors to Mrs. Washington this afternoon were not numerous but respectable."

THE PRESIDENT'S FIRST MESSAGE TO CONGRESS

New Year's Day, 1790 was typically cold, a day for sleeping late and spending the day with family in the living room, before a roaring fire. For the most public man in North America, however, it was business as usual. Washington wrote in his journal: "The Vice-President, the Governor—Senators, Members of the House of Representatives in Town—Foreign public characters and the respectable Citizens came between the hours of 12 & 3 o'clock to pay the compliments of the Season to me—and in the Afternoon a great number of Gentlemen & Ladies visited Mrs. Washington on the same occasion."

The following day, Saturday, January 2, Hamilton presented Washington with a copy of his "Report on Public Credit," which he had just completed. Coupled with appendices and a proposed change to the tax law, the report comprised a total of 20,000 words: some light reading for the president.

Washington and Hamilton were both due to appear before Congress in the coming days: on January 8, Washington would present the first Annual Message to Congress (a.k.a. the State of the Union Address); and on January 14, Hamilton would present to the House of Representatives his "Report on Public Credit."

As Hamilton turned to leave the President asked him to wait a moment. "Alex, I have a favor to ask," said the President. "I want you to write the Annual Message to Congress. Madison is not here, and there is no one else I can trust to do it. Can you write a few words appropriate for the occasion?"

The preceding is conjecture, but something like it probably did occur. Of all the public documents Washington issued as president, authorship of the first Annual Message is unknown. There is no tale-tell correspondence—no smoking gun as it were—to indicate authorship. Hamilton wrote many of Washington's official documents and letters during the Revolution, and Hamilton, Madison and Jefferson wrote many of Washington's state papers while the General was President. Madison was out of town throughout the Fall of 1789, and for much of that time was in Virginia bedridden with illness. He did not return to New York until after the Annual Message was given. Thomas Jefferson was not yet a part of Washington's administration; he didn't accept his appointment as Secretary of State until late February. That leaves Hamilton.

To be sure, Hamilton had his hands full organizing the treasury department, doing research, and composing the "Report on Public Credit." Having completed the report before the first of the year, he had time to write it. The annual message is not long. The two men likely talked, Washington's expressed his ideas, and Hamilton returned to his office to write it. He was known for his quickness with a pen and likely had a draft ready for the president by the following morning. As important, Hamilton knew how to express Washington's ideas better than anyone else.

WASHINGTON'S ADMINISTRATION ON PARADE

Friday, January 8, 1790 was yet another cold day in New York. That morning, waiting outside the Palace Mansion, were horses and coaches, uniformed coachmen and footmen, and the New York State Militia. At 10:30 the front door of the Palace Mansion swung open and out stepped the President and his administrative officers and staff, having previously shared tea and light conversation. Dressed warmly in overcoats, they filed out and took their assigned places.

At the head of the procession, astride two of Washington's finest white horses, were the president's personal secretaries: Colonel David Humphreys and Major William Jackson. Next was President George Washington, seated alone inside a yellow coach drawn by six white horses. Next in line, aboard a chariot, were secretary Tobias Lear, and junior secretary Thomas Nelson. Behind them, on horseback, was presidential aid Robert Lewis. After him, alone inside three separate carriages, were Chief Justice John Jay, Treasury Secretary Alexander Hamilton, and Secretary of War Henry Knox.

At half-past ten the procession proceeded south on Pearl as far as Broad Street, turned sharply right, passed by the Fraunces Tavern, where General George Washington had bid farewell to his army officers at the close of the Revolutionary War, and headed toward what looked like a Greek Temple at the top of the street. This was Federal Hall. At the appointed hour of eleven the procession stopped in front of the Hall. Looking resplendent in dark blue, Washington emerged from the coach and entered the building.

"I was met by the Doorkeepers of the Senate and House and conducted to the Door of the Senate Chamber," Washington wrote in his journal, "and passing from thence to the Chair through the Senate on the right, & House of representatives on the left, I took my Seat. The Gentlemen who attended me followed & took their stand behind the Senators; the whole rising as I entered. After being seated, at which time the members of both Houses also sat, I rose (as they also did) and made my Speech."

President Washington's First Annual Message to Congress took all of ten minutes to read. Eight months earlier, delivering the Inaugural Address, he'd made but one request of Congress—to draw up a bill of rights. This time he asked for a number of things that the Constitution specifically delegated Congress to do: to provide a uniform currency, set a standard of weights and measures, develop a system of patents for inventions, give copyrights in science and literature, ascertain a uniform rule of naturalization, and further develop the postal service and expand the network of postal roads to facilitate "the intercourse between the distant parts of our Country." He then asked Congress to pass without delay Hamilton's financial recommendations as outlined in the "Report on Public Credit." In closing, he made a case for public education: "Knowledge is in every Country the surest basis of public happiness . . . every valuable end of Government is best answered by the enlightened confidence of the people: and by teaching the people themselves to know and to value their own rights. . . ."

Everyone there could feel good about the new government and its many accomplishments: passage of the 1789 Tariff Act, creation of the Supreme Court and federal judiciary system, creation of the Executive Departments of State, Treasury and War, and passage of the Bill of Rights. No Congress ever again would achieve as much as the First Congress had in the first six months. Then, too, no subsequent Congress ever again would feel as compelled to act as the First Congress had, when the very existence of the republic was at stake.

The first session of the First Congress had been a test of unity, and it was that very unity that produced such remarkable results. The second session of the First Congress, beginning in January 1790, would test that unity to the breaking point as congressman debated three highly divisive issues: Hamilton's financial plan, the abolition of slavery, and the Residency Bill.

CHAPTER 17

The Price of Liberty

The day after George Washington delivered the State of the Union Address, Alexander Hamilton informed the House of Representatives that the "Report on Public Credit" was ready for their consideration.

Debate followed on how the report should be presented. A number of Congressmen were opposed to Hamilton making the presentation. Some feared it would blur the separation of power's doctrine, while others feared Hamilton's renowned powers of persuasion would somehow unfairly influence the outcome.

Two days later—on Monday, January 11—Hamilton celebrated his thirty-third birthday. That same day Congress made a decision: a clerk would read Hamilton's report to the House. Like a mere interested citizen, the Treasury Secretary would listen from the gallery.

On Thursday, January 14, a clerk seated himself before the House and read aloud Hamilton's 20,000 word report: it took 90 minutes. The report included eleven appendices consisting mainly of numbers and an itemized draft of a proposed tax revision, which were not read. There was little discussion afterwards. It was a lot of information to take in and most Congressmen didn't know what to make of it. Someone made a motion to have the hand-written report printed so everyone could have a copy to study. The motion carried. That afternoon, the document was sent by courier to a printer in Hanover Square. Three-hundred copies were ordered.

Six days later, on January 20—the day Madison returned from Virginia—copies of Hamilton's report were distributed in the House. Within a few weeks the report was printed or summarized in newspapers around the country. Debate was not scheduled to begin until February 8, time enough for the opposition to make its case against the report. In the interim, the House resumed debate of the controversial Residency Bill.

Political storms were gathering.

REPORT SUMMARY

"The Price of Liberty." That's what Hamilton called the public debt because it financed the successful completion of the War of Independence. The total debt was $76 million, or 40 percent of the nation's GDP (Gross Domestic Product). As a point of comparison, the last time the public debt was 40 percent of GDP (in 1983), the public debt was $1.4 trillion.

The debt fell into three broad categories: Foreign (French and Dutch loans), Domestic (continental securities comprised of bonds, loan office certificates, army pay certificates, indents, etc.) and State (bonds and IOUs). The amounts outstanding were:

Foreign Debt: $11.7 million (10 million plus 1.7 million in unpaid interest);
Domestic Debt: $40.4 million (27 million plus 13 million in unpaid interest);
State Debt: $25 million (Hamilton's estimate of principle and unpaid interest).

Congress was in favor of paying the foreign debt in full. The question was what to do with the rest? Should the domestic debt be paid in full too, or be partially repudiated based on the current market value of continental securities (50 cents on the dollar, or $13.5 million), or be repudiated altogether? Or should the domestic debt be paid off as quickly as feasible (estimates ranged from five to ten years), or, as Hamilton proposed, be funded? And what about states' debt? Should it be assumed by the federal government or be the states' responsibility? And what about unpaid interest? Pay or repudiate?

In Hamilton's mind, the entire amount, while large, was not so large that it could not be properly managed and actually benefit the nation. He wanted to fund everything: foreign debt, domestic debt, state debt, and unpaid interest; to lump it all together, monetize it, and thereby increase the nation's money supply.

Hamilton's "Report on Public Credit" reads like an attorney's summation to a jury. The Treasury Secretary had mastery of the facts, had a plan of action, and now he was going to steer Congress on a course that was best for the nation's prosperity and economic growth. It's no accident that he buried most of the numbers in the attachments. The report was not an accountant's summary of outstanding debts; it was a sales pitch on what should be done. The wording is friendly, easy to follow, the telling of a story of which there can be but one outcome.

"Hamilton explained his policies in well-written, logically constructed arguments that remain a pleasure to read, even two-hundred years later," was how past Federal Reserve Chairman Alan Greenspan described the Report in 1996.

Hamilton began with an issue on which everyone could agree—the importance of maintaining good public credit. Then, one-by-one, he discussed the principle issues: funding, discrimination, assumption, a sinking fund, and a new tax proposal. Each of these issues would be debated in Congress over the next six months.

PUBLIC CREDIT: Essential to national security. "Loans in times of public danger," wrote Hamilton, "especially from foreign war, are found an indispensable resource, even to the wealthiest (of nations)." Under such circumstances, "to be able to borrow upon *good terms,* it is essential that the credit of a nation should be well established."

Hamilton compared the financial habits of a nation with those of a responsible businessman. "By good faith, by a punctual performance of contracts, States, like individuals, who observe their engagements, are respected and trusted: while the reverse is the fate of those, who pursue an opposite conduct." Hamilton provided a laundry list of benefits including, "to restore landed property to its due value; to furnish new resources both to agriculture and commerce; to cement more closely the union to the states; (and) to add to their security against foreign attack."

FUNDING: Not quite the alchemist's dream of converting lead into gold, but close. ". . . in countries in which the national debt is properly funded, and an object of established confidence, it answers most of the purposes of money. Transfers of stock or public debt are equivalent to payments in specie; or in other words, stock, in the principal transactions of business, passes current as specie." (note: it would be only after the Civil War that the word "stock" would come to mean a share of ownership, while "bond" would mean debt; in Hamilton's day the words were largely interchangeable.)

The debt would be funded with a new issue of U.S. treasury bonds. Interest on treasury bonds would be guaranteed by revenue drawn from a new tax. Treasury bonds would then be accepted with bank notes as another form of money, thus increasing the nation's money supply. The benefits would be many. With money in greater supply loans would be easier to get, interests rates would fall, and everyone would benefit: merchants, planters, handicraft manufacturers, laborers, and farmers. In contrast, with much of the nation's money supply tied up in unfunded debt, money becomes scarce making loans costly and difficult to obtain. Hamilton attributed the decrease in land value—as much as fifty percent in the Deep South, twenty-five percent everywhere else—to the scarcity of money. Hamilton also made the case that interest rates would lower as a result of funding.

DISCRIMINATION: An emotional (and political) issue because it dealt with army veterans who were paid with continental securities and who for a variety of reasons sold their securities for pennies on the dollar. Should they be compensated for their loss? And, with the price of securities on the rise, should speculators who purchased these devalued securities be allowed to profit? Discrimination was a means of redress, an effort of determining what was paid, when, and to whom, of compensating soldiers for their loss, and of paying speculators only what they paid for the stock plus accrued interest.

Hamilton agreed what had happened was unfortunate but countered with the argument that a deal was a deal; no one had forced the original bearers to sell their securities. Speculators had "paid what the commodity was worth in the market, and took the risk of reimbursement upon (themselves)." Discrimination, while well-meaning, would only make the matter worse. Discrimination, said Hamilton, "is inconsistent with justice, because in the first place, it is a breach of contract; in violation of the rights of a fair purchaser. The nature of the contract in its origin, is, that the public will pay the sum expressed in the security, to the first holder, or his assignee." Discrimination would not only be a bureaucratic nightmare that could very well create more problems than it solved, it likely would increase the public debt manifold and in the future make the purchase of government securities anything but desirable.

ASSUMPTION: Hamilton proposed that the federal government assume all state debts and, as with the domestic and foreign debt, fund them with a new issue of U.S. securities. The War was national; the debt, whether domestic or state, was therefore national and should be treated as such. Assumption would assure uniform regulation and guarantee the War debt in all its forms would be fairly paid. Some states had made provision for paying their debt already, such as Virginia, while others had not because they were in deep financial trouble, such as Massachusetts. Hamilton wanted no state to suffer or be penalized on account of their individual debt. He wanted all War debts to be paid by the federal government so that going forward the states would be on equal financial footing, at least as far as the public debt was concerned. Hamilton also promised equality among the states when state debts were audited so that the states that had paid their debt would be compensated equally with those states that had not.

While not stated in the report, Hamilton's goal was for all creditors—both those who owned continental securities and those who owned state securities—to be beholden only to the federal government for payment. It was one more way of further strengthening the national government.

SINKING FUND: while interest payments on U.S. Securities would be paid from tax collections, Hamilton proposed paying the principle from a sinking fund, over a prescribed period of twenty years. Revenue for the sinking fund would be drawn from post office receipts. Hamilton had another undisclosed purpose for the sinking fund and that was to cover a bank run on Hamilton's planned federal bank, should a financial panic occur.

TAXATION: Hamilton proposed an excise tax on liquor, salt, sugar, coffee and tea, that would assure that the new government had both adequate spending power and the necessary funds to make quarterly interest payments on the debt.

Hamilton concluded: ". . . the proper funding of the present debt, will render it a national blessing."

Hamilton's idea of "a national blessing" (bonds, banking, commerce, manufacturing) was not everyone's idea of "a national blessing" and therein lay a very large road block to getting his financial plan through Congress.

JEFFERSON KEEPS THE PRESIDENT WAITING

There were two other matters pending action in early 1790: one was the appointment of Thomas Jefferson as Secretary of State; the other was the Supreme Court that was scheduled to sit for the first time on February 1.

George Washington had not heard a word from Thomas Jefferson since writing and asking him to head up the State Department. That was in November. It was now the middle of January and the President was becoming concerned. Acting Secretary of State John Jay was soon to be sworn in as the first Chief Justice of the Supreme Court and Washington couldn't very well ask him to wear both hats while waiting for Jefferson to make up his mind.

What was Jefferson doing that was so important he couldn't pick up a pen and write the President of the United States? At the very least, he could tell him that he was undecided, that his daughter was getting married and that he intended to be at the wedding to give her way.

James Madison recommended Jefferson for the job. No doubt, when Madison arrived in New York in January the first thing Washington asked him was what was Jefferson's decision? Had he accepted or not? If he had, when could he be expected to take office? Madison confessed he didn't know. Yes, he had spoken with Jefferson at length about filling the position, and no, Jefferson had not yet made up his mind. In the weeks that followed, Washington, Madison and Jay each wrote Jefferson urging him to accept.

In the meantime, Washington concerned himself with moving family and staff into an even larger executive mansion. He received word from the Comte de Moutiers that he was making preparations for his return to France and that the home he was renting, the Macomb House at 39 Broadway, would soon be vacant. Washington wanted this house. It was relatively new, large and spacious, and it had a commanding view of the Hudson not unlike the view from Mount Vernon of the Potomac. There was much work to be done, however. New stables needed to be built. Rooms needed to be repainted, new wallpaper put up, new carpet put down, some rooms refitted as offices, some decorated for meetings and social occasions, and myriad of little things the progress of which kept Washington occupied for several weeks—and his mind off Thomas Jefferson.

THE COURT IS NOW SITTING

Monday, February 1. A carriage waited outside the second most impressive house in New York (after the Macomb House), at 10 Broadway. The owner, John Jay emerged and stepped briskly inside the carriage. A footman dutifully shut the door and the carriage was off.

Jay didn't have far to go. It was a two-block ride from Lower Broadway to the old Royal Exchange Building at the intersection of Broad and Water Streets. It was there he would preside as chief justice of the Supreme Court.

A faint smell of animal dung greeted Jay and the other justices as they arrived and entered the first-floor arcade and proceeded upstairs. The Exchange Building was a commodities marketplace where grain and livestock were sold. Today, however, the area was clear of livestock and all sign of commercial activity. The second floor was converted into a makeshift courtroom.

The justices were not sure how they should dress for the occasion. The white judicial wig was out: it was much too British as Justice William Cushing discovered a few days earlier when he arrived in New York wearing one. His appearance on the street caused such a stir that he returned immediately to his lodging, sent for a peruke maker, and purchased a more appropriate covering for his head. Jay and his fellow justices wore flowing black robes as they took their places on the bench. Unfortunately, only three justices of the six Washington had appointed were present on the first day. Without a quorum, the first meeting of the United States Supreme Court adjourned after but a few minutes.

The following day, a fourth justice arrived to make a quorum. The Court crier opened the proceeding with a ritual invocation that has remained unchanged for more than two centuries: "Oyez! Oyez! Oyez! All persons having business before the honorable, the Supreme Court of the United States are admonished to draw near and give their attention, for the Court is now sitting. God save the United States and this Honorable Court."

The courtroom was crowded with attorneys and the curious, but none approached the bench to argue a case. In fact, the Court docket was empty. It would be some time before cases proceeded through the lower federal court system and by appeal come to the attention of the Supreme Court. In the meantime, the four justices occupied their time with the adoption of procedural rules and the admission of lawyers to the Court's bar. Having no cases to consider, at the end of the first week the Supreme Court concluded its first session. It would meet again in August, in quite another location, in Philadelphia.

In the meantime, the justices would ride circuit. This would be the undoing of John Jay. In writing the Judiciary Act, Congress had created a separate federal circuit court for each state. There was no separate staff for these courts so each of them was formed by two Supreme Court justices and one local district judge. Since each circuit had to meet twice a year, at dates and places fixed by Congress, the six justices were required to "ride circuit" twice a year. Given the distances and the condition of the roads in 1790 America, it was not possible to return home between court sessions, so a justice would be away from home several weeks or months at a time. At this point in his life, Jay had no desire to be away from home for extended periods. He hated the hardship of travel, and he didn't find the local cases particularly stimulating. He'd been expecting the Supreme Court to be so much more than it was in the 1790s. After two years, he would resign.

CHAPTER 18

Stocks, Speculators, and Slavery

The mood inside the House of Representatives was not pretty. A number of congressmen were outraged that investors, a.k.a. "speculators," "stock-jobbers," and "bloodsuckers," were making a financial killing at the expense of army veterans.

It was Monday, February 8, the first day of debate on Hamilton's plan to revive public credit. In the gallery above the floor, it was standing room only. People who came to see a show would not be disappointed. Somewhere in the gallery was the Treasury Secretary, who surely looked on with alarm at what was happening on the floor below.

The first issue on the docket was discrimination: whether or not to compensate veterans and suppliers who for a variety of reasons had sold their government bonds and IOUs at deep discount.

Debate was getting underway when the representative from Georgia took the floor. A great bear of a man with a booming voice, James Jackson was a frontier politician known to pack a pair of dueling pistols. He fought bravely in the Revolutionary War, afterwards becoming rich practicing law, and owned a large plantation. Because he was from the Deep South and a known hothead, he was an easy target for Northerners to mock, particularly by those seated in the gallery. Jackson, however, did not like being trifled with. On one memorable occasion he removed his pistols, pointed them up at the gallery, and said, "Begone with you, or I'll shoot you dead, sirs, dead."

On this particular day, Jackson hitched up his pants, cast a threatening eye at the gallery, and declared: "Since (Hamilton's) Report has been read in this House, a spirit of havoc, speculation, and ruin, has arisen, and been cherished by people who had access to the information the report contained . . . Three vessels, sir, have sailed within a fortnight from this port, freighted for speculation; they are intended to purchase up the State and other securities in the hands of the uninformed, though honest citizens of North Carolina, South Carolina, and Georgia. My soul rises indignant at the avaricious and immoral turpitude which so vile a conduct displays."

What he was saying was essentially true. Speculators were headed into the nation's hinterlands to buy public securities from ex-soldiers and war suppliers with the hope of making a sizable profit. While a number of Representatives expressed outrage at the practice, it was hardly news. Speculators were as much a part of New York City as accountants and longshoremen, dating back to the days of Dutch rule. Speculators usually dealt in commodities and conducted their business in the same coffee houses that were frequented by Congressmen. Now several of these Congressmen were expressing outrage at the practice, as if they'd never known about it. In the immortal words of Claude Rains in *Casablanca*, they were "shocked, shocked to see speculating going on. . . ." And like Claude Rains, a number of them were profiting from it, including the man with the pistols, James Jackson.

Speculating in public securities had been taking place since the early 1780s. Merchants and large landowners—anybody with money to invest—began buying them up expecting to make a nice profit—if and when the national government got around to paying the war debt. It was a gamble especially in light of the Confederation government's lack of revenue and general impotence, and for several years the price of public securities remained low. As soon as the U.S. Constitution was ratified, however, demand picked up and the price of securities began to climb on the open market. Even investors in Amsterdam and in London, working through a New York brokerage firm, began buying them. It was a sign of investor confidence in the Constitutional mandate to pay the public debt in full. Hamilton had alluded to this in his "Report on Public Credit":

"A general belief prevails that the credit of the United States will quickly be established on the firm foundation of an effectual provision for the existing debt . . . From January to November (1789), they rose thirty-three and a third percent, and from that period to this time (January 1790) they have risen fifty percent more."

As encouraging as these increases were, continental securities had a long way to go before reaching par, and therein lay the problem. If Hamilton's financial plan was to work, public securities needed to be trading at par. From 10 cents on the dollar, by January 1790 when Congress reconvened, securities were trading at 50 cents on the dollar, which was good but far short of where they needed to be. The rest was up to Congress. Passage of Hamilton's Funding and Assumption Bill, coupled with passage of Hamilton's excise tax from which interest payments would be drawn, would likely do the trick.

INVESTOR CONFIDENCE

The key was investor confidence. Investors could put their money anywhere; Hamilton wanted them to invest in public securities. Call them what you will—"speculators," "stock-jobbers," and "blood suckers"—to Hamilton they were investors who were betting on the success of the federal government. If investors had good reason to believe in the financial integrity of the government, public securities would hold their value on the open market. If they didn't, public securities would fluctuate and Hamilton's plan of converting the debt into liquid capital would not work. In order to monetize the public debt it had to be stable.

Hamilton's plan called for the federal government to redeem all continental and state securities at face value. However, securities would not be redeemable in gold or silver coin but with a new issue of U.S. securities. The advantage of the new securities over the old was that the federal government would begin making regular interest payments on the new issue. In fact, Hamilton viewed public securities as more of an annuity than a stock or bond. He saw them as a financial instrument that guaranteed interest to the holder for however long he held the bond. Public securities would trade on the open market, could be used in business transactions as a form of money (like bank notes), only the government would not redeem them for hard cash. The government didn't have the cash anyway, but that wasn't important. What was important was that investors believed the government stood behind its obligations.

In order for U.S. securities to be as good as gold, the government could never default. For many of the larger investors, living in New York, Philadelphia, London, Paris and Amsterdam, that was what mattered most. Whether or not they were ever paid in specie wasn't important, as long as their stocks held their value, could be traded on the open market, and paid quarterly interest.

To be sure, speculators were buying low—as low as five cents on the dollar in some cases. By January of 1790, the going rate for continental securities was 50-cents on the dollar. Speculators were paying in specie. The originals holders didn't have to sell. Many had been sitting on their government bonds and IOUs for several years with nothing to show for it. Speculators were offering payment in gold and silver coins. Why not take it? A piece of the pie was better than none at all.

Speculators ran the risk of the government defaulting or of repudiating the debt in part or in full, depending on what Congress decided. Hamilton's proposal looked promising, but politics played a part; there was no guarantee Congress would pass the measure. Speculating in government securities was just that—speculating.

Jackson was just getting started with his accusations. He and others opposed to assumption charged that Hamilton's supporters in Congress stood to profit greatly, a charge that eventually would be blown up to an accusation that the whole scheme was a plot to enrich speculators. It was true that several of Hamilton's staunchest supporters in both houses were security holders. Yet the two most ardent champions of assumption, Fisher Ames and Theodore Sedgwick of Massachusetts, held no state securities at all, and five opponents of assumption—opponents, mind you—held more than $1,000 apiece in state securities. In the Senate, seven members who championed Hamilton's proposal held large amounts of securities, ranging from $6,000 to $60,000.

In sum, there is little doubt that a number of congressmen who supported Hamilton were motivated at least in part by personal interests, but not to the extent Jackson imagined—probably eight or nine of the sixty-five members of the House and four of the 24 senators.

While professing indignation, Jackson too was motivated by personal interests. He was speculating in land—buying public land in western Georgia with state securities purchased at ten cents on the dollar, and being credited with full-face value at the time of purchase. He was against assumption because it meant competition in his state's bond market was driving up the price of state securities.

Jackson was not alone. Several representatives from Jackson's home state were in on it, plus representatives from the back country of South Carolina, North Carolina, Pennsylvania, and northern New Hampshire. These frontier politicians were out to make a fortune through the purchase of state-owned lands with depreciated public securities. In turn, they planned to sell the land in 100-acre parcels at great profit. Hamilton's proposed assumption of state securities threatened to spoil their get-rich-quick scheme.

THE MAN IN THE MIDDLE

There was a larger issue troubling southern congressmen and it had nothing to do with speculators. It was the fear that Hamilton's plan would upset the established order. It would enrich the north at the expense of the south. At the same time, it would strengthen the federal government which, by the way, was located in a northern city. Under such a scenario, the balance of power would be altered significantly in favor of the north. With the exception of South Carolina, which was in bad financial straights and favored assumption, the battle over assumption was shaping up as a sectional issue: North versus South.

Once again, the man in the middle was James Madison. He alone had the power to deliver the votes either way, as Hamilton well knew. In the "Report on Public Credit" Hamilton very cleverly quoted the congressional resolution of April 26, 1783—a resolution written by Madison himself—which explicitly pledged there would be no discrimination between original and later holders. That was then. Now Madison favored discrimination. Only the issue wasn't really about discrimination at all; it was about assumption. The debate over discrimination was merely a pretext, a trial balloon, to determine the mood of the House. If the House voted for discrimination, it would be a clear indicator that assumption was dead.

Why had Madison changed his tune? Because he was feeling political heat from back home and was under a lot of pressure to act on behalf of his state. His constituency was angry with funding and assumption and what it represented, but especially with assumption. Virginia was one of the few states to have actually paid off its state's war debt. If assumption passed, Virginians would be taxed for a debt they had already paid. In effect, they would be paying twice. Hamilton met with Madison privately to assure him that Virginia would be compensated—and be compensated well—when state debts were audited. But it wasn't enough. Virginia wanted more—more power, more money, more gravitas. As John Adams put it so well: in Virginia all geese are swans. Hamilton was soon to find this out.

There was yet another reason why Virginia was against Hamilton's plan. Early frosts had wiped out half of that year's tobacco crop, and the bizarre money market prevented tobacco prices from rising enough to make up more than a fraction of their losses. It reminded Virginia planters yet again of why they hated the British and their financial system, with its unscrupulous moneymen, symbolic money, bankers, and institutionalized debt. What was Hamilton's plan but an imitation of the very system they despised?

Such was Madison's dilemma. The stakes were high. To break with Hamilton now was to risk losing influence with the president. Not to do so meant certain defeat in the next election.

After James Jackson's long speech, several congressmen spoke, followed by yet another long speech by Jackson. Elias Boudinot of New Jersey then took the floor. He spoke for many when he said: "I should be sorry if, on this occasion, the House should decide that speculation in the funds are violations of either moral or political law. A government hardly exists in which such speculation is disallowed; . . . (I agree) that the spirit of speculation had now risen to an alarming height; but the only way to prevent its future effect, is to give the public funds a degree of stability as soon as possible."

Debate consumed all of Monday, Tuesday, and Wednesday. On Thursday, February 11, Madison took the floor for the first time. On this day he made his position quite clear: he was for discrimination. Seated not 30 feet away up in the gallery, the implication was not lost on Hamilton. With Madison in opposition, the fight over funding and assumption would be bitter and drawn out with success far from assured.

The last thing Madison wanted was to inflame emotions as Jackson had done. Madison's presentation was low key, his arguments cool and logical, designed to control the debate, and therefore to control the outcome. He spoke at length, building a case for discrimination carefully, point-by-point. Throughout the morning, all went well. Not so in the afternoon. In the afternoon, his determination to control events was challenged by a new issue he had not foreseen, an issue sure to ignite the passions—slavery.

It came without warning. In the afternoon, an ominous sign was a gathering of Quakers in the gallery, then Thomas Fitzsimons of Pennsylvania asked to have the floor, followed by John Lawrence of New York who asked to have the floor. Speaking on behalf of the Quakers in their states, Fitzsimons and Lawrence presented petitions calling for the immediate abolishment of the slave trade.

Reaction was immediate as representatives from the Deep South took the floor to protest vehemently. James Jackson of Georgia spoke first with words that boomed like a canon. He glared up at the Quakers. Who were these people? he asked rhetorically. What right did they have to petition Congress? They did not fight in the Revolutionary War. Their "precious conscience" would not allow it. What standing did they have among veterans, who "at the risk of their lives and fortunes, secured to the community their liberty and property?"

William Loughton Smith of South Carolina, took a quieter and more legalistic approach. He pointed out that the Constitution prohibited Congress from passing a law that abolished the slave trade until 1808. The Quakers' petition, therefore, did not have standing. Put another way, they were asking for something that the Constitution had declared off limits.

Jackson would not let go, however. He detected a sinister plot behind the Quaker petition. "I apprehend, if through the interference of the general governments, the slave-trade was abolished, it would evince to the people a general disposition toward a total emancipation." Translation: the Quaker petition was a mere pretense to achieving their real aim of abolishing slavery altogether. He was right.

The following day, Friday, February 12, another petition was presented, this one from the Pennsylvania Abolition Society. It urged Congress to "take such measures in their wisdom, as the powers with which they are invested will authorize, for promoting the abolition of slavery, and discouraging every species of traffic in slaves." The petition made two additional points sure to excite the fears of southern slaveholders. First, it claimed that both slavery and the slave trade were incompatible with the values for which the Revolution was fought. Second, it challenged the claim that the Constitution prohibited any legislation by the federal government against the slave trade for

20 years, suggesting instead that the "general welfare" clause of the Constitution empowered the Congress to take whatever action it deemed "necessary and proper" to eliminate the stigma of trafficking in human beings and to "Countenance the Restoration of Liberty for all Negroes."

The petition was signed by one of the most esteemed and respected of American patriots: Benjamin Franklin.

THE TRUMPET OF CIVIL WAR

Upstairs in the Senate, meanwhile, William Maclay of Pennsylvania heard a rumor there was "warmth in the House of Representatives on the Quaker memorial," in other words, the House looked on the petitions favorably. Boy, was he wrong. He went to gallery to have a look. What he saw was 60 well-dressed men in a state of near-brawl. "The House have certainly debased their dignity," he later wrote in his journal. "Using base invective indecorous language 3 or 4 up at a time. manifest signs of passion. the most disorderly Wanderings, in their Speeches, telling Stories, private anecdotes &ca &ca. I know not What may come of it. but there seems a General discontent among the Members, and many of them do not Hesitate to declare, that the Union Must fall to pieces at the rate we go on."

One of the angriest protestors was Aedanus Burke of South Carolina (he of the whipped syllabub metaphor). The petitioners were "blowing the trumpet of sedition," he declared. Not to be outdone, James Jackson of Georgia said he could hear the "trumpet of civil war." And so it went until someone called for the question. Over strong southern opposition, a vote was taken and the green light was given to debate the slavery question at once.

Jackson then held up a Bible. Slavery was God's will. Everyone knew that. "Ask any Georgia minister," he said. What's more, the southern economy depended on slave labor for its very survival. "Rice cannot be brought to market without these people," he said.

William Smith of South Carolina concurred. "Such is the state of agriculture in that country, no white man would perform the tasks required to drain the swamps and clear the land, so that without slaves it must be depopulated." Smith pointed out that one of the biggest conflicts among the framers of the Constitution was between those states which depended on slave labor and those that did not. As a result, a sectional agreement had been worked out between northern states and southern states that the newly created federal government would not interfere with southern slavery. The southern states had ratified the Constitution with that understanding as a precondition. "Unless that part was granted they would not have come into the union," Smith said. He added: "We took each other, with our mutual bad habits and respective evils, for better, for worse, the Northern States adopted us with our slaves, and we adopted them with their Quakers."

John Laurance of New York took the floor next. He wanted to know how any Christian could read the Sermon on the Mount and believe slavery was compatible with the Bible. As far as the Constitution, Laurance said slavery was an anomaly that would be tolerated only for a given period of time because there was a clear perception that it was wrong and that eventually it would be abolished. He then pointed to the northern states as a clear example. Half of them had abolished slavery since the signing of the Declaration of Independence. It was time the south got on board and began the process.

And so it went. As with assumption, the battle fell along sectional lines, North versus South, with the future of the American republic hanging in the balance. The Senate, meanwhile, turned a deaf ear by closing their windows to mute the shouting matches taking place in the lower house.

Madison elected to stay out of it. Like George Washington, he was a Virginian who had spent a number of years living in the north, first as a student at Princeton College in New Jersey and later as a Congressional delegate in Philadelphia and in New York. He was familiar with the growing abolitionist sentiments of the north. Despite being a slave owner, Madison believed "the peculiar institution" was morally wrong and a national embarrassment. And, he felt certain, it was dying out. So why risk unity—why risk the republic—over an issue that would die off on its own?

The republic had faced the slavery question twice before: in 1776 while debating independence, and again in 1787 while drafting the U.S. Constitution. In the interest of national unity, the slavery question was side-stepped both times. Now, thanks to the petitions presented by the Quakers and by Ben Franklin, the question was up for debate yet again, and threatening national unity once again.

Late in the afternoon Madison reasserted his control. He moved to have the debate taken up by committee, thereby moving it from the public eye and allowing Congress to continue the debate over discrimination. The motion carried. With that, a very long week of debate ended.

On Monday, February 15, Madison resumed his case for discrimination. The public debt should be paid in full, he said. The government would pay what it owed, of course, but to whom did it owe it? The original holders of government securities had a rightful claim, and so did current holders. "To pay both is perhaps beyond the public ability," he said. "And as it would far exceed the value received by the public, it will not be expected by the world, nor even by the creditors themselves.

To reject wholly the claims of each is equally inadmissible . . . ." The honorable thing, he said, was to compromise: to pay the current holders the present market value and to pay the original holders the difference between market value and face value.

It seemed logical enough and the fair thing to do. As the week wore on and counter arguments were made, however, it became clear that Madison's proposal presented more problems than it solved. Identifying the original holders would be a bureaucratic nightmare, and in many cases impossible. Record keeping was scant at best. As one representative pointed out, the work of tracing the original creditors would fill the land "with discontent, corruption, suits, and perjury."

Another objection was that of simple justice. If an original holder sold his bonds to another, "are we to disown the act of the party himself?" asked Elias Boudinot. "Are we to say, we will not be bound by your transfer, we will not treat with your representative but insist on resettlement with you alone?"

In essence, Madison was saying contract law did not apply to the transfer of bonds. Should anyone be unhappy with the amount he was paid at the time of sale, he had merely to turn to the government for redress, and the government would intervene and make it right. Put another way, the owners of public securities were not responsible legally or otherwise for their action. Such a scheme would make a few people happy but it would frighten away the vast majority of serious investors both nationally and abroad.

Monday, February 22 was Washington's birthday. That same day, in the House, a call for the question was made. A vote was taken and the outcome was not even close—the discrimination bill was defeated by 23 votes—13 for, 36 against. In effect, the government decided it would stand behind the transferability of bonds.

Hamilton was relieved, not only because it bode well for the upcoming funding and assumption debate, but because it insured the desirability of owning public securities. It meant the influx of new money entering the market would stay—money from major investors in Europe and at home—money that was driving up the price of pubic securities, helping the nation recover from financial collapse, and insuring the future welfare of the nation.

After a string of successes, it was Madison's first defeat in the House, and a stinging defeat at that. The soft-spoken Virginian did not accept defeat gracefully. When it became obvious his motion was going to fail, he became argumentative and angry. One of Madison's supporters in the Senate, William Maclay, wrote angrily in his journal: "The obstinacy of this man has ruined the opposition (to Hamilton)."

Madison wasn't giving up. He had devised a new and clever strategy for defeating assumption.

CHAPTER 19

Franklin's Last Public Act

On his 58th birthday, George Washington supervised the move across town to his new residence, at 39 Broadway.

The president wrote in his journal: "Monday 22nd. Set seriously about removing my furniture to my new house. The two gentlemen of the family had their beds taken there, and would sleep there tonight." (The two gentlemen were Col. David Humphreys and Tobias Lear.)

That same day, Washington received word that the House of Representatives had defeated the Discrimination Bill. It was welcome news.

While the president favored Hamilton's financial plan in its entirety, he did not support it publicly. Washington believed the public did not want a mere politician as president; the public wanted a father-figure, a national leader who operated above the fray and didn't take sides politically. As commander-in-chief of the Continental Army, Washington learned his job as military leader was part ceremonial and part administrative. The ceremonial part was what the public saw. It was showmanship—pomp and circumstance. As someone who appreciated the theater, Washington viewed the public side of being president as a role to be played, and the role was that of king. He knew this as well as he knew anything. He dressed and acted the part.

A family friend saw him make the transformation once. It was in the middle of informal dinner at the Executive Mansion. Told that some men were waiting outside to express their respect, Washington "disappeared, shortly thereafter making his appearance in full dress." The "full dress" was his presidential uniform—a dignified blue or black suit, with gold buttons and gold buckles, ceremonial sword, and hat. After exchanging pleasantries, he again retired, changed back into casual clothing and returned to dinner. In the one set of clothes, he was President of the United States, dignified, distant, leader of the nation. In the other, he was General Washington, Virginia gentlemen. Even the press learned to acknowledged the difference.

What the public didn't see was the administrative side of Washington's presidency. This was the business side of executive leadership, of setting expectations, of motivating subordinates by whatever means necessary, and of getting results: sometimes unsavory, always necessary. As administrator, Washington used his advisors and his cabinet officers to find solutions, offer alternatives, write his reports and speeches, deal with Congress, keep him well informed, and do his bidding.

Hamilton saw Washington's role as an aegis, a protective shield, under which the President's staff worked unfettered, and without which the Treasury Secretary's financial program very likely would not have gotten off the ground.

The following day, Washington wrote in his journal: "Tuesday 23rd. Few or no visitors at the Levee today, from the idea of my being on the move. After dinner, Mrs. Washington, myself, and children removed, and lodged at our new habitation." The "children" were his step-grandchildren: George Washington Park Custis and Eleanor Park Custis.

Located a block-and-a-half from Bowling Green park, the four-story Macomb House towered over nearby buildings. Like the previous executive mansion at 1 Cherry Street, it was made of honey-colored brick. The house featured a wide entry hall with large, high-ceilinged drawing rooms on either side that were ideal for entertaining and for receiving foreign dignitaries. These rooms had French doors that opened onto a balcony with a breathtaking view of the Hudson River. Washington could be forgiven if sometimes mistaking the far shore for Maryland instead of Jersey.

Washington's new address was close to everything that mattered. Across the street and down one block was the home of the Supreme Court chief justice John Jay. One block north of the Macomb House were the executive offices of Treasury, State and War. One block up from there, at the corner of Broadway and Wall Street was Trinity Church where the president now attended Sunday service. One block east of Trinity Church, at the corner of Wall and Nassau Street, was Federal Hall. Further east, at the corner of Wall and Water Street, was Merchant's Coffee House, where each day public securities were being sold in what was a bull market. How long the bull market would last depended largely on what Congress did with the funding and assumption bill.

There was one piece of unfinished business bothering Washington and that was the appointment of Thomas Jefferson as Secretary of State. Washington had waited three months for his reply. Finally, on February 14, it arrived in the mail. Jefferson's letter read in part:

"Sir, I have duly received the (follow-up) letter of 21st January with which you have honored me, and no longer hesitate to undertake the office to which you are pleased to call me. Your desire that I should come as quickly as possible is a sufficient reason for me to postpone every matter of business, however pressing, which admits postponement. Still it will be the close of the ensuing week before I can get away, and then I shall have to go by way of Richmond, which will lengthen my road . . . I hope I shall have the honor of satisfying you that the circumstances which prevent my immediate departure are not under my control."

JEFFERSON MOVES NORTH

Jefferson had planned to return to Paris after Christmas. Being minister to France suited him perfectly. The job consumed little of his time or energy. He had plenty of opportunity to study architecture, to travel to the south of France, and on occasion to get over to London and shop. A voracious reader, he was forever buying books on a wide range of subjects. Indeed, among the many items he had shipped from France was a caseload of books. While in Paris, he developed a taste for French cooking (he sent his personal chef to French culinary school) and especially for French wine.

The position of Secretary of State did not suit him and he knew it. Jefferson feared his time would be consumed with mundane details, he would be at the beck and call of the president, and no longer have time to pursue his many interests. Madison assured him that would not be the case, but for the most part that's how it turned out to be. Like most creative people, Jefferson was a free spirit and didn't like being tied to a job. Being highly ambitious, however, he could not resist the allure of being a part of Washington's inner circle. In New York, he would have influence with the president and perhaps be next in line for the nation's top office. Not so in France. For these reasons, he accepted the appointment as Secretary of State.

Jefferson saw his daughter Martha married to Colonel Thomas Mann Randolph on February 23. On March 1, he boarded his phaeton (a coach with a pulldown top—the sports car of its day) and departed for New York. On the way he stopped in Richmond to obtain a two-thousand dollar loan from his English creditors. Like most Virginia planters, Jefferson was perpetually short of cash. A week later he traveled to Alexandria where he was trapped by eighteen inches of snow. He sent his phaeton on to New York by boat and booked passage on the next stage coach bound for New York. In Philadelphia he stopped to see an old friend—Benjamin Franklin.

If everyone wanted George Washington as their king, then everyone wanted Ben Franklin as their uncle. Franklin's bespectacled and wizened eyes tended to ignore people's vices and to see only their virtues. That did not mean Franklin suffered fools gladly, as we shall see. Like Hamilton, he was an Horatio Alger story come to life, the poor boy who overcame a world of obstacles to rise to the top of society. Franklin was America's premier scientist, humorist, business strategist, journalist, statesman and diplomat. Beloved in France, his visage was instantly recognizable throughout North America and in all of Europe. Of all the Founders, Benjamin Franklin was the person most responsible for making the United States a haven of religious tolerance.

Franklin came late to the patriotic cause. He spent most of the 1760s in London attempting to obtain a royal charter for Pennsylvania. As late as 1771 he lobbied for a position within the English government. When he returned to the colonies, however, he was thoroughly disgusted with the English Parliament's handling of the American crisis. He joined the patriotic cause and rose quickly to the top of political leadership. Franklin was the only person to sign all four of the documents essential to the founding of the United States: the Declaration of Independence, the Treaty with France, the Peace Accord with Britain, and the Constitution.

Franklin and Jefferson sat on the committee that drafted the Declaration of Independence. Jefferson wrote the bulk of the document, with an assist from Franklin and John Adams. A decade later, Jefferson replaced Franklin in Paris as minister to France.

Franklin's contribution to the Constitutional Convention in 1787 was modest. His closing speech, however, helped convince the delegates to set aside their differences and sign the document. Among his closing remarks:

"I agree to this Constitution, with all its faults, if they are such . . . I doubt whether any other convention we can obtain may be able to make a better Constitution; for, when you assemble a number of men to have the advantage of their joint wisdom, you inevitably assemble with those men all their prejudices, their passions, their errors of opinion, their local interests, and their selfish views. From such an assembly can a perfect production be expected?

"It therefore astonishes me, sir, to find this system approaching so near to perfection as it does; and I think it will astonish our enemies, who are waiting with confidence to hear that our councils are confounded, like those of the builders of Babel, and that our states are on the point of separation, only to meet hereafter for the purpose of cutting one another's throats.

"Thus I consent, sir, to this Constitution because I expect no better, and because I am not sure that it is not the best."

At the time of Jefferson's visit, Franklin, now age 84, was involved with the final project of his long public life—the abolition of slavery.

Bedridden and near death, he'd been following the slavery debate in Congress in the newspapers. While Jefferson was in transit, a great deal had been taking place in the House.

On March 8, the special committee had announced it was ready to give its report.

Representatives from the Deep South protested immediately. It was neither the time nor the place to be debating slavery, they said. There were Quakers in the gallery. The press was present. It seemed the whole world was watching—standing in judgement. The debate was not for public consumption. If anything, it should be held in private among gentlemen, as it had been on past occasions.

The delegates from South Carolina were particularly outraged. William Loughton Smith pointed up at the gallery and likened the Quakers to "evil spirits hovering over our heads." James Jackson made it his duty to glare threateningly at the gallery whenever there was negative reaction. He made no bones about his feelings: Quakers were lunatics, he said, and then launched into a long and mostly incoherent tirade. The best the press could make of it was that any decision by the House to receive the committee report was tantamount to the dissolution of the union. Despite their protests and their threats, the Deep South did not have the votes to stop the committee report from being aired.

REACTION TO THE COMMITTEE REPORT

On March 16, the committee presented its report. Among the key points:

— Congress had no power to prohibit the slave trade before 1808, and no power to emancipate slaves or to interfere in the states' "internal regulations" of slavery;

— Congress could, however, regulate the slave trade by levying a ten-dollar importation tax referred to in the Constitution;

— Congress also could encourage state legislatures to "revise their laws from time to time, when necessary" with regard to the two issues, and promote the ideals listed in the petitions.

The report concluded "that in all cases to which the authority of Congress extends, they will exercise it for the humane objects of the (petitioners), so far as they can be promoted on the principles of justice, humanity, and good policy."

It was mild stuff, but one would never know it judging by the reaction from the Deep South.

Aedanus Burke of South Carolina denounced the Quakers as spies, traitors, and suppliers of the enemy. He became so unruly he had to be called to order.

Cool as always, William Loughton Smith spoke in a softer voice. To accept the report in its present form, he said, "would excite tumults, seditions, and insurrections." Not only that, it would destroy all that slavery had made possible: the southern economy and the southern way of life, a life of culture, refinement, and valor.

These speeches were warmup acts for the main event: James Jackson.

Jackson stacked a number of books on his desk, including the Bible. The Bible, he said, sanctions slavery in several passages from the Old Testament. Are not the two precepts, "Masters treat your slaves with kindness: Slaves serve your masters with cheerfulness and fidelity . . ." clear proofs?

The most reliable and recent studies of African tribal culture, he said, demonstrated that slavery was a long-standing custom among Africans themselves. Enslaved Africans in America were simply experiencing a condition that they would otherwise experience, probably under more oppressive conditions, in their native land.

Jackson read selected passages from Thomas Jefferson's *Notes on the State of Virginia.* "What is to be done with the slaves when freed?" Jackson read, quoting Jefferson. Either they must be incorporated where they are or they must be colonized somewhere else. The two races cannot live together on equal terms because of "deep rooted prejudices entertained by the whites—ten-thousand recollections by the blacks of the injuries they have sustained—new provocations—the real distinctions that nature has made, and many other circumstances which divide us into parties, and produce convulsions which would never end but with the extermination of one or the other race."

"Perhaps there were a few whites in the North who did not concur with Mr. Jefferson's sentiments," Jackson said. Perhaps the Quaker petitions approved of racial mixing and looked forward to "giving their daughters to negro sons, and receiving the negro daughters for their sons."

Jackson spoke for two hours. After he finished, there was no rebuttal. Not in the House, anyway. A rebuttal would be forthcoming, however, all the way from Philadelphia.

FRANKLIN'S PARODY

Jackson's speech was published in newspapers around the country. From his deathbed in Philadelphia, Franklin read an account of Jackson's speech in the Federal Gazette around the time of Jefferson's visit. Whether or not Franklin and Jefferson discussed the House debate is not known. By the time the Virginian arrived in New York, on March 21, Franklin had penned his response. A satire, it appeared in several newspapers from Philadelphia up to Boston but nowhere south of the Potomac. It was Franklin's last public act.

Wrote Franklin:

"Reading last night in your excellent paper the speech of Mr. Jackson in Congress, against meddling with the affairs of slavery, or attempts to mend the condition of the slaves, it put me in mind of a similar one made by Sidi Mehemet Ibrahim, a member of the Divan of Algiers.... It was against the petition of the sect called Erika, or Purists, who prayed for the abolition of piracy and slavery, as being unjust. Mr. Jackson does not quote it: perhaps he has not seen it. If, therefore, some of the reasonings are to be found in his eloquent speech it may only show that men's interests and intellects operate and are operated on with surprisingly similar circumstances."

Using Sidi Mehemet as a stand-in for Jackson, the Devan of Algiers for Congress, and the Erika, or Purists, for the Quakers, Franklin parodied Jackson's speech in the Algerian speech, which he dreamed up. At the time, Algerian pirates in the Mediterranean were raiding American vessels and making slaves of the captives. Franklin's parody compared the American and Algerian policies and showed there was little to differentiate them. Where Jackson used Christianity to justify enslavement of African-Americans, Sidi Mehemt used Islam to justify enslavement of Christians.

Paraphrasing Jackson, Franklin quoted Sidi Mehemet's fictitious speech: *"If we forbear to make slaves of their people, who, in the hot climate, are to cultivate our lands, who are to perform the common labors of our city, and in our families? Must we not then be our own slaves? And is there not more compassion and more favor due to us Mussulmen, than to these Christian dogs? We have now above 50,000 slaves in and near Algiers. This number, if not kept up by fresh supplies, will soon diminish, and be gradually annihilated. If then we cease taking and plundering the Infidel ships, and making slaves of the seamen and passengers, our lands will become of no value for want of cultivation; the rents of houses in the city will sink one half, and the revenues of government arising from its share of prizes must be totally destroyed."*

If the trade and keeping of Christian slaves be abolished *"who is to indemnify their masters for the loss? Will the state do it? Is the treasury sufficient? Will the Erika do it? Can they do it. . .? And if we set our slaves free, what is to be done with them . . .? Our people will not pollute themselves by intermarrying with them. . . ."*

As slaves *"is their condition made worse by their falling into our hands? No . . . they are brought into a land where the sun of Islamism gives forth light, and shines in full splendor, and they have an opportunity of making themselves acquainted with the true doctrine, and thereby saving their immortal souls. . . ."* Are not Christians *"better off with us, rather than remain in Europe where they would only cut each other's throats in religious wars. . . .? How grossly are (the Erika) mistaken in imagining slavery to be disallowed by the Al Koran! Are not the two precepts, to quote no more, Masters treat your slaves with kindness: Slaves serve your masters with cheerfulness and fidelity, clear proofs to the contrary. . . ?"*

Franklin concluded the paraphrase of Jackson's speech with the Algerian saying: *"The Doctrine, that Plundering and Enslaving the Christians is unjust, is at best problematical . . .* and *. . . that it is in the Interest of the State to continue the Practice; therefore the Petition be rejected."*

The same day Franklin's letter was published in the Federal Gazette, the House of Representatives did as Jackson requested and rejected the Quaker and Franklin petitions.

CHAPTER 20

The Slavery (Un)Resolution

No shouting matches, no brawls, no threats of secession. On the floor of the House of Representatives, all was sweetness and nice.

Several northerners who previously had sided with the Quakers expressed regret that the petition to end the slave trade had gotten out of hand. Fisher Ames of Massachusetts wondered why the House had allowed itself to be drawn into such a divisive debate over what he now called "abstract propositions." James Jackson of Georgia was feeling particularly charitable. He thanked Ames and his northern colleagues for "seeing the error of their ways." He said it was nice to see again the old conciliatory spirit that formerly had united northern and southern interests.

The events in Congress that day, however conciliatory, were among the supreme ironies of the young republic. On the very day Benjamin

Franklin's letter appeared in newspapers making a mockery of James Jackson's justification of slavery—March 23, 1790—the House of Representatives decided to ignore slavery as if it didn't exist. And it did so without so much as a whimper of opposition from northern abolitionists in Congress.

Obviously, something had happened, some sort of deal worked out between factions, done privately and out of public view. Who could have brokered such a deal? While the answer isn't known with certainty, evidence points to the man from Orange County, Virginia.

James Madison was personally embarrassed by the slavery debate, embarrassed that it had gotten out of hand, and embarrassed that it was reported in the newspapers. He found the blatantly proslavery arguments of the Deep South "shamefully indecent," and "intemperate beyond all example and even all decorum." While he lived south of the Mason-Dixon Line, he felt more comfortable operating on the high moral ground of the north, where slavery was fading away. As floor leader and a progressive southerner, he was in a unique position to end the rancor by bringing both sides to the table and brokering a compromise.

SEVEN RESOLUTIONS

In the days leading up to the compromise, the subcommittee that had been meeting behind closed doors reported back to the House with Seven Resolutions in response to the Quaker petition. The Deep South did not want the resolutions aired publicly and asked to have the committee's report tabled. For the moment, Madison agreed. His motive was not merely to table the report—he wanted to render it of none effect. It was at this point that a deal was made that returned unity to the floor.

With a sense of new-found unity—and Madison controlling the outcome—the House went into committee of the whole and addressed the Seven Resolutions. However tepid, the Resolutions were troublesome to slave holders and therefore needed revising. After discussion, the seven resolutions were reduced to three. A proposed tax on the slave trade was dropped altogether, as was the seventh resolution, with its vague declaration of solidarity with the benevolent goals of the Quaker petitioners. The new language of the second resolution read in part: "The Congress have no authority to interfere in the emancipation of slaves, or in the treatment of them within any of the States; it remaining with the several States alone to provide any regulation therein, which humanity and true policy may require." Instead of imposing a moratorium on congressional action against slavery until 1808, as specified in the Constitution, the revised resolutions made it unconstitutional "to attempt to manumit them at any time." In other words, any future effort at emancipation by the federal government was strictly prohibited. Thus, the revised version of the committee's recommendations were a resolution to do nothing. It passed the House easily.

According to historian Joseph J. Ellis, the decision that day in the House of Representatives had the equivalent effect of a landmark Supreme Court decision that prohibited any government effort at ending slavery and the slave trade—forever.

In 1792, when another Quaker petition was presented in the House, William L. Smith of South Carolina referred his colleagues to the earlier debate of 1790. The petition was withdrawn. Some 40 years later, in 1833, Daniel Webster cited the same precedent, when he said: "My opinion of the powers of Congress on the subject of slaves and slavery is that Congress has no authority to interfere in the emancipation of slaves. This was resolved by the House in 1790. . . ."

A number of people with the political clout to have made a difference kept silent. Among the seven most influential people in America, only one spoke out—Benjamin Franklin. The other six were George Washington, James Madison, Alexander Hamilton, John Jay, John Adams, and Thomas Jefferson. While their positions on slavery are similar, their records are remarkably different, as the following illustrates:

GEORGE WASHINGTON

Washington was born at a time when slavery had yet to be questioned anywhere in the colonies. As a young man, he was a tough task master, but as he grew older he began to change. Whippings stopped. He encouraged marriage among slaves, and to keep families together resolved not to sell or trade slaves without their consent. Since consent was rarely given, the General found himself with a growing economic liability—a work force larger than he could employ profitably. The problem was partly due to the high-birth rate among Mount Vernon slaves and partly because he switched from growing tobacco to growing wheat and barley which required fewer workers. Most Virginia planters, when overstocked or in need of quick cash, sold a few slaves. Washington did not.

As commander-in-chief of the Continental Army, Washington spent eight years in the north where slaves were fewer and gradual emancipation was underway. At first, he was shocked to find free blacks serving in his army. As the war dragged on and enlistment fell off, he urged more slaves to be enlisted with the promise of freedom at war's end. As a result, the Continental Army was the most racially integrated American fighting force until the Vietnam War. Being in the north for so long, Washington began to see the advantage of free labor, manufacturing, and financial credit, and to question the economics of slavery. While in Philadelphia over the winter of 1778-79, he seriously considered selling his slaves and using the proceeds as investment capital.

After the Revolution, Washington returned to life as a Virginia planter intent on making Mount Vernon profitable again. He acknowledged that slavery was evil but he didn't see a way of running his large plantation without it. One reason slavery was losing its hold in the north was the endless supply of free labor arriving daily at docks in cities like Boston and Philadelphia and especially New York. The only labor force entering the south was enslaved.

Washington decided the best he could manage was to free his own slaves upon his death. To prepare them for freedom, he intended to have them taught to read and write only to discover Virginia had passed a law making it illegal. In private, Washington was increasingly frustrated with the attitude of his fellow Virginians toward slavery. Should the nation divide along north-south lines, Washington told friends he would side with the north.

JAMES MADISON

The man from Orange County, Virginia seemed to be forever in the middle of two opposing political forces. James Madison was both a nationalist and a Virginian, which were about as compatible as cats and dogs.

Over the winter of 1790, Madison was forced to choose, and he chose to side with his home state, which meant turning his back on the nationalist vision he shared with Hamilton, and siding with a narrow states' rights agenda that included slavery. The decision would prove irrevocable. Madison would go to his grave as a slave owner.

Madison, like Jefferson, Washington, George Mason, and other liberal-minded Virginians, believed slavery was immoral and inconsistent with the ideals of the revolution. In 1783, as Madison was preparing to return home from Philadelphia after living four years in the north, he learned his slave Billey had become "too thoroughly tainted to be fit companion for fellow slaves in Virginia." The usual practice with slaves who resisted returning to the life of a plantation as a slave, was to ship them off to the West Indies. It was cruelty in the extreme, as West Indian slaves were literary worked to death. Madison could not bring himself to do this. Instead, he sold Billey in Philadelphia, where he would be set free in seven years. In a letter to his father, Madison explained his actions: why should Billey be punished "merely for coveting that liberty for which we have paid the price of so much blood, and have proclaimed so often to be right, and worthy the pursuit, of every human being?"

As with Washington, time in the north changed Madison's view and he had trouble readjusting to life on a Virginia plantation. The cruelty and injustice of the slave system so affronted him that he studied law and invested in land speculation as a means of earning a living by other means. It didn't work. He never practiced law and he failed as a land speculator. So Madison returned to elected office. Politics didn't pay well but for extended periods it did keep him away from the evils of his father's slave plantation.

In 1785, as a member of the Virginia Assembly, Madison spoke in favor of a bill (drafted by Jefferson) that called for the gradual abolition of slavery. Reaction to the bill was so volatile that Madison gave up all hope of abolishing slavery in his lifetime. To get elected and to have influence in his state, meant being silent on the slavery issue. Madison's only consolation was to tell himself that eventually slavery would fade away in the south as it was doing in the north. It was wishful thinking.

ALEXANDER HAMILTON

Born an outcast on a tiny Caribbean island, Alexander Hamilton had little trouble identifying with slaves. As a bastard, he couldn't attend a christian school. When he was nine, his father left never to return, and when he was eleven his mother died. At age twelve, he was put to work in the service of others. Because he had a head for math, he was made a clerk in a counting house (his older brother James was made a carpenter's apprentice). A life of "grov'ling" (as he put it) was not what he had in mind for himself. He read Plutarch's "Lives of Noble Grecians and Romans" and dreamed of one day being famous as a nation-founder.

Hamilton saw African slaves arrive daily at the docks in St. Croix, be whipped into submission and be herded like cattle to the sugarcane fields. Many died from the unrelenting heat and intolerable working conditions. Being white, Hamilton knew he had a slim chance of breaking free of a life of drudgery, which he managed to do, while slaves had absolutely no chance of regaining their freedom.

As an officer in Washington's army, Hamilton advocated the enlistment of African slaves as soldiers with the promise of freedom at war's end. "I have not the least doubt the (N)egroes will make very excellent soldiers," he wrote to John Jay. How did he assess their innate abilities? At a time when Jefferson questioned the mental and moral abilities of blacks, and speculated in writing about their inferiority, Hamilton wrote, "For their natural faculties are as good as ours."

When the war ended, northern abolitionists began pointing out the contradiction of a revolution for freedom fought by a society that tolerated slavery. "It always seemed a most iniquitous scheme to me," wrote Abigail Adams in a letter to her husband John, "to fight ourselves for what we are daily robbing and plundering from those who have as good a right to freedom as we have."

Hamilton never owned slaves, and was among more than thirty New Yorkers who, in January 1785, formed the New York Manumission Society. Paradoxically, many members were themselves slaveholders. They rejected a resolution that Hamilton supported, requiring members to free their slaves. Nonetheless, over the next decade the Society worked to make slavery illegal in New York and to protect free blacks from being illegally taken into slavery.

JOHN JAY

As president of the New York Manumission Society, John Jay advocated gradual emancipation and apparently decided such a policy applied to himself. The few slaves he did own—five in all—were not manumitted until late in his life.

By all accounts, Jay was a benevolent master. To a fellow slaveholder he wrote: "Providence has placed these persons in stations below us. They are servants but they are men; and kindness to inferiors more strongly indicates magnanimity than meanness." To an antislavery friend in England he wrote that it was "very inconsistent as well as unjust and perhaps impious" for men to "pray and fight for their own freedom" and yet to "keep others in slavery."

Jay drafted a petition for the Manumission Society arguing for legislation that would prohibit the export of blacks or slaves from New York. "It is well known," he argued, "that the condition of slaves in this state is far more tolerable and easy than in many other countries" (i.e. southern states). While the Constitutional Convention was meeting in Philadelphia in 1787, he drafted another petition, this time to urge the new federal constitution to prohibit the import of slaves into the country. The timing wasn't good as delegates already had decided to remain silent on the issue, and the petition was not submitted.

Within a few years of its formation, the New York Manumission Society opened a school for free blacks, and over the next few decades this school and others sponsored by the society educated more than two thousand African Americans. Many of the graduates went on to become leaders of the black community and leaders of the abolition movement. While Jay was governor of New York (1795-1801), the state passed legislation to end slavery which took many years to implement. It wasn't until 1827 that slaves were given freedom in New York.

JOHN ADAMS

John Adams never owned slaves, nor hired the slaves of others to work his farm, as was sometimes done in New England. Honest John chopped his own wood, planted and harvested his own fields, and rose to prominence as a savvy Boston attorney.

Despite being against "the peculiar institution," Adams appeared in several slave cases—for the master, never the slave. It was in keeping with his character to represent those with whom he disagreed, if they had a worthy case. He defended the commanding officer of the British regiment that fired on patriots in the Boston Massacre, and got him acquitted.

Adams was sent to Philadelphia to represent Massachusetts as a delegate to the Continental Congress. As a persuasive and indefatigable speaker, he could talk a reluctant Congress into declaring independence from England, but he could not talk southern delegates into giving up their slaves.

In throwing off the yoke of monarchy, the colonists were attempting to create the world anew. Someone needed to explain it. Adams picked a brilliant young southerner with a flair for writing to find the right words. Possessing a "canine appetite" for books, Thomas Jefferson had little trouble finding the words that went to the very heart of the issue:

"We hold these truths to be self-evident, that all men are created equal, that they are endowed by their Creator with certain inalienable rights, that among these are life, liberty, and the pursuit of happiness. That to secure these rights, governments are instituted among men, deriving their just powers from the consent of the governed."

And,

". . . when a long train of abuses and usurpations, pursuing invariably the same object evinces a design to reduce them under absolute despotism, it is their right, it is their duty, to throw off such government, and to provide new guards for the future security."

Jefferson's initial draft included passages that called slavery into question, passages that were struck out by the delegation-at-large. Indeed, the biggest stumbling block to independence was slavery. The south would not compromise. The south would have its slaves without condition, or there would be no revolution.

Adams, like all northern delegates, was not about to let southern slavery jeopardize the larger purpose, which was independence. Yes, Adams was against slavery but going forward he would speak not of abolition but of gradual emancipation. Gradual emancipation was underway in the north and nowhere was that more evident than in Philadelphia, where Congress was meeting. No doubt, such evidence convinced delegates that the same thing would happen south of the Mason-Dixon Line—eventually. Among the next generation of leaders,

John Calhoun would speak of slavery as "the scaffolding for the south," support that would be removed, "when the work was done."

"Gradual emancipation" proved to be magical words that brought unity to the Continental Congress and ultimately independence from England. The very idea of gradual emancipation allowed slave owners north and south to live with their hypocrisy. Not everyone was taken in. In London, Samuel Johnson asked: "How is it that we hear the loudest yelps for liberty from the drivers of Negroes?"

THOMAS JEFFERSON

Among the great Congressional orators of 1776, Thomas Jefferson was an anomaly: he was shy and had trouble expressing himself. Adams recalled that "during the whole Time I sat with him in Congress, I never heard him utter three sentences together." What Jefferson lacked in speaking skills, however, he more than made up in writing skills. When it was time to draft the Declaration of Independence, the choice came down to two people: John Adams and Thomas Jefferson. Adams was himself an excellent writer but acknowledged that Jefferson was better, so the task fell to the shy Virginian.

It took Jefferson two days to write the first draft. Adams and Benjamin Franklin made a few stylistic changes then the document went before Congress. It was a painful ordeal for Jefferson to sit through as approximately one-fourth of what he had written was crossed out. While he didn't breathe a word of protest, he lamented the changes for the rest of life. Congress had "mangled" his manuscript.

Jefferson's preamble with its ringing endorsement of universal equality—the part everyone remembers—was left intact. The cuts were to the part no one remembers: the lengthy bill of indictment against King George III, chief of which was the long passage in which Jefferson blamed the King for slavery and the slave trade. As emphatic a passage as any, it was to have been the climax of all the charges made against the king. The passage was removed, Jefferson said later, mainly because South Carolina and Georgia objected. While it condemned slavery as evil, Jefferson's concluding passage stopped short of endorsing outright abolition. Be that as it may, the passage proved controversial and was stricken out. The preamble was allowed to stand, which would become holy scripture for human rights advocates the world over.

While Jefferson was against slavery, like other southern planters he wasn't prepared to release his slaves from bondage. He was counting on gradual emancipation to somehow solve the problem for him. What no one seems to have considered at the time was the vastly greater number of slaves living in the south as opposed to the north, and that the south—particularly the Deep South—was still importing African slaves while the northern workforce was filling its ranks with immigrant European free labor.

Years later, when it was clear that southern slavery was not fading away but spreading into the western territories, Jefferson grew alarmed. In his final years, it awoke him "like a fire bell in the night," filling him with terror. He believed the two races could not live together in harmony. Once freed, Jefferson believed former slaves would take revenge on their former captives. "We have the wolf by the ears," he complained, "and we can neither hold him, nor safely let him go."

Jefferson was not a party to the Slavery (Un)Resolution of 1790 but he would have agreed that silence was the only way of preserving the fragile union. Like the other five, he too believed slavery was morally wrong and would eventually die out, so why risk everything they had struggled to achieve over an issue that was doomed anyway?

FINAL WORD

The founders knew well that the slavery question if left unaddressed might be the ruin of their beloved republic. Never did they dream, however, that by avoiding the issue they were condemning 600,000 yet unborn citizens to die in a war that one day would bring closure to "the peculiar institution." By remaining silent that is, in fact, what they were doing.

CHAPTER 21

"The Most Bitter and Angry Contest"

Thomas Jefferson arrived quietly in New York City on Sunday, February 21 and booked lodging at a tavern on 115 Broadway. The following morning he was sworn into office as Secretary of State. That same day Washington's birthday was celebrated; it's likely this was the time when Jefferson and Hamilton met for the first time.

As Washington was the father of his country, Jefferson and Hamilton were destined to become the fathers of the two-party system. As to which party each represents in our time is not clear. Being pro-business would seem to make Hamilton a Republican, until one digs deeper into his writings and discover a deep-rooted racial tolerance that would put him in good stead with liberal Democrats. While some historians have framed him as an elitist, Hamilton created a financial system that rewarded ingenuity and hard work rather than class and privilege. Jefferson is harder to pin down. Conservative Republicans and Liberal Democrats alike can quote Jefferson for their own purposes, such was the diversity of ideas he expressed over his long lifetime. The man who drafted the Declaration of Independence and initiated America's doctrine of separation of church and state also questioned the intelligence of African Americans and advocated states' rights over the power of the federal government. As the nation's chief executive, however, he expanded the powers of the presidency and doubled the size of the nation, actions more Hamiltonian than Jeffersonian.

Jefferson and Hamilton were the brightest minds of their generation; after that the similarity ends. As a member of the Virginia gentry, Jefferson was born into a life of ease and privilege. Orphaned at age 11, Hamilton had to work hard for everything he achieved. Both men were voluminous readers, trained in the legal arts, good listeners, and quick on the uptake. Where Hamilton tended to share his ideas freely, Jefferson tended to be reserved and spoke freely only among intimates. Both men could be charming when the occasion called for it. Jefferson avoided conflict; Hamilton welcomed it. Hamilton enjoyed talking about economics, law, and politics; Jefferson favored art, music, science, and architecture. Hamilton was a romantic, obsessed with honor, yet highly pragmatic. Jefferson was an artist at heart who saw the world in terms of good and evil, black and while. Hamilton pursued higher learning to advance his career; Jefferson pursued higher learning for the sheer joy of it.

At six-foot-two, Jefferson was unusually tall in an age where the average height was five-foot-seven. He had blue eyes, a long fine nose, a strong jaw, and sandy red hair that he wore tied in a ponytail. On his feet he was square-shouldered and formal in appearance. Sitting he tended to be a sloucher. He bowed to everyone he met, and listened with arms folded across his chest.

Jefferson arrived at mid-point of the First Congress, at the close of the slavery debate and the beginning of the assumption debate. His first task was to find a suitable house to rent, preferably near the State Department.

MADISON GOES PUBLIC

While Jefferson searched for a house, Madison asked to meet privately with Hamilton. He was going public with his opposition to assumption and wanted to pay Hamilton the courtesy of informing him first. By now, Hamilton surely suspected Madison's change of heart. He recalled later that Madison "alleged in his justification that the very considerable alienation of the debt, subsequent to the period at which he had opposed discrimination, had essentially changed the state of the question."

In Hamilton's mind, Madison was turning his back on everything the two of them stood for, including the role of statesman. Sure, Madison had to face his constituency in next year's election, but in the best sense of the word, a statesman didn't worry about elections. He did what was best for his country rather than be swayed by public opinion. Public opinion was fickle. It was motivated by fear and therefore easily manipulated by unscrupulous politicians. At its worst, it was mob rule and quick to trample on individual rights. Madison knew this very well. As the author of the U.S. Constitution, he had designed a government of checks and balances to keep public opinion in check and to protect individual rights. What was Madison doing but giving in to public pressure from back home by opposing Hamilton's financial plan?

To defeat assumption, Madison's strategy was to stall for time, until representatives from North Carolina took their seats in the House.

North Carolina was the latest state to join the union and opposed assumption. If Madison was to defeat the assumption bill, he would need North Carolina's five votes. So he stalled for time. First, he tied up the House for several weeks with debating the merits of discrimination. He hadn't counted on the slavery debate but it ate up more time and therefore served his stalling tactics quite well.

Madison's next move was to divide and conquer. He knew how to count votes, and funding had the votes. Assumption, on the other hand, was controversial and therefore vulnerable. Madison moved to have funding and assumption separated and debated as separate bills. Hamilton, of course, wanted the two programs debated as one, which is how he saw them. In order for his financial plan to work, he needed the $25 million in states' debt and what it represented—state creditors made beholden to the federal government. The matter was debated and put to a vote. Despite a number of Congressmen who supported Hamilton, this time the vote went Madison's way. Funding and assumption would be debated in the House as separate bills.

With assumption first on the docket, the focus now was on state accounts—on how much each state owed creditors. On February 24, Madison moved that assumption be coupled with an "effectual provision" for settling state accounts. After a long debate, Madison's proposal was adopted. A few days later it was moved and approved that the treasury secretary prepare a report on what taxes could be raised to support the state debts if they were assumed by the federal government. Since Hamilton had pointedly avoided this question in his report, many thought the order would either catch him unprepared or uncover a design to impose highly objectionable taxes. Either way, the result would consume more time and thereby serve Madison's overall purpose of stalling for time. Hamilton, however, who had been following the debate closely, was prepared. Within two days he presented the House with a report containing ten painless and easily collected sources of taxation, which together would yield more than $1 million annually and thus service the state debts comfortably.

Several weeks of debate followed, as March gave way to April. Debate was particularly rancorous. Jefferson, who sometimes watched from the gallery, categorized the assumption debate as "the most bitter and angry contest ever known in Congress before or since the union of the states." On April 13, with the five delegates from North Carolina having taken their seats at last, Madison called for the question. A vote was taken and the House defeated assumption by two votes—31 to 29. As Madison knew it would, North Carolina's five votes made the difference.

Over the next six weeks, as the Funding Bill was hammered into shape, repeated efforts to re-insert assumption into Hamilton's financial package were blocked successfully by the man from Orange County, Virginia.

According to Forrest McDonald, Madison's stalling tactics were a godsend to the very people he detested—speculators. It gave them more time to purchase state securities at mere pennies on the dollar—and southern states securities at that. According to McDonald's research, during that time eleven New Yorkers purchased North Carolina securities with a face value of $617,185 for a cash outlay of a mere $80,000. Eight other New Yorkers acquired South Carolina securities with a face value of $606,643 for a cash outlay of $120,000. Another twenty-two speculators bought Virginia securities with a face value of $1,070,077 for comparable outlays of cash. Writes McDonald: "Before he was through Madison would put more profits into the hands of speculators than Hamilton could have done by inviting them to help themselves to the Treasury."

FRANKLIN EULOGIZED

The same day Assumption was defeated Thomas Jefferson celebrated his 47th birthday. Four days later, on April 17, Benjamin Franklin died. The next day word of his passing reached New York. Flags were flown at half-mast. On April 22, a memorial service was held in the House of Representatives. James Madison delivered the final tribute:

"The House, being informed of the decease of Benjamin Franklin, a citizen whose native genius was not more an ornament to human nature, than his various exertions of it have been precious to science, to freedom, and to his country, do resolve, as mark of the veneration due to his memory, that the 169members wear the customary badge of mourning for one month."

Joseph J. Ellis writes of the occasion: "The symbolism of the scene was poignant, dramatizing as it did the passing of the prototypical American and (with him) the cause of gradual emancipation. Whether they knew it or not, the badge of mourning the members of the House agreed to wear also bore testimony to the tragic and perhaps intractable (slavery) problem that even the revolutionary generation, with all its extraordinary talent, could neither solve nor face."

CHAPTER 22

Washington's Second Trip (and Second Illness)

George Washington lacked the common touch. Being a man of few words and emotionally distant made him unapproachable. However, a bit of cow dung clinging to the sole of his polished boots could have a transforming effect. On a farm he would open up and talk shop. Touring Long Island the third week of April, that is what he did—talk shop with farmers and be a regular guy.

It was a part of the president's plan to tour the nation, to see and be seen among the people. Washington wanted to know what common people thought of the new government; what he was doing was taking an informal opinion poll to find out. At the same time, he wanted to know what was being farmed on Long Island and if there was anything he might learn that could improve the farming methods at

Mount Vernon. Being the first planter in Virginia to apply fertilizer to his fields, he was interested to learn that Long Island farmers were using cow dung to fertilize their fields.

WASHINGTON SLEPT HERE

On Tuesday, April 20 Washington set out with his usual entourage of personal secretaries, servants and outriders in a coach drawn by the usual six white horses. Washington traveled well, but he was a man's man. On first sight he could make women blush and cause men to stammer. But to have him spending the night in your house? To the average farmer, this was heaven. "The father of our country ate at this table, slept in this bed, and spent the evening talking about MY farm."

Washington's journal: "About 8 Oclock (having previously sent over my Servants, Horses and Carriage) I crossed to Brooklyn and proceeded to Flat Bush — thence to Utrich — thence to Gravesend — then through Jamaica where we lodged at a Tavern kept by (William) Warne—a pretty good and decent house." While dining at the home of William Barry in Utrecht he complimented Mrs. Barry on her cooking and questioned Mr. Barry about the crops he was growing in his fields. Washington duly noted the types and the yield. "He told me that their average Crop of Oats did not exceed 15 bushls. to the Acre, but of Indian Corn they commonly made from 25 to 30 and often more bushels to the Acre but this was the effect of Dung from New York . . . That of Wheat sometimes got 30 bushels and often more of Rye."

The following day, the Washington entourage traveled east to South Hempstead, then southeast to the old South Road where "we came in view of the Sea & continued to be so the remaining part of the days ride, and as near as the road could run for the small bays, Marshes and guts, into which the tide flows at all times . . . ." Washington took it all in: the weather, the soil, the crop yield. "The Country were more mixed with sand than yesterday, the Soil of inferior quality; Yet with dung wch. all the Corn ground receives the land yields on an average 30 bushels to the Acre. . . . " Washington spent the second night at Apple Tree Neck farm in Islip, at the house of one Judge Isaac Thompson.

Thursday, April 22, Washington struck out at eight o'clock, traveled east as far as Brookhaven, turned north and crossed over to the north shore of Long Island, passing Coram on the way. "The first five Miles of the Road is too poor to admit Inhabitants or cultivation being a low scrubby Oak, not more than 2 feet high intermixed with small and ill thriven Pines," writes Washington. "Within two miles of (Coram) there are farms but the land is of an indifferent quality much mixed with Sand. . . . From then to (Setuaket) the Soil improves . . . but it is far from the first quality." Washington spent the third night in Setuaket, at the house of "a Captn. Roe." The Roe house overlooked Long Island Sound.

From Setuaket, Washington turned toward home. "Friday 23d. About 8 Oclock we left Roes, and (fed) the Horses at Smiths Town, at a Widow Blidenbergs . . . thence 15 miles to Huntington where we dined and afterwards proceeded Seven Miles to Oyster-bay, to the House of a Mr. Young . . . where we lodged." Washington noted again that the soil was poor, and the road "a mere bed of white sand, unable to produce trees 25 feet high." As he journeyed west, the soil improved. On the peninsula between Oyster Bay and Huntington Bay Washington saw what had been an extensive stand of timber that had been reduced to one quarter its original size by the British Army during its occupation of the island in 1776. It was yet another reminder to the general of how fast the cost of war could devour natural resources.

Saturday, April 24. Washington departed at 6 a.m. hoping to reach New York before dusk. According to local lore he stopped at the house of Harry Wilson in Glen Cove and from their porch addressed a group of children. His journal makes no mention of the meeting. In Hempstead, he was served breakfast at the home of Hendrick Onderdonck "where we were kindly received and well entertained. This Gentleman works a Grist & two Paper Mills, the last of which he seems to carry on with Spirit, and to profit. . . ." The paper mill, the president learned, was the first to be built in the state of New York.

From Hempstead, Washington traveled to Flushing, where he dined at noon, and on to Brooklyn, with the sun falling fast on the horizon. "The land I passed over to day is generally very good, but leveller and better as we approached New York. The soil is intermixed with pebble, and towards the West end with other kind of stone which they apply to the purposes of fencing which is not to be seen on the South side of the Island nor towards the Eastern parts of it . . . the Road is very fine, and the Country in a higher State of Cultivation & vegetation of Grass & grain forwarded than any place else I had seen—occasioned in a great degree by the Manure drawn from the City of New York." Washington beat the sun and arrived home before dark.

Two weeks later, on Sunday May 9, Washington began to feel ill.

WASHINGTON'S SECOND BRUSH WITH DEATH

It would be Washington's last entry in his journal for more than a month. It read simply: "Sunday 9th. Indisposed with a bad cold, and at home all day writing letters on private business." Within 24 hours Washington's cold had turned to pneumonia. He was soon bedridden and having trouble breathing.

Three physicians were summoned. In spite of their efforts the president grew steadily worse. On Wednesday, May 12, Dr. John

Jones, a prominent Philadelphia physician who had attended Benjamin Franklin in his final illness, was summoned to New York. Exactly what he prescribed for Washington is unknown. The president was made as comfortable as possible. Outside the Macomb House straw was laid down to deaden the sound of passing carriages.

Despite every effort to keep Washington's illness as private as possible, word got out—death was imminent. Visitors who called at the Executive Mansion hoping to be admitted to the sickroom were gently turned away by Martha Washington, who sat at his bedside knitting hour after hour. "Called to see the President," representative William Maclay wrote in his diary. He was not let in, but joined the despairing group of politicians and friends in the downstairs parlor, with "every Eye full of Tears his life despaired of."

One of those allowed in to see the President was Thomas Jefferson. He arrived as the president's breathe quickened, shallow respirations grew still fainter. Around four o'clock he saw a change. In a letter to his daughter, Jefferson recounted what happened next: "A copious sweat came on, his expectoration, which had been thin and ichorous, began to assume a well-digested form, his articulation became distinct, and in the course of two hours it was evident he had gone thro' a favorable crisis." This was on May 20. The following morning "total despair" gave way to cautious hope. "Indeed, he is thought quite safe," Jefferson then noted.

Some days later, in a letter to his son-in-law, Jefferson wrote: "You cannot conceive the public alarm on this occasion. It proves how much depends on his life."

While the president kept up a cheerful face for Martha, he admitted to friends, more than he had done as a soldier, that he felt he was dangerously risking his life for his country. "I have already had within less than a year two severe attacks, the last worse than the first," he wrote. "A third will put me to sleep with my fathers. At what distance this may be, I know not. Within the last twelve months I have undergone more and severer sickness than thirty preceding years afflicted me with, put it all together." His physicians, he wrote to Lafayette, advised "more exercise and less applications to business. I cannot, however, avoid persuading myself that it is essential to accomplish whatever I have undertaken (though reluctantly) to the best of my abilities."

GONE FISHING

Although he was able to resume most of his duties by the first June, Washington did not recover fully for several more weeks. Despite persistent coughing, shortness of breath and chest pains, he felt well enough to take a three-day fishing trip off Sandy Hook. He invited Thomas Jefferson and Alexander Hamilton to join him. If they discussed funding and assumption or where to locate the nation's capital, it went unrecorded. Instead, the president returned with a large haul of sea bass and much warm praise for his "able coadjutors, who harmonize extremely well together."

CHAPTER 23

The Season for Horse Trading

Everything was coming to a head. On June 2, the House passed the Funding Bill and sent it upstairs to the Senate. If the Senate passed funding without assumption, assumption was dead. If that happened, Hamilton told friends he would resign his post. What would be the point of continuing? Funding alone would not solve the nation's woeful economic predicament. If the republic didn't want to save itself financially, Hamilton wouldn't be a party to it. Besides, he could make far more money practicing law.

To get what he wanted Hamilton was prepared to do what any self-respecting politician would do—some old-fashioned horse trading.

It was the season for horse-trading. Deals were being discussed nightly over dinner among local and state politicians, congressmen and merchants, on the trading of votes for assumption in exchange for votes on where to place the nation's capital. Indeed, after all these months, the Residency Bill was still being debated in Congress. Back in January, at the opening of the second session, the House had adopted a new joint rule by which any business left unfinished at the end of one session must begin all over again at the next session, thereby killing the bill that had selected Pennsylvania for the site of the new capital. Now, the site of the capital was up for grabs again. It was a clever bit of political maneuvering engineered by the ever-resourceful James Madison. The man from Orange County, Virginia was prepared to do whatever it took to move the capital to the Potomac.

JEFFERSON HAS A HEADACHE

It seemed everyone was down with some illness in the Spring of 1790. George Washington was incapacitated with yet another near-fatal illness. Madison was waylaid with dysentery. In John Adam's house, everyone but the vice president had the flu. On any given day, any number of Congressmen might be home nursing some ailment. And for all of May Thomas Jefferson was confined to a darkened room with a severe migraine.

Jefferson had a long history of migraine headaches. According to recent studies, his migraines were brought about by work-related stress. Jefferson's latest migraine may have come with the realization that the United States might be pulled apart by one or two regions seceding from the union. Most southern states were threatening to secede should assumption pass, while South Carolina and the northeast were threatening to secede if assumption wasn't passed. Despite all the progress that Congress had achieved over the summer of 1789, gridlock had set in and nothing was getting done. Talk of secession was a daily occurrence. There were those advocating that the federal government be dissolved as unworkable, and starting over again.

Having spent four years in France, Jefferson knew the success or failure of the United States largely depended on its credit rating in Europe. The impression that the infant republic was prone to crisis did not exactly inspire confidence abroad. While creditors in Britain, in the Netherlands, and in Switzerland saw massive amounts of interest being earned, they were also seeing danger signals should Congress fail to pass the Assumption Bill. Jefferson knew the mere threat of trouble might be as destructive as the fact itself. Should Europe's bankers fear the worst, they would take action—probably by asking some of the smaller states to liquidate what today would be called "subprime loans." If the states stalled or admitted that they were unable to pay, the bankers might allow partial settlements to be made at a discount, accepting less then full payment in order to get back a portion of their money. The spreading action would develop rapidly to get at least partial repayments from larger borrowers. The result would be the end of easy credit. The effect would further cripple America's ailing economy.

There was yet another reason for Jefferson to worry. War was impending in Europe. He knew the United States could remain neutral only if it were strong. Strength and good credit went hand-in-hand. As Jefferson put it: "Our business is to have great credit, and to use it little. Whatever enables us to go to war, secures our peace."

Once Jefferson was feeling better he called for a meeting with Robert Morris. Morris was among the most powerful men in the Senate and the prime motivator behind relocating the capital to Pennsylvania. If a deal could be made, he was the one to make it. On June 15, possibly acting on behalf of the president, Jefferson proposed to Morris a compromise: after the present session of Congress ended, the capital would move from New York to Philadelphia, where it would remain for ten years. After that, it would move to a permanent home on the

Potomac. The first compromise being agreed to, it was now possible for Jefferson to broker a deal with Hamilton and Madison.

On June 20, Jefferson invited Hamilton and Madison to dine with him at his new quarters at 57 Maiden Lane. It was destined to become the most famous dinner in American history.

DINNER AT JEFFERSON'S

Only one account of the dinner was ever recorded, a couple of years after the fact, by Thomas Jefferson. Here's what Jefferson wrote:

"Going to the President's one day I met Hamilton as I approached the door. His look was somber, haggard, and dejected beyond description. Even his dress uncouth and neglected. He asked to speak with me. We stood in the street near the door. He opened the subject of assumption of the state debts, the necessity of it to the general fiscal arrangement and its indispensable necessity toward a preservation of the Union. . . .

"I had not yet undertaken to consider and understand it, that the assumption had struck me in an unfavorable light . . . but that I would resolve what he had urged in my mind. It was a real fact that the Eastern and Southern members (S. Carolina however was the former) had got into the most extreme ill humor with one another. . . . On considering the situation of things, I thought the first step towards some conciliation of views would be to bring Mr. Madison and Col. Hamilton to a friendly discussion of the subject. I immediately wrote to each to come and dine with me the next day, mentioned that we should be alone . . . and that I was persuaded that men of sound heads and honest views needed nothing more than mutual understanding to enable them to unite in some measures which might enable us to get along."

Jefferson's account of how the meeting took place makes for a nice story but apparently is just that—a nice story. Except for Dumas Malone, Jefferson's biographer, historians don't buy it. There are three problems: (1) Hamilton was habitually a sharp dresser and very careful about his appearance; (2) Jefferson would never have been a party to anything he didn't understand fully. On the very day the deal was made, in fact, he wrote a long letter to James Monroe preparing him for news of precisely the kind of compromise that eventually occurred. Monroe, like most Virginians, opposed assumption. Jefferson assured him that he too found the measure objectionable: "But in the present instance I see the necessity of yielding for this time . . . for the sake of the union, and to save us from the greatest of Calamities"; and (3) at the time Jefferson wrote his account of the deal, he was forming a political party in opposition to Hamilton, and wished to explain his part in the deal, that he had been an innocent participant.

While Jefferson's account of how the dinner deal came about was a fabrication, in all likelihood the dinner did take place. In 1792 Jefferson told Washington the deal made that evening with Hamilton was the greatest political mistake of his life. "It was unjust," he said, "and was acquiesced in merely from a fear of disunion, while our government was still in its infant state."

Historians have debated how many people actually attended the dinner, suggesting that five or more were necessary to make a deal of such a far-reaching consequence. Judging by Jefferson's account, only three were present. Charles A. Cerami in his book "Dinner at Mr. Jefferson's" makes a compelling case for three being present—Jefferson, Hamilton, and Madison. A woman who often helped with Jefferson's social planning left this account: "When he dined with persons with whom he wished to enjoy a free and unrestricted flow of conversation, the number of persons at the table never exceeded four—each with a dumbwaiter beside him, containing all the utensils and most of the foods needed for the entire dinner. Not only did the intervention of servants disturb the conversation, Jefferson felt, but much of the public discord that often followed was produced by the mutilated and misconstructed repetition of remarks that were heard by servants or by unnecessary guests."

WHAT WAS SERVED

Jefferson had a sophisticated palette, having lived in Paris for four years. He adored French wines, and prior to leaving Paris ordered 288 bottles for shipment to Monticello. His chef, an African-American slave named James Hemings, was trained in the culinary arts while in Paris. Based on accounts of what Jefferson served on social occasions at Monticello, it is possible to reconstruct what may have been served that night in New York. Credit Charles A. Cerami ("Dinner at Mr. Jefferson's") with the following.

Hamilton and Madison arrived promptly at 4 o'clock (both were known for promptness, and had no patience with those who weren't). A servant led them into the newly appointed drawing room, where Jefferson welcomed them. After being seated, Jefferson served them white wine, which he poured himself. It was one of the esteemed whites, he said, made in the hills near the village of Tains.

Conversation was pleasant. Political discussion before and during dinner was considered strictly taboo.

After half an hour, the three moved to the dining room. There was no prearranged seating at the table, as Jefferson desired an informal atmosphere. Jefferson told his guests to sit where ever they pleased.

Two servants appeared and placed a dumbwaiter beside each guest, placed the salad course on the top shelf, and arranged the silverware that would be needed for the entire meal. The dumbwaiters were on four legs, made of walnut, simple, square, fitted with shelves, on which was placed various dishes. Guests could then help themselves without aid of a servant. Because Jefferson preferred white wines to reds, white wine accompanied the salad course. Jefferson described this wine as a 1786 Bordeaux, much esteemed, which he called Carbonnieux. "I had come upon it on a side trip which I had made through the Duchy of Anjou while returning to Paris from a wine-tasting visit to Bordeaux."

In keeping with the Monticello custom, two main courses were served. The first was a capon (a specially prepared chicken) stuffed with Virginia ham and chestnut puree, artichoke bottoms, and truffles, with a bit of cream, white wine, and chicken stock. It was served with a Calvados sauce, made with an apple brandy of Normandy that Jefferson had brought back from his travels. Because the strong flavor of the sauce might overpower a French wine, he served one of his Italian favorites, a Montepulciano from Tuscany.

The second course was the equivalent of the New York boeuf a' la mode, an elegant beef stew that was a favorite at Monticello. James Hemings had improved upon the Monticello recipe by what he had learned in Paris by adding French ingredients that enhanced the flavor. Jefferson served a rare and very expensive red wine from Chambertin.

Various small sweets were then laid out—macaroons, meringues, bell fritters, etc. Dessert itself was something akin to a baked Alaska, ice cream enclosed within a warm pastry. Jefferson then served what looked like a cloudy white wine. It was in fact champagne without the bubbles, called champagne non-mousseux , meaning non-sparkling.

WHAT WAS NEGOTIATED

Having finished desert, negotiations began in earnest. Wrote Jefferson: "I opened the subject, acknowledged that my situation had not permitted me to understand it sufficiently but encouraged them to consider the thing together. They did so.

"After some discussion, which was not prolonged Madison extended his remarks by saying that Assumption was a bitter bill to Virginia and other states that had already paid most of their wartime debts. Hamilton responded by indicating that he understood Virginia's unusual position, but wondered whether a reasonable adjustment of the amount that Virginia would be assessed might enable it to support Assumption? To which Madison responded that such an adjustment would be a step in the right direction, but that considerably more would be needed to soothe the bitter pain that Assumption represented to most of the southern states."

What could be done to sooth the bitter pain that assumption was causing southerners? For starters, moving the capital from the north to a location on the Potomac. Yes, remove the capital away from the corrupting influence of big cities and northern money-men to a rural setting amidst southern plantations and clean country air. That would do nicely.

Moving the capital south of the Mason-Dixon line "was a just measure," Jefferson concurred in his recounting of the dinner deal "and would probably be a popular one with (the south), and would be a proper one to follow the Assumption. . . . But the removal to the Potomac could not be carried unless Pennsylvania could be engaged in it." Jefferson had Robert Morris's support, which was encouraging, but by itself was not enough. More was needed to insure passage in the Senate. Madison, of course, had the necessary votes to get assumption passed in the House. Did Hamilton have the necessary votes in the Senate to relocate the capital on the Potomac? He assured them he did. Was Hamilton willing to make a trade—assumption for a southern capital?

Yes, he was. The three then toasted the deal.

COMPLETING THE DEAL

In keeping their end of the bargain, Jefferson and Madison would obtain the three or four votes necessary for assumption to be passed in the House. In exchange, Hamilton would help fulfill the terms of Jefferson's compromise deal with Robert Morris. While Morris had already arranged two vote changes that would assure passage of assumption in the Senate, he was having trouble finding the votes necessary to remove the capital from New York. Hamilton must find these votes. He persuaded the only two amenable New Englanders—Massachusetts Senators Tristan Dalton and Caleb Strong. They both strongly favored assumption as the means of rescuing their state from financial collapse. Hamilton convinced them that the only way for assumption to pass was for them to reverse their positions regarding the capital location.

There was something more required of Hamilton, and it had to do with money. As part of the settlement of state accounts, Hamilton arranged to have the sum allotted Virginia under the Assumption Bill increased so that Virginia would end up receiving more than she would be required to pay. The total allotted Virginia ended up being $13 million, or more than half the total of all thirteen states' combined war debt of $25 million. In Virginia all geese ARE swans.

According to historian Forrest McDonald, the Virginians were "extremely artful" in getting what they wanted. "They used the first trade, which would give the south the permanent capital, to provide a cloak of respectability for the second, which was worth a net to their state of more than $13 million in the final settlement. Thus, because only one trade rather than two appeared to have been made, and because the trading appeared to have involved not money but only assumption in exchange for the capital, they avoided giving the impression of having made a corrupt bargain."

Having negotiated a sweet deal for Virginia, why did Jefferson regret the bargain two years later?

While he understood Hamilton's plan better than he would ever have admitted, Jefferson did not fully realize the extent of its impact on the nation. The federal government had captured forever the bulk of American taxing power, thus creating an unshakeable foundation for federal over state power. Had Hamilton withheld vital information? Not at all. The Treasury Secretary had explained his views ad-nauseam. According to historian Ron Chernow, Jefferson "had not been duped but outsmarted by Hamilton, who had embedded an enduring political system in the details of the funding and assumption scheme."

In an unsigned newspaper article published that September, entitled "Address to the Public Creditors," Hamilton gave away the secret of his statecraft that so infuriated Jefferson: "Whoever considers the nature of our government with discernment will see that though obstacles and delays will frequently stand in the way of the adoption of good measures, yet once adopted, they are likely to be stable and permanent. It will be far more difficult to undo than to do."

As president, Jefferson would find this to be true as he tried and failed to dismantle Hamilton's financial system. It was for the best, as Jefferson found out. Later, in making the Louisiana Purchase, he would make the purchase not with the cash (which the federal government didn't have) but with symbolic money—with government bonds—thanks to the financial system created by Hamilton.

POSTSCRIPT

The deal having been made, all that remained now was for Congress to cast the votes. On June 29 Senators Dalton and Strong changed positions and thereby killed a last-ditch effort to keep the temporary capital in New York City. Two days later the Senate passed the bill putting the temporary capital in Philadelphia and the permanent capital on the Potomac. On July 9 the House approved the Senate bill.

On July 14 the Senate amended the House's Funding Bill by reinserting a provision for assumption and by changing the interest rates (in order to be in compliance with a revised set of formulas worked out by Hamilton and Robert Morris). On July 22 the House took up the Senate's amendments. Two days later the votes were cast. Various shifts had assumption advocates outnumbered 29 to 33, but on July 24, four Representatives switched votes (with some arm-twisting by Jefferson and Madison) and the measure carried. By July 29 all differences between the House and the Senate bills had been worked out. Having passed Congress, the final bill went to the President for his signature.

Four separate statutes were passed giving life to the proposals Hamilton advocated in "The Report on Public Credit." One was a Congressional Act for the settlement of state accounts. Another was the Funding and Assumption Act, which provided refinancing and servicing all domestic debts and authorizing a new European loan of $12 million to consolidate and refinance the foreign debt. A third statute provided for the establishment of a Sinking Fund, to insure the public debt was paid off within the prescribed period of 20 years.

The fourth act increased and revised import duties along the lines Hamilton had proposed.

The laws as passed were close enough to Hamilton's original proposals to be acceptable to him. Before adjourning on August 12, Congress gave him two new assignments: the House instructed him to make a further report on the public credit, by which it was understood that he would draw up plans for further taxes as well as the creation of a national bank. Hamilton's new report was to be ready when Congress reconvened in December—in Philadelphia.

The deal that got Hamilton's financial plan through Congress and landed the nation's capital in the Upper South, thereby preserving the fragile unity of states, would be forever known as the Compromise of 1790. It was the first of three comprises that would keep the nation together, up to the Civil War. The other two were the Comprise of 1820, and the Missouri Compromise of 1850.

CHAPTER 24

Washington D.C., The Anti-City

Thomas Jefferson hated cities. Oh, he loved what they had to offer—fine food and drink, fine clothiers, bookshops, theaters, museums, universities, architecture—but he hated more what they also offered—commerce, banks, stockbrokers, factories, crime, filth.

The idea of building a city from scratch—of starting over as it were—appealed greatly to a purist like Jefferson. It had nothing to do with financial gain as, for example, it partly did for George Washington, James Madison and others who had property holdings along the Potomac. For Jefferson, it wasn't about money, it was about an ideal—it was about creating the perfect city. And what better place? The Compromise of 1790 placed the capital in the heart of the Upper South.

There was little question about what to name the city. The name of the nation's first president appeared on the first survey map and that settled it. The undeveloped swamps and woods was then known officially as "Washington City." President George Washington was asked to head up the project. His first task was to appoint Thomas Jefferson as principle advisor; in effect, as the man in charge of quality control. It was, after all, Jefferson's vision they were creating. Jefferson did not want his ideal city sullied with commerce and industry and all that went with it. Let Norfolk be the region's business hub. Jefferson's city would be a shining example of virtuous republican government. It would be an American Athens.

This was not something new that was being attempted. Creating a capital city from scratch had been done before. Peter the Great of Russia had built St. Petersburg where once there had been a swamp. It became a great city because Peter the Great was an absolute tyrant of indefatigable energy, vision and persistence. He brought in the best architects of Europe to design the city's infrastructure, marshaled 40,000 unpaid peasants to build it, and forced the nobility, merchants, traders, government bureaucrats and common folk to pick up and move there.

Louis IV of France had done it as well, with the building of Versailles. The royal palace was a baroque masterpiece, but as a city it had nothing to do with people and how they lived. Commerce had no place. The place was majestic but sterile. The King could command a legion of courtiers to attend to him, but the brightest and most creative men in France preferred Paris. When the French Revolution came, the capital was forcibly returned to Paris.

St. Petersburg and Versailles were made possible by the will of two absolute monarchs. Could a democracy marshal the necessary means to build a city from scratch? The answer is yes, but it wouldn't be fully realized—it wouldn't be an actual city—for at least 150 years.

THE FEDERAL CITY

The architect who had given a facelift to Federal Hall in New York City—Pierre Charles L'Enfant—was hired to design a city layout. The plan L'Enfant submitted was even more ambitious than the preliminary sketches Jefferson had dreamed up. L'Enfant superimposed a radial system of avenues on Jefferson's grid of streets. He added tree-lined walks on either side of broad avenues, several public squares, five grand fountains, expansive parks and gardens, and arranged the public buildings in such a way as to have a sweeping view of the Potomac. One of the noteworthy aspects of the plan was its striking similarity to the layout of Versailles, where, coincidentally, L'Enfant grew up.

The problem was money. From the start, George Washington insisted that financing not come from the Federal government, but from the sale of city lots. Besides, asking Congress for money might reopen the question of residency and the dream of a southern capital might yet be repealed. In any event, what money Congress was spending on government buildings was being spent in Philadelphia, where the temporary capital was located.

The sale of lots proved an utter failure. Out of ten thousand lots in the government's possession less than 100 were actually sold. L'Enfant was so disgusted with the scheme as being beneath the government's dignity that once he completed the city layout, he promptly resigned. A syndicate was formed by three men of acknowledged standing in the financial community, James Greenleaf, John Nicholson, and Robert Morris, "the financier of the Revolution." The syndicate was to purchase several thousand lots, pay for them in seven annual installments, sell a portion to private buyers at the enhanced prices that presumably would be the result of their activities, and negotiate a large loan abroad using unsold lots as collateral. The promoters, however, could not sell their lots, could not meet their installment payments, and could not interest investors, foreign or domestic. The scheme collapsed and by the fall of 1797, the syndicate of three found itself under lock-and-key in debtor's prison.

Meanwhile, the cornerstone was laid for the Executive Mansion in a ceremony hosted by President George Washington. Other than that, nothing much happened. Lots were not being sold, and buildings were not going up, and the grand squares, parks and fountains were never built. Few commercial ships frequented the Potomac. In a final desperate bid to keep the dream city alive, Washington went to Congress for a loan, using unsold lots as collateral. Some collateral: the lots were worthless. What should have been a slam dunk dragged on for four long months before Congress authorized a loan of $500,000.

Three government buildings were then built: the Executive Mansion, the Capitol, and the Treasury Building. James Hoban, an Irishman from South Carolina, designed the President's House, a stately building inspired by the home of the Duke of Leinster in Dublin. It was still unfinished when Jefferson was elected president in 1801. It would remain unfinished until 1833, more than 40 years after it was begun. Inspired by the Roman Pantheon, the capitol was designed by Dr. William Thornton. The initial building contained assembly rooms for the House of Representatives, the Senate, and the Supreme Court. The capitol building would not be completely finished for another 71 years. And who should do the work? With the exception of a handful of Scottish stone cutters, slaves did the lion's share of the work. They cleared trees, drained the swamps, leveled the land, graded the streets, and erected the government buildings. Like ancient Athens of Greece, the American Athens would be built by slave labor.

All roads leading to Washington City were rudimentary and confusing. Coaches spilled over on uneven roads. When the capital moved from Philadelphia to Washington City in 1800, Abigail Adams got lost while en route. As First Lady, she hung the Adams' laundry in the unfinished East Room. With the exception of the President's House and the Capitol, Washington City was not a city at all but a shanty town, occupied four months of the year by Congress. The rest of the time it stood empty and vacant. The only commerce to be seen were boarding houses and bordellos. People would arrive and ask where they could find the nation's capital and be told they were standing in the heart of it.

George Washington wanted the city named after him to have a university, a thriving theater, a retail center, hotels worthy of visiting dignitaries, and commerce: yes, to be as diverse and vibrant as Philadelphia and New York City. What Washington really wanted was a northern city on the Potomac. His dream would not be fully realized for more than 150 years. It wasn't until after World War II that Washington D.C. began to bear resemblance to an actual city. Separated from the commercial, financial, intellectual, and cultural centers of the nation, even today Washington D.C. would not be confused with the capitals of other modern nations, such as Berlin, London, Paris or Rome.

SLAVE CAPITAL

It's tempting to wonder what Jefferson thought of his anti-city. It was totally cut off from the larger world and therefore not unlike Monticello. As president he could preside over the nation in perfect solitude, as he presided over his Virginia plantation. There were no professors from a major university, no benevolent Quakers, and no sophisticated money men to influence the Jeffersonian Democrats who controlled Congress in the first part of the nineteenth century. There was little commercial traffic on the Potomac to give the place a cosmopolitan air.

Washington D.C. was a backwater, but it was the South's backwater, where slavery went unquestioned. Up until the Civil War, slaves were auctioned off within a block of the Capitol. Writes historian Garry Wills: "Can one imagine a succession of twelve slaveholder presidents if the capital had remained in Philadelphia? The southerners got what they wanted, a seat of government where slavery would be taken for granted, where it would not need perpetual apology, excuse, or palliation, where the most honored men in the nation were not to be criticized because they practiced and defended and gave privilege to the holding of slaves."

CHAPTER 25

Unfinished Business

In the Spring of 1790, George Washington looked past the Allegheny Mountains to the continent beyond and saw only trouble.

In defiance of the 1783 Treaty of Paris, British forces still occupied the Northwest Territory. In the southwest, Spain blocked the Mississippi River to American navigation. In between were the Indian nations, vainly resisting the onslaught of American expansion. Washington feared some incident on the frontier would spark an Indian war and draw the United States into conflict with England or Spain. As Washington saw it, the solution was to sign a peace treaty with the Indians and deal with Spain and England through diplomatic channels.

The biggest threat was from the Indians in the Southwest. Comprised of four tribes—Creeks, Cherokees, Choctaws and Chickasaws—they operated as a loosely aligned Confederation, much as the United States had done under the Articles of Confederation. Over time, the four tribes had become dependent on white traders for most of their needs, not only for clothing and luxuries, but for guns and ammunition. Finding it necessary to deal with both the United States and Spain, the tribes tried to play the two nations off against each other to their own advantage. Lacking centralized leadership, they often failed to act effectively. As soon as the Revolution was over, Spain, the United States, and various states acting separately, took advantage of the Indians' lack of centralized leadership and procured contradictory treaties in which presumed representatives of all four tribes would sign on the dotted line induced by whoever was suppling the most liquor and gifts.

In trying to make the treaties stick, Spain had the advantage. Her economic interests were the same as the Indians'. She had no large population lusting after the Indian hunting grounds. In fact, Spain encouraged Indian hunters; the fur trade, which brought the Indians prosperity, also contributed to Spain's prosperity. On the other hand, the treaties negotiated by the United States often involved large land concessions. The Indians immediately repudiated these treaties as having been agreed to by only a few of their nationals. Settlers moved into the disputed areas anyway, and fighting ensued.

As with slavery, Washington's view of the American Indians had changed over the years. During the French and Indian War, Washington believed Indians to be "butchering" and "diabolical" monsters. Now, he saw them as "poor wretches," more sinned against than sinning Where he once ordered secret surveys to be made in lands legally belonging to the Indians, he now saw the white men who sold Indian lands as the true villains.

How can anyone expect peace with the Indians, Washington asked, "so long as the spirit of land-jobbing prevails and our frontier settlers entertain the opinion that there is not the same crime (or no crime at all) in killing an Indian as in killing a white man?"

To establish peace in the southwest, the Washington administration set out to determine the validity of the treaties that had been made during the time of the Articles of Confederation both by the national government and by various states. The only way to bring peace to the frontier, Washington told Congress, was to foster the "happiness" of the Indians and that depends "on the national justice and humanity of the United States." American expansion beyond the Alleghenies was inevitable, Washington knew, but land for that expansion must be purchased fairly and only as needed. Thus, he urged expansion efforts to proceed with "circumspection, moderation, and forbearance" when dealing with the Indians, and peace will have a better chance of prevailing.

THE YAZOO LAND SCANDAL

The Washington Administration had to deal not only with Spain and the Indians, but with opposition in those states that were encouraging and profiting from Indian land-grabs. The United States and specifically Georgia, claimed land that was also claimed by Spain. While the federal government was still forming, the Georgia legislature sold twenty-five million acres to land companies in Virginia, South Carolina, and Tennessee. Most of this land was in disputed areas. The tracts comprised almost all of the land of the Choctaws and Chickasaws and part of the Cherokees. Since much of the territory lay between the Mississippi and Yazoo Rivers, the land scandal has been known forever after by the name "Yazoo." By 1790, the Yazoo land scandal was threatening to plunge the entire Southwest into war. Somehow, Washington had to squash Yazoo before that happened—but how?

Since the Yazoo land grants violated a number of treaties, Washington wondered whether he had the right to place federal authority in opposition to Georgia's official acts. First, he consulted with Attorney Edmund Randolph on the constitutional considerations. Next, he asked Hamilton whether he should denounce Yazoo in a proclamation. Hamilton doubted that he had the right under the Constitution, so the President put the matter to Jefferson. Hamilton, meanwhile, discussed the question with Rufus King of the Senate and reported back that the Senate would likely take up the issue and that, in his opinion, it would be better to let action originate there. Jefferson considered Georgia's behavior unconstitutional, but felt that the state and the Indian tribes should be further consulted before Washington acted. Short of sending in the U.S. Army, which was woefully undermanned, Washington didn't have a lot of options. Even if he issued a proclamation denouncing Yazoo and urging all United States' officers and citizens to observe the treaties, he had no effective means of enforcing it.

Washington did have one trick up his sleeve and that was to lure their leader, Alexander McGillivray, to New York. McGillivray was the son of a Scottish fur trader and a Creek girl of mixed blood descended from an aristocratic Southern family. Now living among the Creeks, McGillivray had lived in Georgia for a time and was familiar with the white man's duplicity in dealing with Indians. This combination, joined with a gift for leadership, made him a dominate figure within the Creek nation. His way of life was extravagant. Living deep in Indian territory, he maintained an estate that rivaled many on the Chesapeake Bay: a mansion house, extensive plantations, even African-American slaves.

THE TREATY OF NEW YORK

Washington sent a personal invitation to McGillivray to come to New York and negotiate a peace treaty acceptable to both the Indian nations and the United States. That McGillivray would profit from the deal was encouraged. Washington's timing could not have been better. A crisis in the waters off North America's Pacific Coast, in Nootka Sound, had brought Spain and England to the brink of war. McGillivray, who was dependent on Spain for subsistence, was flattered by Washington's letter. Realizing he might need a new source of supply, he willingly accepted the President's invitation. He gathered twenty-nine Indian warriors around him, and headed northward from Georgia. If he feared trouble along the way, he was mistaken. Rather, he was received with a flattering welcome in town after town. Sailing up from New Jersey to Manhattan, the largest crowd since Washington's arrival gathered to see him. His appearance and that of the Creeks made a sensation. Abigail Adams described the visitors as "the very first savages I ever saw." They were conducted by Secretary of War Hugh Knox and uniformed members of the new Society of St. Tammany to the Executive Mansion where Washington greeted McGillivray warmly.

"I am glad you have come, Colonel. I have long felt we had much in common."

"I cannot flatter myself that much, Mr. President," replied McGillivray, "but it has long been my ambition to shake your hand in friendship."

Washington left the actual negotiations to Knox, who crafted the treaty. Much of the text was likely proposed by McGillivray. The two parties pledged lasting peace and friendship. All but three million acres of the land in dispute was ceded to Georgia. Creeks within the boundaries of the United States would be subject to federal laws, rather than Georgia state laws. British right to passage through Creek lands was also restricted, and Creek prisoners were to be returned from American custody. The Creeks also ceded the land belonging to the allied Oconee Indians, which had been a contentious issue. For their part, the Creeks were granted an annual payment. In addition, Creeks within American territory and Americans within Creek (and American) territory would be subject to U.S. law, but Americans settling in Creek territory would forfeit federal protection. In an effort to encourage Creeks and Seminoles to take up agriculture, the U.S. government offered to provide domestic animals, agricultural tools, and up to four interpreters, intended to act as farm advisors.

The Treaty of New York as it was called contained six articles, set forth in a separate document, and kept secret. The first laid out the structure of future commerce between the United States and the Creek Nation, including shifting the traffic in trade goods through American ports and away from Spanish territory and ports-of-entry. The United States also agreed to pay select Creek chiefs a $100 yearly stipend and a commission to McGillivray as a brigadier general with annual pay of $1,200. This last gesture was aimed at encouraging the white Creek leader to promote U.S. interests and policies among Creeks. Finally, should the fur trade by way of Spanish possessions be stopped by war, as compensation $50,000 worth of goods would be imported to the Creek country through the United States without duty.

The Senate wasted no time in approving the treaty over the strident objections of Georgia's lawmakers. Infuriated by the government's concession of three million acres, pistol packin' James Jackson was likewise apoplectic that Washington should treat Indian "savages" as his diplomatic equals.

On August 7, Washington appeared in the House chamber of Federal Hall and addressed an assembly that included Knox, McGillivray, and two dozen Creek Indians. After signing the document, Washington gave McGillivray books and an epaulette from his wartime uniform. To the other Indians he presented strings of beads, representing perpetual peace, and tobacco to smoke in remembrance of the occasion.

McGillivray and the Creeks then filed past Washington, each giving him the handshake of peace. A native song concluded the ceremony.

The Treaty of New York was Washington's first great diplomatic triumph. His policy of "circumspection, moderation, and forbearance" had paid off.

EVERYONE UNDER HIS OWN VINE AND FIG TREE

On August 4, 1790, Congress authorized the first issue of U.S. Treasury Bonds thereby setting in motion Hamilton's economic program.

On August 12, Congress adjourned. Legislators wasted little time packing and getting out of town.

President George Washington, meanwhile, had one final piece of unfinished business to deal with—Rhode Island. Rhode Island was not only small—37 miles wide by 48 miles long—but a source of considerable grief for the Union. Under the Articles of Confederation, it had been the only state to vote against the Tariff Bill, thereby blocking the government's best hope of creating a revenue stream. In 1787, Rhode Island was the only state NOT to send delegates to the Constitutional Convention in Philadelphia. And in 1788 the Rhode Island legislature put the brakes on a scheduled ratifying convention thereby denying the people of that state the right to decide whether or not to join the Union.

Well, Rhode Island had been a thorn in the nation's side long enough. It was time they joined they Union. The surest way of getting their attention was to hit them where it counted—in the pocket book. Word went out that if they didn't join the Union their exports would be taxed as if they were a foreign nation. Being heavily dependent on trade with New York, Philadelphia, and South Carolina, they got the message. On May 29, 1790, Rhode Island ratified, becoming the thirteenth state to join the Union.

Rhode Island had been a thorn in Washington's side as well. He had avoided the state while touring the Northeast the previous Fall. Now, he wanted to personally welcome the Ocean State into the fold. On August 15 the President boarded a packet ship and journeyed there by sea. Joining him were Secretary of State Thomas Jefferson, New York Governor George Clinton, Judge Blair of the United States Court, three members of Congress, and three of Washington's staff. They were merely window dressing. Washington was the main event, the one everyone wanted to see.

If there was any resentment about being coerced into joining the union, Rhode Islanders didn't show it. On the morning of the 17th, they turned out in droves to cheer the President's arrival in Newport. After the usual round of speeches, Washington made a tour of the city. Fully recovered from his illness and feeling fit and strong again, he walked with the briskness of a young man. Those walking with him had trouble keeping up. In the evening he attended a dinner in his honor at the State House.

The following morning, while listening to various city officials and religious leaders welcoming him to their city, Washington was particularly touched by a letter read aloud from the Newport Hebrew Congregation. The members were descendants of Portuguese Jews who had suffered persecution during the Spanish Inquisition and sought refuge in America. Their letter read in part:

"Permit the children of the stock of Abraham to approach you with the most cordial of affection and esteem. . . .

"With pleasure we reflect on those days—those days of difficulty, and danger, when the God of Israel who delivered David from the peril of the sword—shielded Your Head in the day of battle: and we rejoice to think, that the same Spirit, who rested in the Bosom of the greatly beloved Daniel enabling him to preside over the Provinces of the Babylonish Empire, rests and ever will rest, upon you, enabling you to discharge the arduous duties of Chief Magistrate in these States.

"Deprived as we heretofore have been of the invaluable rights of free Citizens, we now with deep sense of gratitude to the Almighty disposer of all events behold a Government, erected by the Majesty of the People—a Government, which to bigotry gives no sanction, to persecution no assistance—but generously affording to all Liberty of conscience, and immunities of Citizenship: deeming every one, of whatever Nation, tongue, or language equal parts of the great government Machine:

"This so ample and extensive Federal Union whose basis is Philanthropy, Mutual confident and Public Virtue, we cannot but acknowledge to be the work of the Great God, who ruleth in the Armies of Heaven, and among the Inhabitants of the Earth, doing whatever seemeth him good. . . ."

A LETTER WORTHY OF LINCOLN

As president, Washington had written any number of letters to various churches and congregations around the country, but his response to the Hebrew Congregation is particularly profound. The style is lean, direct, Lincolnesqe. His allusion to everyone sitting in safety "under his own vine and fig tree" is from the Bible.

Washington's letter:

"While I received with much satisfaction your address replete with expressions of esteem, I rejoice in the opportunity of assuring you that I shall always retain grateful remembrance of the cordial welcome I experienced on my visit to Newport from all classes of citizens.

"The reflection on the days of difficulty and danger which are past is rendered the more sweet from a consciousness that they are succeeded by days of uncommon prosperity and security.

"If we have wisdom to make the best use of the advantages with which we are now favored, we cannot fail, under the just administration of a good government, to become a great and happy people.

"The citizens of the United States of America have a right to applaud themselves for having given to mankind examples of an enlarged and liberal policy—a policy worthy of imitation. All possess alike liberty of conscience and immunities of citizenship.

"It is now no more that toleration is spoken of as if it were the indulgence of one class of people that another enjoyed the exercise of their inherent natural rights, for, happily, the Government of the United States, which gives to bigotry no sanction, to persecution no assistance, requires only that they who live under its protection should demean themselves as good citizens in giving it on all occasions their effectual support.

"It would be inconsistent with the frankness of my character not to avow that I am pleased with your favorable opinion of my administration and fervent wishes for my felicity.

"May the children of the stock of Abraham who dwell in this land continue to merit and enjoy the good will of the other inhabitants—while every one shall sit in safety under his own vine and fig tree and there shall be none to make him afraid.

"May the father of all mercies scatter light, and not darkness, upon our paths, and make us all in our several vocations useful here, and in His own due time and way everlastingly happy."

G. Washington

That same day, Washington re-boarded a ship and after seven hours at sea was greeted in Providence with a salute of cannon fire, the ringing of church bells, and the singing of songs. After the sun set he visited the local college (the future Brown University) which on this special occasion was all aglow in candlelight. The next morning was cold and rainy. When the weather cleared Washington was given a walking tour of the city, including a visit to the local shipyard where he was reminded that Rhode Island depended on trade for its livelihood. That afternoon he attended yet another dinner in his honor. After a number of toasts and speeches by local dignitaries, Washington's party boarded a packet ship and returned to New York.

CHAPTER 26

A Fit Expression of the American Republic

The show was over. It had made for high drama and low comedy, with heroes and villains aplenty, but it had come to an end. Like some theatric troupe, the federal government was packing up and taking its act to another city.

While in New York, the executive and legislative branches had completed the work left unfinished at the Constitutional Convention, averted the breakup of the Union, and made provision for the public debt. The infant republic was on firmer ground now. Everyone deserved a bow.

Unlike Congress, which had assigned the work of packing and shipping to clerks and departmental secretaries, George Washington took it upon himself to supervise moving the contents of the Executive

Mansion. He personally saw to it that crates were packed properly, loaded onto wagons, and safely shipped off to Philadelphia.

On August 28th, the Governor of New York, the Mayor and City Aldermen were invited to the Macomb House for a farewell dinner. Martha Washington was finding it difficult to suppress her tears. She had not expected to be happy in New York, but found living there to her liking. "I contrive to be as happy here as I could be at any place except Mount Vernon," she wrote to a friend. "In truth I should be very ungrateful if I did not acknowledge that everything has been done which politeness, hospitality or friendship could suggest to make my situation as satisfactory and agreeable as possible."

Two miles away, at Richmond Hill, Abigail Adams was having similar feelings. "It will not be Broadway," she wrote to a friend about the move to Philadelphia.

On Monday, August 30, the President and First Lady rose early, hoping to get out of town without notice. Waiting outside, however, were the Governor, Chief Justice John Jay, and various state and municipal officials. Washington shrugged, and said to Martha simply, "They must have their way."

"PARTING IS SUCH SWEET SORROW"

Washington's departure was very much like his arrival. New Yorkers turned out in droves. Canons fired a thirteen gun salute. As Shakespeare wrote in "ROMEO AND JULIET, "Parting is such sweet sorrow." The President waved his hat; Martha wiped her eyes. The presidential barge slipped from its moorings, struck out into the bay, and somewhere off near the Jersey Shore disappeared in the glare of afternoon sunlight.

"THOSE CHARMING MEN"

The last to depart were Thomas Jefferson and James Madison. The two left New York on September 1. Riding in Jefferson's phaeton, it's likely they stopped in Princeton to see Madison's old Scottish professor, John Witherspoon, who was now nearly blind, and then spent a week in Philadelphia.

In Philadelphia they arranged lodging for the coming session of Congress. Madison secured a room at a boarding house. As he had in New York, Jefferson leased a house and planned a number of renovations to accommodate the elegant furnishings he was expecting from France. With the exception of President George Washington, no member of the federal government lived as extravagantly as the Secretary of State. In Philadelphia, he would maintain a household of five servants, a maitre d'hotel imported from Paris, and a stable of four horses.

The late-summer weather was pleasantly mild so the Virginians took a more leisurely route home by traveling down the eastern side of the Chesapeake, as far as Chestertown. From there, they sailed across the Bay to Annapolis, where they met up with Thomas Lee Shippen, whom Jefferson had befriended in France. While awaiting the arrival of the phaeton on a slower boat, they borrowed small boats and rowed about the rivers and inlets, and at a local inn were served "delicious crabs." In Annapolis, the travelers climbed to the top of the state capitol (still standing and in use today) to view the panorama of bays, rivers, and islands. Before leaving the next day, they dined on what Shippen described as the most perfectly prepared turtle soup he had ever eaten. In contrast, the following evening at a country inn the food was atrocious and "mosquitos, gnats, flies and bugs" pestered them throughout the night. In the morning, they refused breakfast.

They stopped next in Bladensburg, at an inn kept by "an old black woman," where a few nights earlier President Washington, on the way to Mount Vernon, had stayed. Local townspeople, upset that Washington had shown this woman's inn preference, took out their anger on her outhouse which they smashed to pieces.

Having spent all his money from the high style in which they traveled, a day or so later Shippen parted company with "those charming men Jefferson and Madison."

Jefferson and Madison spent the next couple of days exploring the swamps and woods that was to become the nation's capital. No doubt, the two Virginians were still congratulating themselves on the dinner deal that would bring the capital into the sphere of Virginia's influence, and away from the corrupting influence of stock-jobbers, merchants, bankers, and industry. Washington City would be a slice of Virginia—rural, clean, and virtuous—where men of good character could go about the business of running the nation far from the corrupting influences "of any overgrown commercial city."

The southern capital would give physical form to Jefferson's vision of what the republic should be. Everything would be carefully controlled and under Virginia's watchful eye. Strict building codes would insure a tasteful uniformity in the city's domestic architecture. Public buildings would be designed with an imaginative sweep and nobility of scale. Sandstone, marble, and granite would be the building materials of choice.

THE BAROQUE CITY

Alas, the city Jefferson dreamed of creating had nothing whatsoever to do with democracy. The plan he and L'Enfant dreamed up was for a baroque city—the essence of baroque being absolutism, regularity, and display of grandeur. It had nothing to do with people or how they lived.

According to American historian Lewis Mumford, the ruling principle of the Baroque design is the abstract figure, the execution of which no obstruction can be allowed to interfere. The plan has for its focal points edifices and monuments which are visible symbols of majesty and authority. As with Versailles, it is stunning to behold, but ultimately cold and lifeless.

The grand avenues that L'Enfant designed—160 feet wide, coupled with a network of tributary streets—would take up a total of 3600 acres, more than all the remaining land that was available for private residences and public buildings combined. A population of half-a-million would have been required to justify them, whereas in fact they left room for a population of about a hundred thousand. To pave them would have required a sum equal of perhaps a quarter of the entire national debt. (For the most part the streets, including Pennsylvania Avenue, would remain unpaved for nearly a century.)

Far more fundamental than the grid of streets was the question of what, besides the activities of government, was to sustain the city's life? What was there to attract people, resources, prosperity, refinement, vitality? This was never a concern of L'Enfant or Jefferson. In the baroque city people have no purpose other than to bear witness to the grandeur of buildings, and to watch the coming and going of the ruling elite. Of course, this was never the intent of L'Enfant or Jefferson. Jefferson, for one, would have been horrified at such an idea. They hoped to make the nation's capital a fit expression of the American Republic. In ordering up such a place, however, they reverted to past symbols, to cities and buildings that recalled democratic and republican government—ancient Athens and Rome—but were built on the backs of slave labor. Ironically, Washington City would be no different.

The people who created Washington had no feelings for cities at all, had little sense of what a city was, and little experience of what urban life meant. According to Medieval historian Henri Pirenne, a city is not a city without commerce. In the middle ages, it was the city with all its perceived vices that gave birth to democracy in Europe, created public education, universities, and hospitals, and eliminated slavery. Serfs found refuge in cities, learned a craft and gained their freedom. The expression, "The air breathes freer in cities" is from this time.

Historically, cities have not been created at all; sparked by trade they just happened. In the middle ages, most cities began within castle walls. Merchants set up shop under the watchful eye of kings, and as commerce increased the city expanded outside the walls. As work became more specialized, guilds resulted, and within the guilds democracy began. Because the traditional forms of leadership—the nobility and the clergy—were of no help at all but a hindrance—town councils were formed to better manage the city's needs and growth. In time, the town councils grew powerful and began talking back to kings. A struggle for supremacy resulted, and bribery played a big part in city councils winning their independence. It should be remembered that castles and churches were cold, lifeless places until merchants began paying off kings and clergymen with silks, tapestries, furnishings, and artwork, the very luxuries commerce made possible. All the great Renaissance painters and sculptors, and the soaring gothic cathedrals, would not have been possible without the rise of the merchant class. In time, the merchant class grew and became the middle class.

THE CITY AS SOCIAL CENTER

It's remarkable how much of the building during the middle ages and later was carried out—not by kings, who were preoccupied with petty wars—but by the merchant class. The important guilds were represented in the town councils, and projects of planning and construction were usually supervised by master builders acting as municipal officials. "From the thirteenth century onwards," writes Fritz Roring, "it was a municipal building committee that constructed the whole of Bruges in the subsequent centuries. It fixed the rows of buildings with a deliberate, even exaggerated stress on differences in balustrades; it looked after the paving of the roads and the water supply of the town; it encouraged the replacement of thatched roofs in favor of tiled roofs through a kind of bonus system; and in short it intervened in everything."

At the heart of such planning was the recognition that cities were for people and how they lived. A good example is the piazza of the Italian Renaissance city. The piazze of Florence, Siena, Pisa, and Venice served a wide variety of social needs. The city square, lined with restaurants, food and clothing marts, and shops where craftsmen worked under the eye of passersby, was at once a marketplace, a meeting place to mingle and gossip, a playground for children, a promenade for lovers, and a stage for civic pageants and religious processions.

Bankers set up tables and did their business in the piazza. Yes, moneymen were a part of the scene, and fueled the city's culture. Florence, for example, while producing and trading much of Europe's cloth, also produced Alberti, Dante, Donatello, Michelangelo, da Vinci, Machiavelli, and Galileo. Education itself became a commercial commodity, indispensable in trading centers as, for example, Genoa, where illiteracy was virtually unknown. It was in the cities and towns, not in the countryside, that the medieval universities took root and grew.

The similarity is striking, of the southern slave plantations of Virginia with the feudal estates of medieval Europe. Both were agrarian and largely self-sustaining, managed by overlords and worked by people inextricably bound to the land. Serfs who escaped the feudal estates were pursued with the same zeal as slaves who fled the plantations. The difference was serfs found freedom in cities while slaves found freedom in the free north.

Whether they would have admitted it or not, Jefferson and Madison had cities to thank for the quality of their education, the cultural refinements they enjoyed, and the republican government they cherished and helped to establish in America. Like the clothes they wore, everything they held dear was attributable to cities. The northern cities they deplored were in fact the true symbol of the American republic, where the air breathed freer.

CHAPTER 27

Transition to Philadelphia

The Masters-Penn-Morris House at 190 Market Street in Philadelphia seemed palatial to George Washington when he stayed there in 1787 during the Constitutional Convention.

Now, having stopped in Philadelphia on his way to Mount Vernon, he realized the three-story house, while elegant and well-situated (it was one block from Congress Hall), was too small for his needs. Unfortunately, no other suitable house was available in the city. Compromises would have to be made, such as placing the president's office up on the third floor. Washington prepared a list of alterations for his personal secretary Tobias Lear to carry out in his absence: the addition of a new, larger servants' hall, the conversion of the "cow-house" into additional stables, the installation of larger bow windows in the front of the house, and a number of minor but personal changes to make the First Family feel at home. While on vacation at Mount

Vernon, Washington would write nine letters to Lear with additional tasks to be carried out prior to the President taking possession in late November.

Browsing through a Philadelphia newspaper, Washington saw an advertisement for the sale of three farms not far from town. He would need an open space for the daily exercise of his horses and perhaps to amuse himself with some casual farming. He wanted to buy one of the farms but didn't have ready cash. He offered instead to exchange land that he owned in western Pennsylvania for one of the farms. None of the sellers expressed the slightest interest. Three thousand acres of undeveloped frontier land was not considered a fair exchange for even as little as sixty acres within easy distance of Philadelphia. The alternative was to accept one of the farms as a gift from one of Philadelphia's wealthy citizens. A man of infinite pride, Washington graciously refused the offer.

Washington reached his beloved Mount Vernon in mid-September, in time to enjoy one full month of warm autumn weather. He spent several days on horseback inspecting various projects he had been monitoring by mail from New York. Settling back into the routine of Virginia planter brought him some pleasure, but the responsibility of the presidency weighed heavily on his mind. His biggest concern was with Britain's continued occupation of the Northwest territory. Rumor had it that British forces were planning to march south from Fort Detroit down to the Gulf of Mexico where they planned to overrun the Spanish stronghold at New Orleans.

Prior to leaving New York, Washington sent a secret communication to Jefferson, Hamilton and Adams with what he knew of the planned operation. As Washington saw it, should the British carry out their mission the only conceivable outcome would not be favorable for the United States. British takeover of Spain's North American possessions would put the British "on both our flanks and rear, with their navy in front." In effect, the United States would be surrounded. Washington posed two questions: (1) should the United States permit British troops to use its territory as a staging ground from which to attack New Orleans? and (2) with a bushfire already raging in the Northwest Territory between American frontiersmen and a number of Indian tribes could the United States prevent the British from advancing on New Orleans?

Thomas Jefferson saw the potential crisis as a means to coerce Spain's peaceful surrender of New Orleans and Florida to the United States. He urged delay during which time Lafayette and other friends of the United States at the French court might pressure Spain into acquiescence. Washington liked the idea, and sent Col. David Humphreys to Lisbon as a first step toward establishing better relations with Spain and to open negotiations that would open up the Mississippi to American navigation.

Hamilton also favored working through diplomatic channels, but with England rather than with France and Spain, and awaiting the unfolding of events.

Vice President John Adams favored a somewhat more aggressive approach. Should the British seek permission to march its forces south from Detroit, Adams said their request should be refused "in terms clear and decided, but guarded and dignified, in a manner which no power has more at its command than the President of the United States."

While awaiting word from Humphreys, Washington decided to send in the Army, not to actually block British advancement south but as a show of force—as a bluff. While there, the Army would punish hostile Indians who were attacking American settlers in the Northwest Territory. Between 1783 and 1790, raiders from the Wabash and Miami Indian tribes were believed to have killed 1,500 settlers in Kentucky alone and taken 20,000 horses. Prior to leaving New York, Washington ordered an invasion force under the command of General Josiah Harmar. Unbeknownst to the President, Harmar was a hard-drinking general. Entrusted with 300 regular soldiers and 1,000 militia from Pennsylvania and Kentucky, Harmar was given orders to attack harassing Indians north of the Ohio River.

AT THE PRESIDENT'S DISCRETION

While awaiting the outcome of Harmar's expedition, Washington spent twelve days on horseback inspecting the swamps and woods north of the Potomac in search of the ideal location for the nation's capital. Congress had decided that the District of Columbia, which could be as large as a hundred square miles, was to be located on the Potomac somewhere between the Eastern Branch and the confluence of the Potomac and the Conococheague Rivers; the exact location at the President's discretion.

Beginning at Georgetown, Washington rode north through Frederick, Maryland; on through Shepherdstown, Virginia; and then through Sharpsburg and Elizabethtown (later Hagerstown), both in Maryland, and lastly through Williamsport, on the Conococheague River. Wherever he rode, promoters would suddenly appear and put the hard-sell on him as to the benefits of their particular area. According to Richard Norton Smith, Washington's survey "illustrated both the glories of the American countryside and the cunning of its inhabitants." The President maintained a poker face and divulged little. His decision wouldn't be announced to the public until after the first of the new year. As it turned out, the capital would be placed on the most southerly part of the authorized tract, that nearest Mount Vernon and close to the Eastern Branch of the Potomac.

Near the end of his Mount Vernon vacation, the President became increasingly irritable. He had yet to hear back from General Harmar. Washington's worries were further compounded when he learned that Harmar had an unquenchable thirst for strong drink. Fearing the worst, on November 17 Washington instructed Secretary of War Henry Knox to prepare a full justification of Harmar's campaign and to have it ready when Congress returned in early December. "I expected little from the moment I heard he was drunkard," Washington wrote on November 19. "I expected less as soon as I heard that on this account no confidence was reposed in him by the western country. And I gave up all hope of success, as soon as I heard that there were disputes with him about command." Washington continued to be gloomy when he arrived in Philadelphia on November 27. It didn't help that work on the Executive Mansion had yet to be completed.

Washington wasn't the only one having trouble with his new residence. Finding no firewood in the vice president's house, Abigail Adams spent her first night at City Tavern. In the morning, she returned to her new house to find damp rooms and the overpowering smell of newly-applied oil-base paint. Congressmen arriving in the city voiced their displeasure over a scarcity of affordable housing as labor shortages slowed the remodeling work on public buildings and private homes.

LONDON ON THE DELAWARE

Philadelphia was the most livable city in America. If New York was a high-energy city fueled by caffeine, Philadelphia was a place where people knew how to relax over a glass of wine. It was a city of readers, supported by ten newspapers and thirty bookstores. Thanks to Benjamin Franklin, the City of Brotherly Love boasted a number of cultural and civic institutions, including two theaters, a university, the nation's first public library, a volunteer fire department, and a hospital. It was a clean well-lit place, with paved streets and an oil-burning lamp on every corner. One highborn Englishman described Philadelphia as "One of the wonders of the world." Another English visitor compared the city favorably with London, and the Delaware as far cleaner than the River Thames.

Philadelphia was also the nation's financial capital (New York would assume the title in 1836), with Chestnut Street as the city's financial district. It was there, one block south of Market Street, that Robert Morris opened the nation's first bank. It was there, too, in the State House (renamed Independence Hall), that both the Declaration of Independence and the U.S. Constitution were drafted. Next door to the State House was the Philadelphia County Courthouse, a two-story red-brick building renamed Congress Hall. It was there the federal legislature reconvened, on December 6, 1790. As with Federal Hall in New York, the House of Representatives met on the first floor and the Senate met on the second floor.

Two days after Congress reconvened, President Washington climbed a flight of stairs to the Senate chamber and delivered his Second Annual Address before both houses of Congress. Written by Hamilton and Madison, it was a relatively short speech. Washington began by acknowledging the nation's recovering prosperity. "The abundant fruits of another year have blessed our Country with plenty, and with the means of a flourishing commerce." The price of government securities continued to rise on the open market, at home and abroad. Washington renewed calls for a uniform militia, national mint, national postal system, highway improvements, and a standardized system of weights and measures. He also urged the construction of more American ships to avoid dependence on European shipping, especially in times of war.

Washington then made public the military incursion in the Northwest territory, and offered this justification: "The aggravated provocations rendered it essential to the safety of the Western Settlements that the aggressors should be made sensible that the Government of the Union is not less capable of punishing their crimes, than it is disposed to respect their rights and reward their attachments." Congress accepted Washington's decision without question.

If Washington feared the worst, his suspicions were confirmed five days later when news arrived of a complete route of Harmar's army. In what is now Vincennes, Indiana, a Shawnee warrior named Little Turtle had dealt Harmar two devastating blows that killed 200 men and sent the remainder of his forces scurrying into Kentucky. Harmar was recalled; his military career over. It's probable that the President's full disclosure to Congress prevented Harmar's selection to lead the force and his subsequent defeat from being the subject of a Congressional investigation.

In keeping with the Constitution, the next expedition against Northwest Indian tribes would be authorized by Congress, with a larger force commanded by General Arthur St. Clair. And what of the British forces in the Northwest Territory and of Spain's occupation of New Orleans? In 1795, under the terms of the Jay Treaty, the British would finally evacuate Fort Detroit and Fort Lernoult, 13 years after the Treaty of Paris. That same year, the Treaty of Madrid would open up the Mississippi to U.S. navigation. Both treaties would be ratified on President Washington's watch.

CHAPTER 28

A Clash of Visions

Alexander Hamilton wasted little time relocating the Treasury Department from New York to Philadelphia. He rented two buildings on Third Street, between Chestnut and Walnut Streets, within short walking distance of the Executive Mansion and Congress Hall.

A visitor described Hamilton's office thus: "His desk was a plain pine table covered with a green cloth. Planks and trestles held records and papers, and at one end was a little imitation Chinese vase and a plate of glasses. . . ." Hamilton's office may have been modest, but his department was the largest of the federal government. The 1791 directory lists 93 employees. Also reporting to the Treasury Department were an additional 122 customs collectors and surveyors employed in various ports up and down the East Coast. In comparison, Knox at the War Department had 12 civilian employees and Jefferson at State had six, plus two ministers in Europe.

Prior to the government's formation, U.S. securities had been valued on the open market at less than $15 million. By the end of 1790, with Funding and Assumption in place, the total value had risen to $45 million—an increase of $30 million. Before people could heap praise on Hamilton, he reminded them that increasing the market value of public securities was only the first step. Three more steps were necessary before the nation would be on firm financial ground: (1) the establishment of a mint, (2) a revision of the tax system, and (3) the creation of a national bank, to be called the Bank of the United States (forerunner of today's Federal Reserve). All three were interrelated and important, but the bank was the linchpin of Hamilton's master plan. In order to fully monetize the public debt, a national bank was crucial.

CAPITALIZING THE BANK

To reach his economic goals, Hamilton aimed high. He set the bank's capitalization at $10 million, more than all the gold and silver specie then in circulation. Not a problem, as most of the bank's assets would be comprised of symbolic money. The United States government would subscribe $2 million of the stock, payable in specie. It did not have near that amount of cash, so it would borrow the amount from the bank itself, and pay it back in ten equal payments over a period of ten years. The remaining $8 million in stock would be offered for public subscription, the purchases being payable one-fourth in specie, and three-fourths in U.S. Treasury bonds bearing 6 percent interest. Subscribers would make their payments in four equal installments spaced six months apart.

The bank would have $500,000 in specie, plus the deposits it attracted. It could safely issue notes and take on other obligations up to $10 million, as if it actually had that much in cash; and it was certain to generate a profit. The interest on its loans, at 6 percent, would be augmented by the additional 6 percent it received on the government bonds that formed most of its capital. Subscribers would rush to invest in the bank, and their avidity would send the government's 6 percent bonds soaring. The government bonds, supported in the first instance by the prospect of sinking fund purchases financed by loans from the bank, as a result would be able to form the capital of the bank, which in turn would make the bonds even more valuable than expectations had already made them. In that manner the very creation of the bank would establish the public credit on an enduring basis—even if the bank should never make loans to the sinking fund that started it.

According to historian Forrest McDonald, Hamilton "had found banking's equivalent of the philosopher's stone, whereby base elements are turned into gold."

Hamilton's bank was closely modeled after the Bank of England, with one crucial difference. The Bank of England bought and sold government securities. The Bank of the United States—after purchasing all the original continental and state securities—would be expressly forbidden from buying government securities. It could only sell them. It's primary function would be to provide a money supply for the financing of ordinary business and general economic development. Hamilton stipulated that the bank be operated for the private profit of its stockholders, thus making it in the interest of the stockholders to run it as efficiently as possible. The bank would be chartered for twenty years, the time it would take to pay off the principle.

The bank would need additional tax revenues to service interest payments. Import duties, while sufficient at the outset, would fall short once the assumed state debts would begin falling due at the end of 1791. Therefore, Hamilton recommended an excise tax on spirits to cover the shortfall. It was—that's right—a sin-tax. Public drunkenness was common and worried several legislators. It was thought a tax on liquor might actually limit drinking; that was the idea. In any event, non-drinkers would have no argument against it. On the other hand, distillers' on the American frontier would, and the result would be the so-called Whiskey Rebellion of 1795.

The third part of Hamilton's proposal was a national mint. While not nearly as important as the first two proposals, a national mint was important as a symbol of fiscal orthodoxy, and as a symbol of America itself. Hamilton wanted coins minted in large and small dominations, down to the penny. He pointed out that the lowest price for any commodity would often sell for less if coins were available in smaller domination. Also, he wanted everyone—rich and poor alike—to have easy access to coins; the lower denominations would make this possible. Thomas Jefferson made the call on basing coin denominations on the metric system. Because the early American mints had trouble meeting demand, foreign coins would continue to be widely circulated until after the Civil War.

The excise tax was presented to Congress on Monday, December 13, and the national bank proposal was made the following day. This time, there was a decided lack of skepticism and hostility, and something akin to understanding and acceptance of Hamilton's financial plans for the nation.

HOW CONGRESS VOTED

After debate, the bill for the excise tax was put to vote on January 12, 1791. It passed easily, giving the Treasury Department a second revenue stream to manage.

The National Bank Bill fared almost as well, despite minor opposition from below the Potomac. Some southerners—Madison included—feared the National Bank and the City of Philadelphia would somehow become intertwined and therefore be difficult to separate, thus making it impossible for the federal capital to move to the Potomac when the time came.

To have it both ways—to have the bank and to be assured the capital moved to the Potomac—Madison proposed an amendment. The amendment would limit the bank's charter from 20 years to 10 years, to coincide with the limit of the Bank charter and the capital's move to the Potomac. Few supported the idea. When the amendment failed to carry, Madison withdrew his support of the Bill on the ground the Bank was unconstitutional. Madison's opponents considered his claim for what it was—a smokescreen designed to cover his real intention of protecting the Residency Act. When the matter was put to a vote, the Bank Bill passed both Houses by substantial majorities.

Madison, however, wouldn't let go. Before Washington could sign the bill into law he met with the president not once but three times in a last-ditch effort to convince him the Bank was unconstitutional. At the same time, Madison tried to convince the president that should he sign the Bill into law the National Bank and Philadelphia would be forever wedded and the capital would never move to the Potomac.

While Washington respected Madison's advice, he decided to get a second opinion. In fact, he got two, one from Attorney General Edmund Randolph, and the second from Secretary of State Thomas Jefferson. They agreed with Madison's strict-constructionist's interpretation of the Constitution. Randolph's and Jefferson's written opinions rehashed much of Madison's arguments, while Jefferson added a bit of legal mumbo-jumbo about the Bank violating laws of mortmain, alienage, descents, forfeiture, escheat, distribution, and monopoly.

Now it was up to Hamilton. Washington sent copies of Randolph's and Jefferson's opinions to the Treasury Secretary for rebuttal. At the same time, the President asked Madison to prepare a veto message for Congress, should Hamilton's rebuttal fail to convince. On top of that, he didn't give the Treasury Secretary much time. On February 25, Washington planned to either sign the bill into law or issue a veto. Hamilton spent a number of days in preparation but didn't sit down to actually write his opinion until the evening of February 22. He worked throughout the night and in the morning handed his 13,000-word opinion to the president.

NECESSARY AND PROPER

The Virginians' argument that the Bank was unconstitutional was based on two key issues. The first was that the Constitution was founded on the principle as declared in the Tenth Amendment, that "all power not delegated to the United States by the Constitution nor prohibited to it by the states are reserved to the states or to the people." No one could argue with that, Hamilton wrote in his rebuttal, for "it is nothing more than a consequence of the republican maxim, that all government is a delegation of power." No one could argue that there were not implied powers as well as expressed powers, the implied powers being the legitimate means of obtaining the expressed end. The Virginians contended that the creation of a national bank was an end, not a means. Nonsense, said Hamilton. A bank was merely a way of doing things. The only question was whether or not the bank was being created for a proper end. Does it have "a natural relation to any acknowledged objects or lawful ends of the government"? For example, Congress could not form a corporation to supervise the

Philadelphia police department, "because they are not authorized to regulate the police in that city." On the other hand, it could create a corporation related to tax collection "because it is the province of the federal government to regulate those objects."

The second issue was Jefferson's narrow interpretation of the "necessary and proper" clause of the Constitution. Jefferson saw the clause as highly restrictive, that by "necessary" it meant literally and indispensably necessary. By Jefferson's definition, a bank was merely incidental to government business and not indispensably necessary. Hamilton countered: every government was confined to passing only such laws as were deemed necessary and proper "to accomplish the objects entrusted to it, for no government had the right to do merely what it pleases." For example: no state constitution expressly authorized the creation of a corporation. Could it be argued that incorporating towns was absolutely necessary? No one questioned that states had the power to create them. Indeed, no one questioned that the federal government had the power to create lighthouses, beacons, buoys, and public piers. Under Jefferson's narrow interpretation, creating a harbor would be incidental to regulating commerce, and not indispensable, and therefore unconstitutional. Hamilton also made the point that virtually every European government had created corporations incidental to the collection of taxes and the regulation of commerce.

A bank was the most advantages means of fulfilling the government's powers, Hamilton said. He cited an example sure to get Washington's attention—financing an army. "A nation is thwarted with war (and) large sums are wanted on a sudden to make the requisite preparations. Taxes are laid for the purpose, but it requires time to obtain the benefit of them. . . . If there be a bank the supply can at once be had. If there be none, loans from individuals must be sought (but) the progress of these is often too slow." Under such a scenario, it would be indispensable for the government to create a bank. As president,

James Madison would find this to be true during the War of 1812 when he was forced to resurrect the national bank in order to pay the U.S. Army.

Hamilton easily dealt with Jefferson's pettifoggery about the Bank violating laws of mortmain, alienage, descents, forfeiture and escheat, distribution, monopoly and the like. In the words of Forrest McDonald, Hamilton exposed Jefferson's legalese as "a mixture of bad law, non-law, and irrelevant law."

IMPLIED POWERS DOCTRINE

In making his case for the Bank, Hamilton had created "the implied powers doctrine" which future presidents would rely upon when making decisions that weren't expressly enumerated in the Constitution, including Jefferson himself when he authorized the Louisiana Purchase. Under Jefferson's strict constructionist interpretation, the federal government could not have made the purchase because the buying of territory wasn't expressly stated in the Constitution. As historians have pointed out ever since, had the federal government's actions been limited to enumerated powers, it would have sunk quickly to a level of complete and utter incompetence. Hamilton's interpretation rendered the Constitution a living, breathing document easily adaptable to meet whatever crisis might lay ahead, for generations to come. (Even Jefferson's biographer Dumas Malone and Madison's biographer Irving Brant admitted that Hamilton was right and their man wrong.)

Having completed his rebuttal, Hamilton handed it to the President before noon on Wednesday the 23rd. Washington sat down to read it on the 24th. Swayed by Hamilton's cogent analysis, Washington signed the Bank Bill into law on February 25.

Congress had one final piece of business, admitting two new states into the Union—Kentucky and Vermont. On March 3, 1791, the First Congress of the United States adjourned for the last time, and passed into history. A widely reprinted newspaper article, in recounting the First Congress's many accomplishments, concluded: "The establishment of the federal government completed the revolution in America." It did so through the efforts of 95 elected government officers working without the aid of support staffs or standing committees and for a total cost, including salaries, travel, printing, supplies, and wood for their fireplaces, of less than $374,000. Never let it be said that Americans don't love a bargain.

EPILOGUE

For Thomas Jefferson, it was the "Aha!" moment. It confirmed everything he believed to be true about the Treasury Secretary. Alexander Hamilton was a closest monarchist!

It happened at a dinner about two months after Washington signed the Bank Bill into law. Jefferson was speaking casually with John Adams and Hamilton. Adams said that if the British government were somehow purged of its corruption and if representation in the House of Commons were made more democratic, "it would be the most perfect constitution ever devised by the wit of man." Hamilton disagreed. If the British government were purged of corruption and representation were equalized, he said, "it would become an impracticable government: as it stands at present, with all its supposed defects, it is the most perfect government which ever existed."

One can imagine Jefferson listening intently with arms folded. Heretofore he had thought of Hamilton's financial policies as smacking of England's "corrupt financial system" but as necessary, a bitter pill to be swallowed if the patient was to survive. Now, however, he could see what Hamilton was really after: he wanted to turn America into a monarchy, and to make George Washington king, or, more likely, himself.

The account of the conversation was recorded in Jefferson's "Anas" and nowhere else, written several years after the fact. Was what Hamilton said—if he said it—that revealing? Was he a monarchist? Hamilton had said the same thing at the Constitutional Convention. It should not have come as a news flash to Jefferson. Hamilton was, in fact, quoting David Hume with whose writings Jefferson was quite familiar. Hamilton and Madison drew on many of their political and economic ideas from this highly respected Scottish philosopher. To be sure, Hamilton was ambitious; but so too was Jefferson. Since becoming Secretary of State, he'd had his eyes on the presidency.

Closer to the truth, perhaps, was that Jefferson had become jealous of Hamilton's influence within the Washington administration. It didn't help that the president seemed to be always favoring Hamilton over Jefferson and Madison. To be sure, the president's decision on the Bank Bill was a stinging defeat for the two Virginians. Adding insult to injury, Hamilton's legal brief seemed to be "shouting with a schoolboy's fun at the idea of . . . teaching the Virginia democrats some law" (to quote Henry Adams). Going forward, on nearly every issue of consequence, Washington would side with the Treasury Secretary. On several occasions, Jefferson tried to convince Washington that Hamilton's policies were autocratic and elitist, but Washington wasn't buying it.

What Jefferson and Madison had failed to realize was the special relationship that had developed between Washington and Hamilton during the Revolution. They knew what it was like to conduct a war without food, clothing, adequate medical supplies, ammunition, and money to meet payroll; to be let down time and again by a feckless government. Neither Jefferson nor Madison had ever served a single day in the Continental Army, never mind having suffered the hardships of the winter at Valley Forge. Hamilton's call for a strong national government with strong financial underpinnings rang true for Washington. If the infant republic was to step up and become a world power, it needed a world-class economy. It was liquid capital, not land, that had made the British Isles the most powerful nation in the world. Hamilton's call for the creation of a financial system that rewarded ingenuity and hard work rather than privilege and hereditary wealth, rang equally true for Washington. Hamilton saw America's future in commerce, manufacturing, and liquid capital. To the dismay of Jefferson and Madison, so did Washington.

Jefferson saw the nation's future in agriculture. He wanted America to be a nation of yeoman farmers, where everyone worked his own 50-acre plot of land, and with his own hands created everything he needed. Let Europe be the manufacturing center of the world. "Those who labor in the earth are the chosen people of God," Jefferson said. Bankers and stockbrokers were paper pushers; they didn't create anything and therefore were unnecessary in Jefferson's scheme of things.

A political divide was in the making, not from Jefferson's fear of Hamilton being a monarchist, but over a clash of visions: Jefferson's agrarian utopia versus Hamilton's mercantile mecca. Battle lines having been drawn, the party wars of the 1790s were as vicious as any shooting war. That there was no actual shooting—no political assassinations—stands as a testament to England's enduring legacy in America—the rule of law. When the smoke cleared, Jefferson emerged as victor, having won the 1800 presidential election. It proved to be something of a pyrrhic victory, however. Hamilton's policies were too ingrained to be completely dismantled, and as chief justice of the

Supreme Court John Marshall was forever overruling the Jeffersonian states' rights agenda. On top of that, to be an effective president, Jefferson was forced to adopt many of Hamilton's policies, including the doctrine of implied powers.

In the end, Jefferson's dream of a second American revolution, whereby the republic was recast in Virginia's image, never materialized. It was hijacked by Hamilton's mercantile vision. As historian Stephen F. Knott put it: "The America that explored the outer reaches of space, welcomed millions of immigrants, led the effort to defeat fascism and communism, produced countless technological advances, and abolished slavery and Jim Crow is Hamilton's America."

None of it would have been possible, of course, without the man from Mount Vernon. George Washington made it all attainable: victory over the British, the writing of the U.S. Constitution, the astonishing output of the First Congress, and Hamilton's economic vision for America. There's a reason the Washington Monument stands taller than everything else in the nation's capital.

- END -

BIBLIOGRAPHY

It was an interesting question.

President John F. Kennedy wanted to know how a country of four million people could have produced the three greatest geniuses of the eighteenth century—Franklin, Hamilton and Jefferson?

It was the summer of 1961, and at the Kennedy compound in Hyannis Port, Jack Kennedy had just finished playing backgammon with writer Gore Vidal. Vidal did not have an answer. Said Kennedy: "You know in this, uh, job . . . I get to meet everybody—all these great movers and shakers and the thing I'm most struck by the lot of them is how second-rate they are. Then you read all those debates over the Constitution . . . nothing like that now. Nothing."

Perhaps. Leaders of this or any age are human after all, with human failings. According to historian Joanne B. Freeman of Yale University, that's what makes them interesting.

"Myths dehumanize, removing the uncertainty, the excitement, the ambiguities, and the emotions of the unfolding of history," writes Freeman. "We seek to clearly identify the ‘good‘ and the ‘bad.‘ We try to create better, more logical reasons for the events of history. We endow historical figures with more knowledge, absolute confidence, and ulterior motives than they ever possessed."

Continues Freeman: "But what is truly fascinating about Hamilton, Washington, Jefferson, and their contemporaries is that they were real people, with their good and bad sides, living during a turbulent period, blessed with the talents to take part in the creation of a nation, but like any person faced with challenges, unsure of how to proceed and doubtful about the success of their actions. The history of the United States is a human story. To truly understand it, it is important to preserve its humanity."

In our time we are benefited with a number of excellent books that reveal more of the humanity of the Founders than perhaps the books Kennedy read. A number of these newer books inspired me to write this book.

GEORGE WASHINGTON

All the Founders acted like jerks from time-to-time, with one exception. George Washington doesn't register on the "jerk-meter," which tends to make him as one-dimensional as his portrait on the dollar bill. The myth-making following his death didn't help. For me, it's not so much what Washington wrote or said that reveals his character, but what he did. Washington was an incredible physical presence, and a man of action. Action, not words, go a long way in fleshing out the man. These are the books that helped me gain a better understanding of who he was, what he did, and the world in which he lived:

Washington: The Indispensable Man (1969) by James Thomas Flexner

George Washington and the New Nation: (1783-1793) (1969) by James Thomas Flexner

His Excellency: George Washington (2004) by Joseph Ellis

The Presidency of George Washington (1974) by Forrest McDonald

George Washington: Founding Father (1996) by Richard Brookhiser

Patriarch: George Washington and the New Nation (1993) by Richard Norton Smith

Washington's Crossing (2004) by David Hackett Fischer

The Diaries of George Washington Vol. 6 edited by Donald Jackson and Dorothy Twohig

George Washington's Diaries: An Abridgment edited by Dorothy Twohig

Washington: Writings (1997) edited by John Rhodehamel

Martha Washington: An American Life (2005) by Patricia Brady

Cincinnatus: George Washington & The Enlightenment (1984) by Garry Wills

The American Presidents — George Washington (2004), by James MacGregor Burns and Susan Dunn

ALEXANDER HAMILTON

A number of revealing biographies of Hamilton have appeared in recent years. The one by Forrest McDonald is not so much a biography as an analysis of what he read and how he applied it to government and finance. Unlike Washington, actions don't tell the whole story. You must read Hamilton's writings to fathom his character.

Alexander Hamilton: A Biography (1979) by Forrest McDonald

Alexander Hamilton: American (1999) by Richard Brookhiser

Alexander Hamilton: A Life (2003) by Willard Sterne Randall

Alexander Hamilton (2004) by Ron Chernow

Alexander Hamilton (1982) A Biography by Jacob E. Cook

Hamilton: Writings (2001) edited by Joanne B. Freeman

Alexander Hamilton and the Persistence of Myth (2002), by Stephen E. Knott

Tracks the ups and downs of Hamilton's reputation since the days of our nation's founding.

JAMES MADISON

Next to George Washington, James Madison is tough to get a fix on. His contemporaries found him stiff and humorless, and the books I studied did little to dispel that image. He could be both brilliant and petty. His break with Hamilton appears motivated partly by jealousy.

His take on government was infinitely more realistic than that of fellow Virginian Thomas Jefferson.

James Madison: A Biography (1971) by Ralph Ketcham

James Madison and the Struggle for the Bill of Rights (2006) by Richard Labunski

THOMAS JEFFERSON

Jefferson's reputation has taken a beating in recent years. His writings, like his actions, are often contradictory. Like all successful presidents, he spoke of small government as virtuous (a Jeffersonian ideal) while he expanded the powers of the presidency (Hamiltonian real-politick).

Jefferson & the Rights of Man (1951) by Dumas Malone (1784-1793)

American Sphinx: the Character of Thomas Jefferson (1996) by Joseph Ellis

Jefferson and Monticello: The Biography of a Builder (1988) Jack McLaughlin

Mr. Jefferson's University (2002) Garry Wills

AND THE REST

John Jay: Founding Father (2005) by Walter Stahr

Twice Jay stared greatness in the eye—as Superintendent of Foreign Affairs, and as Chief Justice of the Supreme Court—and both times came up lacking. He was indispensable to the American cause, however, and therefore a great American.

John Adams (2001) by David McCullough

Feisty, fussy and his own worst enemy, Adams managed to offend nearly everyone he encountered. He was correct when he predicted, "Mausoleums, statues, monuments will never be erected to me." The more you learn about honest John Adams, however, the more you respect him.

Benjamin Franklin (1938) by Carl Van Doren

Simply stated, a classic. Who doesn't love wise and kindly Ben Franklin?

A Benjamin Franklin Reader (2003) edited and annotated by Walter Isaacson.

Founding Father: The Life of Oliver Ellsworth (2011) by Michael C. Toth. If you're going to have a revolution, when it's over you're going to need the nuts-and-bolts guys to make the new government work. That was Oliver Ellsworth, a New England pragmatist and one of the most influential delegates at the Constitutional Convention in 1787. Ellsworth is among the Founding Fathers (James Wilson is another) who have been overshadowed by the sheer star-power of Benjamin Franklin, Thomas Jefferson, Alexander Hamilton, James Madison, and George Washington. "Founding Father: The Life of Oliver Ellsworth," by Michael C. Toth, puts Ellsworth's contributions in perspective.

James Wilson, Founding Father (1956) by Page Smith. Unless you've read about the creation of the U.S. Constitution, it's unlikely you're familiar with James Wilson. With the exception of James Madison, Wilson was arguably the most influential member at the

Constitutional Convention in Philadelphia. He was also a signer of the Declaration of Independence, and one of the original six justices to sit on the first United States Supreme Court. In 1956, historian Page Smith wrote a long-overdo biography of Wilson who is perhaps the most neglected member of the Founding generation. Smith does a nice job of blending important details with colorful anecdotes to flesh out Wilson's analytical and somewhat dry character, and to illustrate his many contributions to the creation of our federal government.

Novus Ordo Seculorum: The Intellectual Origins of the Constitution (1985) by Forrest McDonald.

Indispensable in understanding what the Founders read on law, government, and economics and how they applied it to nation-building.

E. Pluribus Unum: The Formation of the American Republic 1776-1790 (1965) by Forrest McDonald

Indispensable to understanding the make-up and politics of the early republic.

The American Presidency: An Intellectual History (1994) by Forrest McDonald

Think you understand the American presidency? This book will open your eyes. Mainly about the ceremonial and administrative roles of heads of state with particular focus on the presidencies of Washington and Jefferson.

The Age of Federalism: The Early American Republic, 1788-1800 (1993) by Stanley Elkins and Eric McKitrick. Don't let the thickness and scholarly appearance fool you. This book is imminently readable. My copy is badly dog-eared from repeated use.

Founding Brothers: The Revolutionary Generation (2000) by Joseph Ellis

It's all here: the Hamilton-Madison dinner deal; why the Founders turned a blind eye toward slavery; Jefferson and Adams' famous correspondence; the collaborative effort with Hamilton that produced Washington's masterful Farewell Address.

Something That Will Surprise the World: the Essential Writings of the Founding Fathers (2006) edited by Susan Dunn

A selection of political writings by Washington, Hamilton, Adams, Jefferson, Madison.

Birth of the Nation: The First Federal Congress 1789-1791 (2002) by Charlene Bangs Bickford and Kenneth R. Bowling. Brief, factual, and to the point.

The House: The History of the House of Representatives (2006) by Robert V. Remini

Invaluable to understanding the First Congress's many accomplishments.

Affairs of Honor: National Politics in the New Republic (2001) by Joanne B. Freeman. Freeman reveals a very human side of the Founding Fathers, warts and all.

Dinner at Mr. Jefferson's: Three Men, Five Great Wines, and the Evening That Changed America (2008) by Charles A. Cerami. Everything you want to know about the most famous dinner in American history, including what they ate and drank.

What Kind of Nation: Thomas Jefferson, John Marshall, and the Epic Struggle to Create a United States (2002) by James F. Simon

An unflattering portrait of our third president coupled with a flattering portrait of our fourth chief justice.

Hamilton, Adams, Jefferson: The Politics of Enlightenment and the American Founding (2005) by Darren Staloff. Ever wonder what it would be like to spend an evening chatting with Hamilton, Adams and Jefferson? Staloff delivers.

The First Salute: A View of the American Revolution (1988) by Barbara W. Tuchman. One of the greatest historians of our time turns her attention to the American Revolution.

Miracle at Philadelphia (1966) by Catherine Drinker Bowen

How the U.S. Constitution was written, and by whom. Should be required reading in public schools.

The Federalist Papers by Alexander Hamilton, James Madison, and John Jay.

The U.S. Constitution operating manual. According to Newt Gingrich, should be required reading for everyone elected to Congress.

Explaining America (1981) by Garry Wills

A primer on "The Federalist Papers" and its authors. Wills' writing can be a bit scholarly but not here.

Fame and the Founding Fathers (1974) essays by Douglas Adair

Historian Douglas Adair never got around to writing a book. This handy tome contains his A-List essays on the Founders. His analysis of Federalist No. 10 (written by Madison) is worth the price of admission.

Inventing a Nation: Washington, Adams, Jefferson (2003) by Gore Vidal.

Vidal shows restraint in this short take on the Founders.

To Begin the World Anew (2003) by Bernard Bailyn

The noted Harvard professor delivers five essays, including an analysis of how the U.S. Constitution was designed to protect minority groups and individuals from the domination of majorities in control of a powerful, freely elected government.

How the Scots Invented the Modern World (2001) by Arthur Herman

Could be titled "How the Scots Invented the U.S." A fair portion is devoted to how Scottish writers influenced the shaping of the Declaration of Independence, the U.S. Constitution, the Supreme Court, and American capitalism.

The Island at the Center of the World (2004) by Russell Shorto

How New York City evolved from a Dutch outpost to the center of the financial world.

Washington: The Making of the American Capital (2008) by Fergus M. Bordewich

How sordid politics resulted in a contemporary version of the Greek Acropolis on the banks of the Potomac River.

Hamilton's Blessing: The Extraordinary Life and Times of the National Debt (1997) by John Steele Gordon

America has been a debtor nation from the beginning. Hamilton created a system to manage it, Andrew Jackson destroyed it, and in the 20th century it was resurrected as The Federal Reserve. Gordon asks a timely question: how much debt is too much?

The First Wall Street: Chestnut Street, Philadelphia, and the Birth of American Finance (2005) by Robert E. Wright

Before Wall Street there was Chestnut Street in Philadelphia, where it all began.

The White House: An Illustrated Architectural History, by Patrick Phillips-Schrock (2013) — Everything you want to know about the six houses that served our presidents, from the Franklin-Osgood House at 1 Cherry Street in New York City, to the White House at 1600 Pennsylvania Avenue, in Washington, D.C.

Manias, Panics, and Crashes: A History of Financial Crises (1978) by Charles P. Kindleberger

Ever hear of the South Sea Bubble? Our Founders had. Hamilton designed a financial system to avoid a repeat.

Essays Moral, Political and Literary (1752) by David Hume

Hume's ideas fueled both Madison's government of checks and balances and Hamilton's economic policies. Those ideas are contained in this single volume.

The Wealth of Nations (1776) by Adam Smith

Smith's classic on economics was widely read by the Founders and has never gone out of print.

On the Wealth of Nations (2007) by P.J. O'Rourke

O'Rouke's take on Smith's classic. Informative and entertaining.

PERIODICALS:

"Financing the American Revolution" by Udo Hielscher, Museum of American Financial History (2003)

"The President's House Revisited" by Edward Lawler Jr., and "Six Houses for the President" by Damie Stillman, The Pennsylvania Magazine of History and Biography, October 2005

"Shall we have a king? John Jay and the Politics of Union" by John P. Kaminski, New York History, Quarterly Journal of the New York State Historical Association, January 2000

"Honor and Interest: John Jay's Diplomacy During the Confederation" by John P. Kaminski, New York History, Quarterly Journal of the New York State Historical Association, Summer 2002

"A lively look at the Founders—John Marshall" by Richard L. Strout, The Christian Science Monitor, June/July 1976

"The American Enlightenment's Other Side," an interview with Richard Brookhiser, The Atlas Society

"What Hamilton Wrought" by Richard Sylla, Leonard Stern School of Business, New York University, 2/1/2006

"The Bank that Hamilton Built" by Phil Davies, The Region, September 2007

Extract from an Address to the people of the state of New York, on the subject of the federal constitution, by John Jay, Library of Congress (1788)

"Washington's Fourth Visit to Rhode Island," by John Williams Haley, Best of Rhode Island, Rhode Island's Monthly 2007

"The Great Debate: Hamilton, Jefferson and the Fight over Assumption" by Robert Sloan, Financial History: The Magazine of the Museum of American Finance, Winter 2010.

"Alexander Hamilton: the Man and the Myths," by Joanne B. Freeman, Paper Money: Official Journal of the Society of Paper Money Collectors, January/February 2007.

Curator's Corner (about the Executive Mansion at 1 Cherry Street, New York,) by Norma Calderhead, Dacor Bulletin, May 2001

CD

"Alexander Hamilton" - (PBS - American Experience) 2007 - A Wonderful video about the life and contributions of Hamilton, with commentary by a number of scholars, including Joanne Freeman, whom I quote.

APPENDIX

I

The Washington Monument

It's the most famous room in the world. It's where Presidents address the nation, especially in times of crisis. It's the room where history is made. It's the Oval Office in the West Wing of the White House.

At one end of the Oval Office, filling in the southern curve, behind the President's desk, are three great windows, each eleven and-a-half feet tall, with special layered glass designed to stop an assassin's bullet. Visible through the windows is a great white marble obelisk that towers over the capital and stands as a silent reminder to every President of what Democracy is about. The obelisk is the Washington Monument.

Unlike the Jefferson and Lincoln Memorials in the nation's capital, the soaring white walls of the Washington Monument are blank. It seems fitting. Words defined Thomas Jefferson and Abraham Lincoln but not George Washington. As a general, as a President, as the Father of his

Country, it wasn't what Washington said but what he did that made him a great leader. Actions, not words, defined the man.

The Jefferson memorial was built 135 years after he left office as president. The Lincoln Memorial was built 57 years after he was assassinated. The Washington Monument, on the other hand, was being planned before Washington even took office as president.

The idea for a Washington memorial was first voiced in the aftermath of the American Revolution. In August, 1783, the Continental Congress, then meeting in New Jersey, resolved unanimously "That an equestrian statue of George Washington be erected at the place where the residence of Congress shall be established." Later, after Congress had voted to build the new seat of government on the banks of the Potomac, President Washington approved the spot assigned by city planner Pierre L'Enfant. It should stand on the Mall, they agreed, at an intersection of lines west and south of the future Capitol building and the President's Mansion.

The new nation had more pressing problems, and Washington himself felt that the low state of the treasury scarcely warranted such an unessential expense. It was not until Washington's death in 1799 that Americans suddenly realized that they had failed to provide a monument in appreciation of the Virginia statesman. As hundreds of impassioned eulogies rang out from pulpit and podium across the land, Congress passed another resolution. The new bill was sponsored by Representative John Marshall, who was himself destined for greatness as the Chief Justice who established the power of the Supreme Court.

Marshall's proposal called for a marble memorial inside the Capitol building, to which Washington's remains were to be transferred when—and if—permission could be obtained from the family. Martha Washington agreed, reluctantly. Eventually, after years of Congressional debate, resolutions, and correspondence with Washington's heirs, a mausoleum was built under the Capitol Rotunda.

It was never happened. Washington's grandnephew and Mount Vernon's owner at the time, John Augustine Washington, refused to allow the General's remains to be moved, citing the General's will, which had directed his burial on the Virginia estate. Henceforth the Capitol tomb would remain a tourist curiosity.

Congress remained determined to honor Washington in some way. In 1832, it authorized the then-huge sum of $5,000 for a statue to be displayed in the Capitol Rotunda. Horatio Greenough, an American sculpture working in Italy, won the commission. Working with a 20-ton block of marble, Greenough's image of Washington as a seated, bare-chested Adonis horrified rather than gratified Congressman and public alike. The General appeared, it was said, as if "entering or leaving a bath." Rather than being placed in the Rotunda, the statue was put outside amidst the shrubbery—and forgotten. Today, the statue can be seen in the exhibit halls of the Smithsonian.

At this point, George Washington's old friend John Marshall, now 78 and full of honors, was called to the rescue, as head of a new civic organization calling itself the the Washington Monument Society. The Society had but one goal—to build the Washington Monument without further delay. They had no way of knowing that repeated delays would mark the Monument's construction, and that few of the founding members would see its completion.

MAGNIFICENT INTENTIONS

A competition was held for a new design. The winner was Robert Mills, onetime draftsman for Thomas Jefferson. Mills had already won acclaim with his memorial to Washington commissioned by the City of Baltimore, and completed in 1829. Appointed U.S. architect by President Andrew Jackson, he designed many public buildings, among them the U.S. Treasury, the Patent Office, and the General Post Office.

Mills' plan for the Washington Monument in D.C., as he described it, outlined a "grand circular colonnaded building . . . 100 feet high, from which sprang an obelisk shaft . . . making a total elevation of 600 feet." Above the central portico, a colossal toga-clad George Washington drove a chariot drawn by six Arabian steeds, all of it carved from marble, of course.

The Monument Society never warmed up to the chariot idea or the ornate base, concentrating instead on raising money to construct the obelisk. That was in 1836, not a good time to be raising money. Andrew Jackson had shut down the Second National Bank, money was in short supply, and an economic depression soon set in. As a result, construction didn't begin for another 12 years. Charles Dickens visited D.C. around this time and described the unfinished capital as "a city of magnificent intentions."

Construction finally began in 1848. On hand for the ground-breaking ceremonies were President James K. Polk; a little-known Congressman from Illinois named Abraham Lincoln, together with two other future Presidents, James Buchanan and Andrew Johnson; George Washington's grandson, George Washington Parke Custis; and the widows of two of the nation's Founding Fathers, Dolly Madison and Elizabeth Hamilton (still active at age 91).

For the first few years, the Monument grew like a marble beanstalk. Then, having reached a height of 152 feet, construction stopped. A political faction calling themselves the Know-Nothings seized control of the Monument Society by an illegal election. After several years, having added only a few feet of inferior stonework that had to be removed, the Know-Nothings returned the project to its legitimate leaders. Now, the Civil War loomed. All work on the monument ceased, despite the Society's redoubled efforts to raise money by placing collection boxes in post offices and at voting polls—including those for the national election that brought Abraham Lincoln to the Presidency.

All during the war, the unfinished Monument stood as a reminder of the break between the states. Soldiers in blue drilled under the United States flag that waved over its flat top. Cattle grazed at the depot set up on the grounds to help feed the Army. Across the way, meanwhile, workmen raised the Capitol's new iron dome—a sign that the Union would go on, as Lincoln said.

The Monument was still unfinished when Mark Twain worked as a Washington newspaper reporter in 1867. "It has the aspect," he wrote later, "of a factory chimney with the top broken off... Cow-sheds about its base ... contented sheep nibbling about its base ... tired pigs dozing in the holy calm of its protecting shadow."

By the centennial of Independence in 1876, the sorry state of the Monument had needled the conscience of Capital officials. Congress passed a law, signed by President Ulysses S. Grant, providing for completion and maintenance of the Monument. After a 25 year hiatus, work resumed.

Army engineers soon discovered the Monument's foundation could not support its proposed height. Before building further, they removed weak sections of the original masonry foundation and strengthened, broadened, and deepened the rest by filling in subterranean tunnels with poured concrete. The memorial's dimensions were changed too as result of research by the U.S. Minister to Italy, George Marsh. A true obelisk, he reported, should have a height of about ten times its base: hence the Monument's final summit of 555 feet, 5 $^{1}/_{8}$ inches, to a base of 55 feet, 1 $^{1}/_{2}$ inches square. (The finished Monument would be the equivalent height of a 55-story building.)

THE LEANING TOWER OF WASHINGTON?

The push to the top started with the laying of second cornerstone by President Rutherford B. Hayes in August, 1880. Construction was completed when the capstone was set in place on December 6, 1884. The Monument was dedicated in 1885 and opened to the public in 1888. To reach the top, visitors either climbed the stairs or rode the slow steam hoist. An electric elevator replaced the steam lift in 1901, then gave way to improved models in 1926 and 1959. Today's elevator reaches the top in about 70 seconds. The stairs were closed to the public in 1971, due to congestion and exhausted climbers needing rescue.

In 1901, the Senate's McMillan Committee for civic development recommended a landscaping project in line with L'Enfant's original plan for a grandly scenic mall. The Monument area was to be cut into a series of terraced gardens, embellished with trees, fountains, and a great circular pool. Since large-scale shifting of earth loads was involved, engineers made deep borings to test soil conditions. They discovered the Monument itself would be endangered by the excavations, producing a "Leaning Tower of Washington." The project was abandoned.

The Monument's surroundings have nonetheless improved since then, when the Mall area was an unsightly clutter of railroad tracks, haphazard buildings, animal pens, and marshes. Massive Government buildings and the Smithsonian Institute complex of buildings now enclose a broad, grassy swath. More recent construction includes a new wing to the National Gallery of Art, the National Air and Space Museum, and the Hirshhorn Museum and Sculpture Garden.

While not a part of L'Enfant's original plans, the Lincoln and Jefferson Memorials completed the intersection of lines the city planner envisioned, with the Capitol and Lincoln Memorial on opposites ends of the east-west line, the White House and Jefferson Memorial on opposite ends of the north-south line, with the Washington Memorial near the center where the lines intersect.

In a city where Government buildings sprawl, the Washington Monument soars. As with the man himself, there is nothing in sight to rivals its majestic height. Shimmering in the sun by day, a pillar of light by night, it reaches peak display once a year when Fourth of July fireworks trace the pointed silhouette "in shooting stars and showers of pyrotechnic flowers."

Had the Washington Monument been commissioned by a tyrant, it would have been built quickly and efficiently. Because it wasn't, it took halting steps to achieve, like the achievements of the government itself. Democracy is often slow to act, and slow to get results. Mistakes are made, the process is maddening and wasteful, but like the Committee that built the Washington Monument, the job gets done and in the end we call the results miraculous. The same can be said of the Washington Monument. The process took nearly a hundred years to complete, but the result is miraculous.

Enduring all manner of storms, symbolic of democracy itself, the Washington Monument stands tall for all the world to see.

- END -

I am indebted to "Washington: Man and Monument" a pamphlet by Frank Freidel and Lonnelle Aikman, in composing this piece.

II

The Great Awakening

It was after the American Revolution, after everything had been settled and the future of the new republic looked promising. Thomas Jefferson wrote that he was not expressing new ideas or principles when he wrote the Declaration of Independence. No indeed. He was expressing ideas that already had become settled in the American mind.

John Adams said much the same thing. "What do we mean by the American Revolution? The Revolution was in the minds of the people... a change in the religious sentiments."

What they were referring to was the Great Awakening, a religious revival that swept the American colonies in the first half of the 18th century. In the decades preceding the War of Independence, revivalism taught people that they could confront religious authority when that authority wasn't living up to the believer's expectations. As a result many Christians broke with the Church of England and formed their own church. It was the democratization of religion and overnight a number of new denominations sprung up across the land, especially in New England.

Thanks to the Great Awakening, Colonists realized that religious power resided not with the established church but rather resided in their very own hands. After a generation or two passed with this kind of mindset, Colonists came to realize that political power did not reside in the hands of the English monarch, but in their own desire to be self-governed. By 1775, even though Colonists did not all share the same theological beliefs, they did share a common vision of freedom from British authority. Thus, the Great Awakening created a climate that made the American Revolution possible.

III

Ordering up a New World

They were 18th-century Scottish philosophers, and what they did was order up a new world that became the United States. Fittingly, they're the subject of a recent book, "The Infidel and the Professor." The "infidel" is David Hume and "the professor" is Adam Smith. The author is Dennis C. Rasmussen, associate professor of political science at Tufts University.

Hume was born in Edinburgh and spoke with a decided Scottish burr, while Smith, who was born a few miles to the north, in Kirkcaldy, Fife, did not. Both were highly gifted students. Hume attended Edinburgh University, but did not graduate. Smith attended Glasgow University, and did. Both suffered temporary breakdowns as a result of overstudy. Hume did not teach, and spent most of his adult life writing, which came easily to him. Smith taught at Glasgow U, and struggled with the pen. Neither married (few great philosophers do), although Hume did fall madly in love with a lady of Parisian society but ended the relationship fearing it would draw him away from his true passion, study and writing.

Hume wrote about human behavior, ethics, religion, political theory, economic theory, and authored a stellar six-volume history of England. Smith wrote two books, one concerning political theory, and one concerning economic theory.

Unlike a number of Enlightenment writers, neither Hume nor Smith were radicals. They did not advocate grand schemes for radically restructuring society. They embraced the benefits of the rule of law, limited government, religious tolerance, freedom of expression, private property, and commerce, while insisting that necessary societal changes should be implemented in a gradual, measured way. Unlike other revolutions to come, this was exactly the result of the the American Revolution—gradual rather than sweeping change.

"The Infidel and the Professor" is almost as much about Hume's and Smith's friendship as it is about their books. The author devotes approximately two chapters to Hume's writings and two chapters to Smith's: one to "The Theory of Moral Sentiments" and one to "The Wealth of Nations." Of the two, "The Theory of Moral Sentiments" was more popular in Smith's day. Meanwhile, across the Atlantic, Hume's and Smith's books were widely studied in America by the Founding Fathers, particularly by Alexander Hamilton and James Madison. Thanks to the scholarship of historian Douglass Adair, we know that Madison was greatly influenced by the political theories of David Hume. Writes Adair: "It was David Hume's speculations on the 'Idea of a Perfect Commonwealth' . . . that most stimulated James Madison's thought on factions." He goes so far as to say Madison had a copy of Hume's book at his side while writing Federalist No. 10.

For his economic ideas, Madison drew upon Smith's "The Wealth of Nations."

According to historian Forrest McDonald, it was the opposite with Hamilton. Hamilton drew more on Hume's economic theories, and for his political theories drew more on Smith's "Theory of Moral Sentiments." Unfortunately, Rasmussen does not discuss in any depth the actual influence Hume and Smith had on America's founding. That said, I enjoyed his book, and recommend it to anyone desiring to know more about two of the greatest and most influential writers of the 18th-century Enlightenment. To learn more about their impact on America's founding, I suggest "Novus Ordo Seclorum: The Intellectual Origins of the Constitution" by Forest McDonald; "Explaining America: The Federalist" by Garry Wills; and "Fame and the Founding Fathers" by Douglass Adair.

IV

The Spirit of Liberty

The influential jurist with the unlikely but appropriate name Learned Hand served as a presiding judge of the Second Circuit Court of Appeals from 1939 to 1951. What follows is a short speech he gave at an "I Am an American Day" ceremony in New York City's Central Park toward the end of World War II. The speech is titled "The Spirit of Liberty," but the underlying theme is the need of humility, of common decency, and of respect for our fellow man regardless of race, religion, and place of origin, if our republic is to long endure. What follows is a slightly edited version of the speech.

Judge Learned Hand:

We have gathered here to affirm our faith, a faith in common purpose, a common conviction, a common devotion. Some of us have chosen America as the land of our adoption; the rest have come from those who did the same. For this reason we have some right to consider ourselves a picked group, a group of those who had the courage to break from the past and brave the dangers and the loneliness of a strange land. What was the object that nerved us, or those who went before us, to this choice? We sought liberty—freedom from oppression, freedom from want, freedom to be ourselves. This we then sought; this we now believe that we are by way of winning.

What do we mean when we say that first of all we seek liberty? I often wonder whether we do not rest our hopes too much upon constitutions, upon laws, and upon courts. These are false hopes; believe me, these are false hopes. Liberty lies in the hearts of men and women; when it dies there is no constitution, no law, no court that can save it; no constitution, no law, no court can even do much to help it. While it lies there, it needs no constitution, no law, no court to save it. And what is this liberty which must lie in the hearts of men and women? It is not the ruthless, the unbridled will; it is not freedom to do as one likes. That is the denial of liberty, and leads straight to its overthrow. A society in which men recognize no check upon freedom soon becomes a society where freedom is the possession of only the savage few—as we have learned to our sorrow.

What, then, is the spirit of liberty? I cannot define it; I can only tell you my own faith. The spirit of liberty is the spirit which is not too sure that it is right; the spirit of liberty is the spirit which seeks to understand the minds of other men and women; the spirit of liberty is the spirit which weighs their interests alongside its own without bias; the spirit of liberty remembers that not even a sparrow falls to earth unheeded; the spirit of liberty is the spirit of him who, nearly two thousand years ago, taught mankind that lesson it has never learned, but has never forgotten—that there may be a kingdom where the least shall be heard and considered side by side with the greatest.

And now in that spirit, that spirit of an America which has never been, and which may never be—nay, which never will be except as the conscience and courage of Americans create it. Yet in the spirit of that America which lies hidden in some form in the aspirations of us all; in the spirit of that America for which our young men are at this moment fighting and dying. In that spirit of liberty and of America so prosperous, and safe, and contented, we shall have failed to grasp its meaning, and shall have been truant to its promise, except as we strive to make it a signal, a beacon, a standard, to which the best hopes of mankind will ever turn. In confidence that you share that belief, I now ask you to raise your hands and repeat with me this pledge:

I pledge allegiance to the flag of the United States of America, and to the Republic for which it stands—one nation, indivisible, with liberty and justice for all.

V

Thomas Jefferson, on Religious Freedom

At his request, Thomas Jefferson's headstone says nothing of the fact that he was Governor of Virginia, America's first Secretary of State, or third President of the United States. It says simply:

"Here was buried Thomas Jefferson, Author of the Declaration of Independence, the Statute of Virginia for Religious Freedom, and Father of the University of Virginia." These three achievements brought him the most satisfaction. The Declaration of Independence was an obvious first choice, and the handsome buildings that surround the quad at the University of Virginia were designed and built under his supervision, which makes this choice understandable as well. But why the Virginia statute for religious freedom? Why was separation of church and state so important to him?

For one, Europe had been roiled in religious conflict and persecution for the past 500 years, where separation of church and state was unknown. One of the longest and most destructive religious conflicts was the Thirty Years War (1618 to 1648) that resulted in eight million casualties, devastation of entire communities including farms and forests in Central Europe, and bankrupted the treasuries of the competing powers. The war began when the newly elected Holy Roman Emperor, Ferdinand II, tried to impose his religious beliefs on the northern Protestant states. The conflict evolved into a long and bloody war of attrition marked by widespread atrocities, disease, and famine. Exhaustion, not victory, drove the participants to sign the treaties of Osnabruck and Munster, part of the wider Peace of Westphalia that restored peace to Europe.

In America, in the decade before independence, the authorities of church and state in Virginia had responded with persecution and violence to the evangelical challenge posed by the growing number of Baptists moving into that state. Jefferson, very much aware of Europe's long and bloody religious conflicts, strongly opposed such intolerance. To Jefferson, a man barred from office for his religious opinions was a gross violation of his "natural right" to civic participation. "Our civil rights have no dependence on our religions opinions," he said, "any more than our opinions in physics or geometry." Nor was it necessary for the state to protect the sacred truths of Christianity. "It is error indeed which needs the support of the government," he wryly observed. "Truth can stand by itself."

Ahead of his time, Jefferson's efforts were bitterly opposed by his fellow Virginia planters. Notwithstanding, he continued to insist on an immediate and strict separation of church and state. "The time to guard against corruption and tyranny," he said, "is before they shall have gotten hold of us." When Jefferson's efforts finally bore fruit in the

1780s, with passage of the Statute of Virginia for Religious Freedom, he considered it one of the greatest accomplishments of his life.

The heart of the Virginian Statute is inscribed on a marble wall inside the Jefferson Memorial in Washington, D.C. The inscription reads: "Almighty God hath created the mind free. All attempts to influence it by temporal punishment or burdens . . . are a departure from the plan of the Holy Author of our religion . . . No man shall be compelled to frequent or support any religious worship or ministry or shall otherwise suffer on account of his religious opinions or belief. But all men shall be free to profess and by argument to maintain, their opinions in matters of religion. I know but one code of morality for men whether acting singly or collectively."

Jefferson believed that in a democracy the best way to support and encourage religion in general was for the government to be completely neutral and impartial concerning religions in particular; and the best way to give religious freedom to all is to deny religious freedom to none, even those whose faith appears strange, suspicious, or just plain silly.

Largely because of Jefferson's prestige and persuasive power, the system that America's founders finally adopted and incorporated into the Bill of Rights in 1791 was the complete disestablishment of religion. The first one-third of the First Amendment reads: "Congress shall make no law respecting an establishment of religion, or prohibiting the free exercise thereof." With these sixteen words, Congress effectively tied its own hands with respect to showing religious favoritism.

Of the three inscriptions Jefferson chose for his epitaph, only one is an actual physical accomplishment. The other two are ideas, ideas that are at the core of the experiment in democratic government we call the American Dream—freedom from religious intolerance, and freedom from arbitrary rule that is the heart of the Jeffersonian doctrine that all people are created equal and "endowed by their Creator with certain unalienable Rights, that among these are Life, Liberty and the pursuit of Happiness."

VI

JEFFERSON'S HOLY TRINITY

The three men I admire most . . .

To Thomas Jefferson, they were Francis Bacon, John Locke and Isaac Newton. They were, the Virginian proclaimed, "the three greatest men who have ever lived, without exception."

Strong words. Who were "the three greatest men who have ever lived, without exception?"

Francis Bacon (1561-1626) - To some, Francs Bacon was the real author of Shakespeare's plays. He was himself a noted playwright, and a player in Queen Elizabeth's court, by turns in and out of favor with the Queen during Elizabeth's 44-year reign. Under King James I who followed, Bacon advanced swiftly, from knight to lord chancellor. In

1621, he pleaded guilty to accepting bribes, was barred from office, and spent his last years in retirement.

Besides being a playwright and statesman, Bacon was a highly acclaimed philosopher and essayist. He is credited with having created the English essay. In one essay he coined the phrase, "Knowledge is power." He established and popularized an inductive methodology of scientific inquiry that was his greatest contribution to philosophy.

In his novel "Atlantis" he envisioned a utopian state where there would be greater rights for women, the abolishment of slavery, an end to debtors' prison, separation of church and state, and freedom of religion and political expression. Some scholars believe that this was his vision for the North American colonies which, as an insider in the English court, he helped create.

John Locke (1632-1704) - Locke wrote the phrase "life, liberty and property" which Jefferson rewrote as "life, liberty and the pursuit of happiness." The Declaration of Independence draws heavily on Locke's Second Treatise.

If Francis Bacon was a government insider, John Locke (1632-1704) was a government outsider—extreme outsider, as in having to leave England in a hurry as a suspect in the Rye House Plot to overthrow tyrannical King James II. When William and Mary replaced King James II during the bloodless Glorious Revolution in 1688, Locke returned to England and began publishing his works on government, education, religion and philosophy.

In his Two Treatises of Government, Locke justified the Glorious Revolution in his doctrine that government requires the consent of the governed, and may be overthrown by revolution if it violates individual rights. Such notions made Locke a "must read" among 1776 American patriots looking to justify their own revolution.

Isaac Newton (1642-1727) - Newton has gone down in popular lore as the guy who discovered the laws of gravity when an apple fell on his head. In fact, he merely observed an apple falling in his garden. Not content to merely attribute it to the earth's gravity, he reasoned that the same force which caused the apple to fall to the earth must extend to the moon and to the planets. His "Philosophie Naturalis Principia Mathematica," published in 1687, described universal gravitation and the three laws of motion, laying the groundwork for classical mechanics, which dominated the scientific view of the physical universe for the next three centuries and is the basis of modern engineering.

Newton invented the reflecting telescope (which is still used today) and developed a theory of color based on the observation that a prism decomposes white light into a visible spectrum. He also formulated an empirical law of cooling and studied the speed of sound. In mathematics, Newton shares credit with Gottried Leibnet for the development of calculus. In a 2005 poll of the Royal Society of who has had the greatest effect on the history of science, Newton was deemed more influential than Albert Einstein.

Bacon, Locke and Newton wrote a great deal about religion, each declaring God to be a rational being. John Locke was the first Deist (several Founding Fathers were Deists, including Jefferson). As much as he wrote about science and mathematics, Newton wrote more about religion, dedicating much of his scientific and mathematic breakthroughs to the revelations contained in the Biblical books of Daniel and Revelation.

Jefferson's "three greatest men who ever lived" were all Englishmen, which is curious for a guy who loathed the English and worshipped the French.

VII

The King James Bible —on its 400th Anniversary

The year 2011 marked the 400th anniversary of the King James Bible, a classic of English literature, and the most quoted book at the Constitutional Convention of 1787. Indeed, the very ideals that exalted the Declaration of Independence were Biblical in origin: all men are created equal and "endowed by their Creator with certain unalienable Rights, that among these are Life, Liberty, and the pursuit of Happiness." The debates at both the Continental Congress of 1776 and the Constitutional Convention of 1787 were, at their core, a pursuit of truth. The truth they were seeking was grounded in Scripture, Scripture that supported the right of people to question their leaders, supported the legitimacy of the democratic process, and supported the idea that individuals were capable of discovering truth for themselves, without the need of clergymen or kings.

The idea that there was a higher, unchanging law that governed the universe appealed greatly to the founders. Where else could they find a code as brief and comprehensive as the Ten Commandments? These Mosaic Laws were designed to meet a specific set of local conditions. Yet, they cover the whole field of human behavior and after three-thousand years are still relevant. The first commandment establishes the nature of God, the oneness of God, as the creative and governing power of the universe. The second commandment establishes man's relationship with God. Commandments three though ten, often called the social commandments, establish man's relationship to man. The commandments appear in three places: Exodus 20, Exodus 34, and Deuteronomy 5. The three accounts differ somewhat. For example, the relative material which follows the fourth commandment, "Remember the sabbath day, to keep it holy," differs in Exodus from that in Deuteronomy. The latter bases the command to grant rest to laborers and animals for Israel's own deliverance from bondage in Egypt. It places a limit on the hours of labor, making it the first labor legislation in history.

THE MOST DEMOCRATIC PEOPLE OF THE ANCIENT WORLD

Classic Greece is credited with having been the world's first democracy. Overlooked, perhaps, is the fact that Moses established representative government that included courts of law, 500 years earlier. It was Moses' father-in-law who suggested the idea. ". . . .thou shalt provide out of the people able men, such as fear God, men of truth, hating covetousness; and place such over them, to be rulers of thousands, and rulers of hundreds, rulers of fifties, and rulers of tens." (Exo 18: 21) These rulers were known as the Judges, and rotation in office was the rule. What this new form of government did was free Moses from the day-to-day cares of his people to concern himself with the direction and welfare of the nation as a whole and, like our Supreme Court, to adjudicate disputes that exceeded the experience and authority of the Judges. "With the advent of the Judges, the Israelites were, as nearly as can be discovered, the most democratic people of the ancient world." (Marchette Chute: THE SEARCH FOR GOD)

After the era of the judges, David, the shepherd boy who slew Goliath with his sling, and rose up to become king of Israel. Yet, his beliefs were much like that of the Judges. He believed the king was under the same moral law as his most humble subject.

When Israel began to stray from Mosaic law and adopt the pagan rites of Persian religions, prophets rose up to act as the conscious of the nation. The greatest of them was Isaiah. Isaiah's message was clear: spiritual growth of the individual was the key to a nation's well-being and prosperity, and not the beliefs of its priests and the military power of its king. If Isaiah was the greatest of the Old Testament prophets, Jeremiah was a close second. He underscored Isaiah's dictum in proclaiming that the understanding of God was not a matter of ecclesiastical organization but of individual responsibility. This was an idea the American founders would seize upon: a nation can only be as great as its people. "The nation of Israel had never been the keeper of the covenant; it had always belonged to the people," writes Chute. In the United States, the covenant was the Constitution, which begins with the words, "We the people. . . ."

THE PATRIARCHAL FAMILY VS. THE INDIVIDUAL

In the New Testament, the idea of true equality among men emerged with the ministry of Jesus and his disciples, and notably with the apostle Paul. In his book, INVENTING THE INDIVIDUAL, historian Larry Siedentop writes: "Followers of Jesus began to claim that his sacrificial life and death amounted to a dramatic intervention in history, a new revelation of God's will. Understanding that revelation would, in due course, provide crucial underpinnings for what we understand as the nature and claims of the individual. . . . Previously in antiquity, it was the patriarchal family that had been the agency of immortality (i.e. ancestral worship). Now, through the story of Jesus, individual moral agency was raised up as providing a unique window into the nature of things, into the experience of grace rather than necessity, a glimpse of something transcending death. The individual replaced the family as the focus of immortality."

Paul's conception of the Christ overturned the assumption on which ancient thinking had hitherto rested, the assumption of natural inequality. Paul said we can and should see ourselves in others, and others in ourselves. Writes Siedentop: "Paul's vision on the road to Damascus amounted to the discovery of human freedom — of a moral agency potentially available to each and everyone, that is, to individuals. This 'universal' freedom, with its moral implications, was utterly different from the freedom enjoyed by the privileged class of citizens in the polis" (cities of Rome).

Paul used Jesus' emphasis on the fatherhood of God to insist on the brotherhood of man. In Galatians Paul writes: "There is neither Jew nor Greek, there is neither slave nor free, there is neither male nor female; for you are all one in Christ Jesus." Says Siedentop: "Through his letters, Paul provided an ontological foundation for 'the individual', through the promise that humans have access to the deepest reality as individuals rather than merely as members of a group."

These ideas of equality were adopted and expanded by Augustine in the fourth and fifth centuries, and began to influence secular law in the 12th and 13th century. If Christianity declared all men equal in the sight of God, should not they be equal in the sight of secular law? Unlike the ancient cities of Rome, liberty was being claimed, not merely for the medieval towns, but for the individuals who lived and worked there. "It is to Jesus Christ that we owe the development of the laws and advantages of our city," proclaimed the citizens of Marseilles in 1219.

The reach of Kings did not extend to the merchant cities of medieval Europe, thanks to hard won town charters that guaranteed self rule. It was from these cities that capitalism, the middle class, and democracy emerged in the middle ages. But what of the Christian church that fostered the ideals of equality and individual freedom enjoyed in the merchant towns? "The church was both present and absent at the birth of a new form of society, something that has confused discussions of the nature of secularism ever since," writes Siedentop. "Christian beliefs provided a sanction for the individual as the fundamental social role, an egalitarian understanding of justice. But in most other aspects, the church did not seek to shape urban institutions directly. Its influence remained indirect."

Ironically, as the medieval towns were increasingly tolerant of differing religious beliefs, the church became increasingly intolerant, going so far as to decree the very safety of the Catholic religion "lay in ignorance of the text," and thereby put a stop to translations of the Bible from the original Greek and Hebrew text into the popular languages of the people. By Papal decree, the average church-goer was forbidden from reading the very book that had been the source of his freedom—the Bible. What was in the Bible and its meaning became the domain of priests. Just how far the European world had strayed when reading the Bible could mean a date with the executioner. During the Spanish Inquisition, the first question asked was: Do you read the Bible in your native tongue? The rack and the stake awaited the wrong answer.

FOOD OF THE SOUL

Enter Erasmus (1466 -1536) who called the Bible "the food of the soul." He pointed out that the evangelists themselves had translated into Greek what Christ Himself had spoken in Aramaic. In fact, to be widely understood, Christ had spoken in the broadest possible terms, in similitudes and parables. Why not translate such language into the native tongues of everyone? William Tyndale (1495-1536) took Erasmus' words to heart. A Cambridge scholar of very great gifts, he set out to translate the Bible into English so that everyone could read and understand it. ". . .I will cause a boy that driveth the plough shall know more of the Scriptures than (the Pope.)"

Tyndale succeeded beyond his expectations, and paid the ultimate price. He was tried for heresy and burned at the stake. Threat of death for reading Tyndale's translation did not stop the English Bible from circulating secretly among the masses. It wasn't allowed in the churches, so it was shared and read wherever common people gathered—in pubs, in coffee houses, and in people's homes. Translations of the Psalms and the four Gospels were the first to be circulated. With the arrival of Gutenberg's printing press, the Bible in full became available to everyone. Public education was a direct result of people's desire to read the Bible.

The English people gradually came to realize that religious power resided not with the established church but in their very own hands. This led to the Protestant Reformation in England, as we'll as in Germany and the Netherlands where for the first time the Bible was translated into the native tongues of these countries. After a few generations of this mindset, people realized that political power did not reside in the hands of the Monarch, but in their own desire to be self-governed. In England, this led to the Glorious Revolution of 1688, and eventually to the American Revolution of 1776.

Seventy years after Tyndale's death—on the order of King James—a committee of 60 Cambridge and Oxford scholars translated the Bible into English, based mostly on Tyndale's ground-breaking translation. This translation became known as the King James Version, or KJV, which was published in 1611.

"The idea of equality before the law is rooted in religious concepts about the dignity of each individual before a divine being. For centuries, this concept has been steadily adopted around the world, challenging the social impositions of race, position, and wealth." (Christian Science Monitor, 11-7-16)

VIII

The “‘Why?” of American Exceptionalism: “Rutgers v. Waddington”

What is American Exceptionalism? According to Ronald Reagan, who used the term often while campaigning for president, it was America’s divine chosen-ness and moral superiority. The term, however, originated with a French visitor to America, Alexis de Tocqueville, who coined the term in his 1835 travel account, writing that “The position of the Americans is therefore quite exceptional, and it may be believed no democratic people will ever be placed in a similar one.” Sociologist Seymour Martin Lipset, took this idea a step further when he wrote in 1997: “Being an American is an ideological commitment . . .” a commitment in which “law is the only sovereign.”

What does American Exceptionalism have to do with a court case that was decided before creation of the U.S. Constitution? A great deal, actually. The case is "Rutgers v. Waddington."

In Peter Charles Hoffer's compelling book about the case, the better part of American Exceptionalism is the legal forgiveness of one's former enemies.

At the center of Rutgers v. Waddington is Alexander Hamilton, who argued for the defendant in 1784. The war with Britain was over by then, but the infant Republic was embroiled in something of a cold war between Patriots and Loyalists, in what the author calls "the first American civil war." At issue was property, property that had been abandoned during the war. Much of it was in upstate New York and owned by Loyalists who had fled the country. Now that the war was over, they wanted their property back.

In the case of Joshua Waddington it was the opposite. He was a Loyalist who during the war had rented a brewery house in New York City from Elizabeth Rutgers, a Patriot who had fled the city. New York City was occupied by the British up to their departure in 1783, and Waddington had paid rent to the British, who in turn donated the money to various charities throughout the city. Now that the war was over, Anthony Rutgers, acting on behalf of his mother, wanted back payment for the rent. A dispute ensued over the exact amount to be paid. The dispute turned ugly during negotiations when the brewery house mysteriously burned down. Suspecting the worst, Rutgers upped the amount to what today would be one million dollars, and turned to the courts for redress.

Prior to this, the New York state legislature had passed the Trespass Act, which tilted the advantage heavily in favor of the Patriots. Nonetheless, Hamilton saw an opportunity for himself and took up the study of law.

Many of the Loyalists seeking redress were wealthy and able to pay healthy legal fees to regain possession of their property, which was considerable. In the immediate postwar years, where tensions still ran high, taking sides with the Loyalists was not the most popular thing for a Patriot to do, but Hamilton had a motive. He wished to create a lucrative law practice while redressing Loyalists' grievances caused by The Trespass Act. Many were wealthy merchants with overseas business connections with ample investment capital that Hamilton believed was critical to jumpstarting the nation's ailing economy. Rutgers v. Waddington was Hamilton's first big case, and something of a test case at that. Should he win, it would set a legal precedent in the courts that favored Loyalists' return to their former place in the American business world, and generate considerable new business for Hamilton's law practice.

The odds of winning were stacked against Hamilton. The terms of the Peace Treaty were vague concerning the welfare of Loyalists, and the Trespass Act outright hostile. Hamilton turned to the writings of Blackstone and Vattel to buttress his case while arguing that the sovereignty of the people was not in the state legislature or the state constitution, but in Congress under the Articles of Confederation. "The first act of our government adopts it as fundamental law . . . these reflections teach us to respect the sovereignty of the union and to consider its constitutional powers as not controllable by any state." This was heady stuff Hamilton was proclaiming, at a time when state power was considered equal if not greater than that of the Confederation Congress. Fortunately for Hamilton, he had a friend in the Mayor's Court which tried the case, in whom he may or may not have shared his legal brief prior to the court's judgement. Whatever actually did occur (the author is uncertain), Hamilton's legal arguments were persuasive and carried the day for his client. Waddington paid a significantly reduced rental fee.

The case has since been considered an early milestone in developing the American doctrine of judicial review. Yet, there was more to the case than meets the eye. It set the tone for what it means to be an American—what "American Exceptionalism" is really about. Writes the author: "(Rutgers v. Waddington) stood for a commitment to resolve differences, even the most violent of differences, under the rule of law. It stood for the autonomy of the judicial branch in a system of checks and balances. It stood for basic fair play. In 1784 and 1865, the sense of fair play had been severely tested by civil warfare. But Rutgers and its legacy envisioned a polity in which former enemies could find neutral forums to resolve disputes and then willingly accept the decisions of these forums. To load all of this on one case in New York's Mayor's Court may seem overreaching, but at the time, contemporaries thought the case of great importance. If, in the course of nearly two and a half centuries of legal and political change, Rutgers's significance has diminished, it is surely long past time to restore its place in the canon."

IX

Washington's Greatest Asset--Character

It seems astonishing what we Baby Boomers were taught in grammar school about George Washington—the story about the cherry tree and not telling a lie. Eventually we learned the story itself was a lie, as surely as we learned Santa Claus was a myth. Some myths die harder than others and the story of George Washington and the cherry tree persists to this day, so much so that the latest generation of Washington biographers must continue to debunk the tale. In "Cincinnatus: George Washington and the Enlightenment," historian Garry Wills has a completely different take on the story, as he does with so much of what he writes about.

The tale of the cherry tree was the creation of one of Washington's early biographers, Parson Weems. It was rewritten later for the McGuffey

Reader to illustrate a simple moral: "Never tell a lie." According to Wills, this was not the point of the story. The moral does not concern young George but George's parents. Weems' anecdote occurs in a chapter that praises Washington's father for teaching his son to never tell a lie. Later, when young George chops down the cherry tree and confesses the deed, his father embraces him for telling the truth, rather than punishing him for cutting down the tree. Says Wills: "In Weems, all the exaggeration is of affection, calling the boy a hero, and so making him one. Praise is the proper stimulant of virtue." In a world where praising children was equated with "spare the rod, spoil the child," Weems, an ordained minister, was saying praise was more effective—and George Washington was the proof.

That said, much of Wills' book is of how artists have portrayed Washington's rock-ribbed character in their work. The most famous example is Gilbert Stuart's oil portrait from which Washington's face on the One Dollar Bill is taken. The portrait itself is a full-length color portrayal: Washington is shown standing beside a desk. Behind him can be seen the regalia of office, "the column of order, the drapes of court, the seat of authority, the opening onto vistas of power," as Wills describes it. "Yet Washington's chair gives the literal basis of his authority—(on it are carved) thirteen stars for the thirteen states of the Union, woven together with the binding yet being ribbons of federal connection." Under the table are three books. Two of the books are histories of Washington's military career—his General Orders, and a history of the American Revolution. The third book is the Constitution, marking the limits of power. On the desk, where Washington is portrayed as having been attending to official correspondence, are signs of law that bind him: the "Federalist Papers" and the "Journal of Congress." Says Wills: "He sits here to execute the will of others, not to impose his own."

THERE IS NO SUBSTITUTE FOR CHARACTER

The symbols in the Stuart portrait are not of a dictatorship but of a democracy; not of the rule of kings and tyrants but of the rule of law. Above all, Washington was a man ever attentive to the law of his country, whether administered by the Continental Congress during his eight-and-a-half years as Commander-in-Chief, or imposed by the U.S. Congress during his eight years as president. There were several moments in Washington's career when he could have made himself king, with the full support of the Continental Army and most of his fellow countrymen. He refused to do so. After the Revolution, he resisted the forces that wanted to make him king, and instead returned to his plantation. In doing so, he was following the example of Cincinnatus, the Roman citizen who left his plow to lead the republic against an invading force. After the invaders were crushed he resisted the temptation to make himself dictator and returned to the plow.

There is no substitute for character. The following quote, by Anthony Harrigan, president of the U.S. Business and Industrial Council, while not specifically about George Washington, sums up the importance of character: "The role of character always has been the key factor in the rise and fall of nations. And one can be sure that America is no exception to this rule. We won't survive because we are smarter or more sophisticated, but because we are—we hope—stronger inwardly. In short, character is the only effective bulwark against internal forces that lead to a country's disintegration and collapse."

X

A Short History of the White House

The White House is a symbol of American democracy and freedom. While it has changed significantly over the past 215 years, it remains what it has always been, the President's House. What follows is a brief history.

Did you know there were five presidential mansions prior to the White House? George Washington lived in three of them. Indeed, he is the only president NOT to have lived in the White House. Like everything else about his presidency, however, Washington set the precedent for how future presidents would conduct the affairs of state, which was from a house rather than from a palace.

The White House was designed by an Irishman named James Hoban who modeled it after a Georgian-style mansion in Dublin, Ireland. With the exception of a half-dozen Scottish stonemasons, and a few journeymen carpenters, it was built entirely by slave labor. The main entrance faced north while the south faced the languid and murky waters of the Potomac.

The second U.S. President, John Adams (1797-1801), moved in before the house was finished, in the fall of 1800. He thought the large two-story house too grand. The original house was lit by candlelight, lacked indoor plumbing (free-standing wash basins and chamber pots were de regueur), and was heated by 39 fireplaces located throughout the house. A bathhouse and icehouse were located in outside dependency buildings while the kitchen and pantry were located in the basement. Water was carted in from a well five blocks away. The first Oval Office, known as the Yellow Room, was located on the second floor. Servants, most of whom were slaves, were quartered in the basement rooms. First Lady Abigail Adams hung the laundry out to dry in the unfinished East Room.

Thomas Jefferson (1801-1809), our third president, took possession of the mansion in March of 1801. Being an artist at heart and an amateur architect, he designed colonnades for the west and east ends to hide the stables and storage rooms. He had a green thumb and planted a vegetable garden for the kitchen's needs. Tomatoes and peas were his particular favorite; also grown were lettuce, squash, radishes, cucumbers, and a wide variety of herbs. He preferred taking his bath indoors and brought a portable tub from Monticello and placed it in a room on the first floor. Servants carried hot water up from the basement kitchen.

During the war of 1812, James Madison (1809-17) and all of Washington were forced to flee to the countryside by the advancing British Army. British soldiers dined on the 3 o'clock dinner Dolly Madison laid out prior to dashing out the door. Having consumed all the wine, the British soldiers set fire to the house. All that remained standing afterwards was the sandstone walls.

The house was rebuilt by the time James Monroe took office in 1817. He spent a small fortune on new furniture he felt was necessary to match that of the European elite (which, after a great deal of bickering, Congress reluctantly paid). He added the South Portico as a shady place to sit and sip juleps while watching the slow-passing Potomac. His presidency was known as "The Era of Good Feelings."

John Quincy Adams (1825-29) added the North Portico (including the porte cochere) that lent a stately elegance to the main entrance. That, coupled with the South Portico, created the appearance of the White House we know today. Adams did not activity seek the presidency. Quoting Shakespeare, he said: "If chance will have me king, why, chance may crown me, without my stir." Andrew Jackson did actively seek the presidency and swept him from office four years later.

Andrew Jackson (1829-37), the nation's first populist president, invited the world into the White House on inauguration day, and the world accepted. They tracked mud onto carpets and upholstered furniture, smashed dishes and broke tables and chairs, and wouldn't leave until Jackson moved the spiked punch outdoors. Jackson didn't trust bankers or stock brokers. He paid off the nation's debt and shut down the Second United States Bank. He had two mini-balls lodged in his chest, the result of various duels. He threatened to personally hang the first Southerner to openly advocate secession. He wasn't a complete ruffian. He built a hothouse to grow orchids year round, and had a permanent bathtub installed with a hand pump that drew water from an outside cistern. When he left office, he returned to his Tennessee home aboard America's newest creation, the passenger train.

Jackson's hand-picked successor, Martin Van Buren (1837-41), entered office just as the nation's longest depression set in, which couldn't be stopped without a lender of last resort (i.e. the Second United States Bank). With the economy in shambles, Van Buren didn't stand a chance of being reelected. But he did keep warm thanks to the latest White House comfort, a coal-fired central heating system.

William Henry Harrison (1841) lasted but one month in office. Prior to dying of pneumonia, he made his presence known among the dairy farmers of Washington D.C. Harrison set off on foot one morning to see about buying a milk cow. The farmer he met did not believe the man who wished to buy his cow was the President of the United States. Harrison led the man and his cow back to the White House, paid him for the cow, and asked him to stay for breakfast.

John Tyler (1841-45) didn't make any improvements to the White House, or leave much of a mark on history, but with 15 children he managed to fill all the bedrooms.

Like Andrew Jackson, James K. Polk (1845-49) was a workaholic and a activist president. He extended the nation's western boundary to the Pacific Ocean with the addition of the Oregon Territory, California, New Mexico and Texas. With the installation of gaslights, he could work longer hours in the Oval Office and get even more done.

Zachary Taylor was another short-term president (1849-50). His successor, Millard Fillmore (1850-53) established the first White House library. Franklin Pierce (1853-57), though considered a failure as president, installed the first hot-water heater and created a second-floor bathroom with hot and cold running water. James Buchanan (1857-61) was yet another failure. He replaced Jackson's hothouse with a long greenhouse where the West Wing now stands. A bachelor-president, his niece doubled as First Lady.

Abraham Lincoln (1861-65) watched the completion of the Capitol dome while guiding the nation through its first cataclysm. What he needed was a communications center to monitor the war's progress. What he got was a telegraph office located several blocks from the White House, which he walked to daily to receive and send dispatches. His wife Mary Todd was heavily criticized by Congress for exceeding budgeted household expenditures which she said was necessary because of the poor condition of the president's house. If we can believe the movie "Lincoln," she discovered mushrooms growing on the ceiling. Lincoln is the only president to have a room named after him—the Lincoln Bedroom. And he was the first President to welcome free Black Americans into the White House.

Andrew Johnson (1865-69) had a miserable time as Lincoln's successor, but he never ran out of water. Municipal water service arrived in Washington in1865, and to maintain good pressure Johnson had a 2000-gallon water tank installed in the White House attic, and plumbing routed throughout the house.

Ulysses S. Grant (1869-77) enjoyed the first use of water closets in the White House, which put an end to chamber pots and close stools, no doubt adding to the party atmosphere the Grant Administration was known for.

Rutherford B. Hayes (1877-81) was the first president to have the telephone at his finger tips, which was installed during his first year in office. To ring up the White House you dialed "one."

James Garfield (1881) was the second president to be shot while in office. He lingered 80 days in bed before expiring. His successor, Chester A. Arthur (1881-85) held the first (and only) White House yard sale.

Grover Cleveland (1885-89 and 1893-97) has the distinction of being the first two-term president not to serve consecutive terms. During his first term, his daughter Ruth had a candy bar named after her ("Baby Ruth"). During his second term, another daughter, Esther, was the first (and so far only) President's child to be born in the White House.

Benjamin Harrison (1889-93) was the last president to wear a beard. On Harrison's watch, electric wiring was installed throughout the White House, making electric lights (and electric shavers) possible.

THE TWENTIETH CENTURY

William McKinley (1897-1901) is considered the first "modern president." He led the winning side of the Spanish-American war, traveled the nation extensively by train, and made the White House the communications center of Washington D.C. by holding regular press conferences thereby shifting the spotlight from Congress to the Presidency. He was assassinated in the first months of his second term. After this, it was no longer possible to stroll the White House grounds or walk through the front door and shake the President's hand. Those days were over.

When Theodore Roosevelt (1901-1909) entered office, the President's House, as it was known, was one hundred years old. According to Mrs. Roosevelt, the house was dark and dismal and had soot-darkened ceilings. The upstairs bedrooms, she said, were akin "to living over a store." The overcrowded offices were separated from the living quarters by a glass screen. Pleading cramped space and no privacy, Roosevelt got Congress to appropriate $540,000 to remodel the house and to build the West Wing extension in place of the now-dilapidated Buchanan greenhouse. Roosevelt had the words "White House" printed on presidential stationary which caught on with the press and forever after the house at 1600 Pennsylvania Avenue has been known as "The White House." One afternoon, Roosevelt saw the press standing outside in the rain and invited them in and, as the story goes, they never left. Ever vigorous, Roosevelt was the first president to ride in a car, fly in an airplane, and plunge beneath the sea in a submarine. A lover of the great outdoors, he placed into the public trust 230 million acres of land, created scores of national parks, forests, and monuments.

William Howard Taft (1909-1913) had a tough act to follow and, some would say, didn't try. He much preferred his next job, as Chief Justice of the U.S. Supreme Court (1921-30). As president, he enjoyed listening to music on the graphonola, an early version of the record player: arias of Puccini's operas sung by Enrico Caruso were a particular favorite; he also favored the music of a young upstart named Irving Berlin. He oversaw the purchase of the first motorized presidential limousine and had the carriage house and stables converted into a garage. "(Mine was) a very humdrum, uninteresting administration," he said later.

Woodrow Wilson (1913-21) was the first and only president with a doctorate degree. Despite having little experience in government, he proved an effective leader. He created the Federal Reserve, set up the Federal Trade Commission, tried and failed to create the League of Nations, and became the first president to deliver the State of the Union in person, rather than in writing, which had been the practice. His wife planted a garden that became famous as the White House Rose Garden.

Warren G. Harding (1921-23) was the first president to address the nation by radio. He also suffered the ignominy of the first major presidential scandal—Teapot Dome (after the site of one improperly granted oil-drilling lease). While never personally implicated, Harding never recovered from accusations and passed away while in office.

Calvin Coolidge (1923-29). Silent Cal has the distinction of lighting the first White House Christmas tree, and overseeing the building of the East Wing extension. He is the only president to be sworn into office by his father, a local notary in Vermont, where Coolidge happened to be when he learned of Harding's death.

Herbert Hoover (1929-33) suffered two calamities while in office: one was a fire that burned down the West Wing, and the second was an economic fire that caused the Great Depression and forced him out office after one term.

Franklin Delano Roosevelt (1933-45). While leading the nation out of the Great Depression and winning the Second World War, FDR had a swimming pool installed in the West Wing basement, addressed the nation on radio with his weekly "fireside chats," and redesigned the Oval Office. The Resolute Desk, made famous by a photo of President Kennedy's young son John peaking out of an open kneehole panel, was made possible because FDR had hinges put on the panel so it would open and close. The desk has been used by a number of presidents since Queen Victoria presented it as a gift to President Rutherford B. Hayes in 1880.

Harry Truman (1945-1953) did not learn of the existence of the atomic bomb until sworn in as president. Later, he learned the second floor of the White House was on the verge of collapse. He, his family and White House staff moved across Pennsylvania Avenue to Blair House while the White House was rebuilt from the ground up. When work was complete, the president's house had forced-air heating and cooling,132 rooms, 35 bathrooms, 28 fireplaces, eight staircases, and three elevators. Truman inaugurated the first televised press conference.

Dwight Eisenhower (1953-61) enjoyed golfing and had a putting green built outside the West Wing. Much to the annoyance of his successor (Kennedy), the spike marks from his golf shoes were still evident on the Oval Office floor in 1961 when he took office.

John Kennedy (1961-63). As a result of the Bay of Pigs and Cuban Missile crises, JFK created the Situation Room in the basement of the West Wing, as a communications center where his advisors, the JCS, and CIA directors could meet in times of crisis. Mrs. Kennedy, meanwhile, redecorated the White House and restored the Rose Garden to its former glory.

Lyndon Johnson (1963-69) had telephones installed in the White House bathrooms while the nation was learning to spell "Vietnam."

Richard Nixon (1969-74) had the basement pool covered over to make room for a bowling alley; he created a big stir by visiting China, and created an even bigger stir by becoming the first president to resign from office.

Gerald Ford (1974-77) had the distinction of locking himself out of the White House late one night while out walking his dog, and of pardoning Nixon from prosecution. He also built an outdoor swimming pool.

Jimmy Carter (1977-81) popularized the term "micromanager" and brought the first personal computer into the White House.

Ronald Reagan (1981-89): having seen "Dr. Strangelove," as president the first thing Reagan wanted to see was the "war room." He was shown the Situation Room (which was the same thing). Everyone thought he was naive to ask Gorbachev to take down the Berlin Wall, until the Soviet Premier did exactly that.

George H. W. Bush (1989-93) put a hex on broccoli while advocating a gentler, kinder America.

Bill Clinton (1993-2001) was the first president assigned an email address.

George W. Bush (2001-09) was sent aloft Air Force One during the 911 attacks. Until more was known, the presidential jet served both as a safe haven and Situation Room from which to monitor events on the East Coast, across American and throughout the world.

Barak Obama (2009-2016). While Obama had the distinction of being the first African-American elected president, his wife Michelle planted the first White House vegetable garden since the 1840s.

While living in the White House has lots of perks, residents complain its tantamount to living in a fish bowl. The only rooms that cannot be seen from the street are located in what used to be the attic. Added in 1927, the attic rooms have windows concealed from the street; its where the White House kids find privacy and love to hang with their friends.

Finally, these words by John Adams written after his first night in the White House: "May none but honest and wise Men ever rule under this roof."

note: I am indebted to "Our White House: Looking In, Looking Out" (2008) (created by the National Children's Book and Literacy Alliance with 110 Renowned Authors and Illustrators) with an introduction by David McCulloch. That book coupled with "The White House: An Illustrated Architectural History," by Patrick Phillips-Schrock (2013) inspired me to write this piece.

XI

Hamilton, the Musical

After buying tickets and waiting almost a year, we finally got to see "Hamilton," the smash Broadway musical. It was midweek, and the line of ticket holders waiting to get in stretched halfway around the Richard Rodgers Theater in New York City. The music is hip-hop, the cast is young and multiracial, and the wry and witty lyrics are delivered in faultless diction. But that alone doesn't explain its magic, or the effect it's been having on audiences since it first opened off-Broadway. The day we went, the white, middle-class, middle-aged audience rose to its feet and roared approval at the close of each scene as if it were a rock concert.

Even more radical than employing hip-hop as the means of conveying the story is "Hamilton's" reckoning with our country's creation myth. Says Rolling Stone magazine: "There's an almost indescribable power in seeing the Founders, in an otherwise historically rigorous production, portrayed by a young, multiracial cast."

"It is quite literally taking the history that someone has tried to exclude us from and reclaiming it," says Leslie Odom Jr., who plays Aaron Burr. "We are saying we have the right to tell it too."

"Hamilton" is the brain-child of Lin-Manuel Miranda, who got the idea for the musical after reading Ron Chernow's 2004 biography "Alexander Hamilton" while on vacation in Mexico. He was drawn to Hamilton's up-from-the-bootstraps immigrant story, which reminded him of his own Puerto Rico-born parents' experience. He also saw in Hamilton's headstrong personality and rhetorical prowess, links to such modern-day rappers as Tupac Shakur. It seemed only fitting that Hamilton's story be told using the music and vernacular of hip-hop—"the language of youth and energy and rebellion," he says.

Miranda wrote the show's first song for a performance at the White House in 2009, part of an evening celebrating the American experience. His rapping tribute to Hamilton—"The ten-dollar Founding Father without a father / Got a lot farther by working a lot harder / By being a lot smarter / By being a self-starter"—received an enthusiastic reaction from the White House crowd. Encouraged, Miranda set about expanding it into a full-scale musical.

Once Miranda felt he had a viable script, he asked Chernow to read it for accuracy. "You mean you want me to tell you when something is in error?" asked Chernow. "Yes, I want historians to take this seriously," replied Miranda. "Well, that was music to my ears," Chernow said later. "I think very often when Broadway or Hollywood does American history, they start out with the assumption that it's boring and that it has to be spiced up for the contemporary audience. Whereas Lin realized that the most dramatic way to tell this story was to stick as closely to the facts as possible."

While other Founding Fathers were born into privilege and wealth, Alexander Hamilton grew up in a tropical hellhole of dissipated whites and fractious slaves. Says Miranda: "I guess the direct line I can pull on the most is between Hamilton's life story and the immigrant narrative in our country. The fact immigrants have to work twice as hard just to get here, but that also, at some point, it's going to be thrown in your face as a negative. In Hamilton's case, it was Jefferson and Madison writing basically the same things you would hear about Obama during the election cycles: 'How do we really know where he's from?'" Hamilton also had to deal with being taunted as a bastard throughout his life—"my birth is the subject of the most humiliating criticism," he wrote in one pained confession. He turned his early family history into a taboo subject which he wouldn't discuss and never wrote about.

Which brings us to the other thing that drew Miranda to Hamilton—his skill as a writer. As with Miranda, Hamilton distinguished himself with the pen. Says Chernow: "Hamilton didn't have a lot of formal schooling. Still, he was one of those people who seems to have read everything, can remember everything and is able to retrieve everything . . . he could write a 10,000 word memo overnight, without needing to make any changes to it when he was done. By the end of the process (researching and writing Hamilton's biography) I felt that compared to him I was a tongue-tied idiot."

FROM NEVIS TO NEW YORK

Here's what we do know about Hamilton's early life: he was born on Nevis, a tropical island in the Caribbean. His father vanished, his mother died, his cousin and supposed protector committed suicide, and his aunt, uncle, and grandmother all died. At age 12, Alexander and his brother James (age 14) were then stripped of their meager inheritance in a court of law, and left to fend for themselves. James apprenticed as a carpenter while Alexander—with a head for numbers—went to work in a counting house on the island of St. Croix. When the island was ravaged by a hurricane, he wrote an essay about the experience which was published in the local newspaper. Impressed by Alexander's writing ability, a Scottish tutor arranged a scholarship that sent him off to a college in New York (today's Columbia University). A month shy of graduation, Hamilton quit school to form a regiment for duty in the American Revolution. Within a year, he was invited by General George Washington to join his inner circle. Hamilton was a part of the beleaguered Continental Army during the devastating winter at Valley Forge, and the even more devastating winter two years later at Morristown. Two years after that, with bayonet in hand, he led a charge into the battle lines at Yorktown that helped turn the battle and win the day.

Two things happened to Hamilton during the war: (1) he married the daughter of a prominent wealthy New York family, Elizabeth Schuyler (together they would have eight children), and (2) he made an exhaustive study of economics that brought him to the attention of Robert Morris, "the financier of the American Revolution." Later, after Washington was elected president, Hamilton was one of the few people—perhaps the only one—with the financial knowledge to solve the riddle of the skyrocketing public debt. More about this in a moment.

After Yorktown, Hamilton studied law and after one year was on his way to becoming the number one attorney in New York City. He did a stint in Congress (where he met James Madison) and quickly realized the Confederation Congress, without the power to tax, was little more than a debating society. Something had to be done or the young Republic would go the way of the carrier pigeon and vanish from the face of the earth. In 1786, he and Madison called for a Constitutional Convention in Philadelphia to be held the following summer. The new Constitution that emerged was not what Hamilton had hoped for, but he put 100 percent of his support behind it, including writing 51 of the 85 essays that comprised "The Federalist Papers," written to convince New Yorkers to ratify the Constitution.

FOUR STATE PAPERS

When Hamilton was appointed Treasury Secretary in September 1789, no one had any idea how much the nation owed its foreign and domestic creditors. A three-man treasury board under the Articles of Confederation had spent three years going over vast amounts of data and failed to come up with a number. It took Hamilton but three months to determine the total amount ($76 million). Many people saw the debt as a national curse, something to be repudiated and forgotten. Not Hamilton. Having made a study of Britain's deft management of public debt, which had underwritten the island nation's rise to power, he drafted a somewhat similar plan but with several key differences and presented it to Congress as the best means of addressing the debt. "A national debt, if it is not excessive, will be to us a national blessing," he wrote. "It will be a powerful cement of our union."

The paper was the first of four state papers he would write that would become the blueprint for the America we know today. The state papers are: (1) Report on the Public Credit (Jan. 1790), which made provision for the public debt; (2) Report on a National Bank (Dec. 1790), which created the Bank of the United States, forerunner of today's Federal Reserve; (3) Opinion on the Constitutionality of a National Bank (Feb. 1790) written in response to Jefferson's contention that such bank was unconstitutional; Hamilton's rebuttal originated "the implied powers doctrine" which every president of consequence has cited in justifying expansion of presidential powers, including Jefferson himself; and (4) Report on the Subject of Manufactures, a bold plan for making the U.S. a manufacturing powerhouse, and perhaps Hamilton's most ambitious paper.

Years ahead of his time, Hamilton viewed an American manufacturing capability as a means of rendering the United States "independent (of) foreign nations," particularly "for military and other essential supplies," and thereby completing the task begun in 1776. Hamilton noted in his report that "to cherish and stimulate the activity of the human mind, by multiplying the objects of enterprise, is not the least considerable of the expedients, by which the wealth of a nation may be promoted. . . . Every new scene, which is opened in the busy nature of man to rouse and exert itself, is the addition of new energy to the general stock of effort." Though Congress refused to adopt this last state paper, he alone among the founders championed an American spirit of enterprise that eventually transformed a Third World nation into the greatest economic power ever known.

Says conservative columnist George F. Will: "There is an elegant monument to Thomas Jefferson in Washington, but none to Hamilton. However, if you want to see Hamilton's monument, look around. You're living in it. We honor Jefferson, but live in Hamilton's country, a mighty industrial nation with a strong central government."

XII

The Two-Party System

The two-party system was not written into the plan. Indeed, the framers of the United States Constitution worked hard to create a government of checks and balances that would discourage the formation of political parties. Why? Because political parties were the result of factions, and factions had been the bane of every republic since, well, the Roman Republic. Madison, Hamilton, and Washington believed that political parties would divide the nation and ultimately cause the downfall of the nation they had labored so long and hard to create. Madison famously expressed these views in THE FEDERALIST nos. 10 and 51. And wouldn't you know it? Within two years of the creation of the Federal Government, a political party began to take shape under the guidance of Thomas Jefferson and, incredibly, James Madison. The party was created in opposition to George Washington's presidency. Jefferson and Madison feared that Washington's nationalists policies (and those of his Treasury Secretary, Alexander Hamilton) exceeded the limited powers prescribed in the U.S. Constitution and, if not checked, would be ruinous to the Spirit of 1776 and return the nation to the clutch of monarchy. As they saw it, King George III of England would be replaced by King George I of Virginia.

Did Jefferson and Madison actually believe this? No. Of course not. It was politics, where truth is the first casualty of political partisanship. In fact, Jefferson and Madison were government insiders and members of Washington's inner circle. Why after two years would they distance themselves from the Washington administration and form an opposition party? A lot of it had to do with where they were from—Virginia. Virginia was a state without cities, where agriculture held sway and the ruling class was comprised of owners of large plantations worked by slaves. Virginia's planter elite was a veritable gentleman's paradise where everybody of means knew everybody else of means, and saw eye-to-eye on what was best for Virginia, and therefore best for the nation.

As a planter himself, Washington was a member of Virginia's ruling elite, but he had undergone a transformation during his eight-and-a-half years as commander-in-chief of the Continental Army. He no longer saw the nation through the eyes of a Virginia grandee, but as an American. If America was going to be politically and financially strong, and—oh-by-the-way—avoid repeating the deprivation and hardship the Continental Army had suffered during the long war, it would need a strong federal government with the power to tax, a central banking system to manage the pubic debt, a business and manufacturing economy, and a standing army and navy. In other words, something that approximated the British Empire that the former colonies had rebelled against. Jefferson and Madison favored exactly the opposite: states' rights, state banks, no public debt, no taxation other than a mild impost on goods entering the country, local militia, and an agrarian economy. In other words, a return to what

North America had been prior to the Revolution—a turning back of the clock to a simpler and more dignified Arcadian past, where men of reason and good breeding oversaw a limited national government, much as the Northern patroons oversaw their large estates in Upstate New York and the Virginia squires oversaw their vast plantations south of the Potomac River. It was a dream with roots deep in English history, and remains alive and well in today's politics.

TOWN vs. COUNTRY

The dream began with the Anglo-Saxons, who farmed the river valleys, tended their flocks in the highlands, and traded with towns along the northern coast of Europe. It was an idyllic existence, interrupted every century or so by invading Scandinavians who after the fighting was over settled down as farmers and assimilated into the population. That changed in 1066 with the invasion of the French-speaking Normans. The Normans conquered but did not assimilate—they took over. They turned the sleepy village of London into a mighty fortress and capital city of their empire that included most of northern France. The lines were drawn. The Norman ruling elite presided in London and consolidated their wealth in the towns, while the Anglo-Saxons lived in the countryside, farmed the land, and paid exorbitant taxes to a distant king whose court spoke French. Centuries passed, the Magna Carta was signed in 1215, the Glorious Revolution of 1688 ousted one king only to be replaced with another, and all the while the farming class fumed while increasing in prosperity and political power. The wealthiest among them became squires, earls, dukes and viscounts. But always the distrust of central authority remained, a distrust of the king and his court, and, by the 17th century a distrust of their corresponding class of moneymen—bankers, brokers, and speculators. And always there remained among the landed gentry a longing for the halcyon days before the Norman invasion.

The landed gentry became known as Whigs, or the Country party, while the members of the British ministry became known as the Court party. By the late 17th century, the dissenting Country party saw themselves as truly virtuous and the Court party as truly corrupt. In the early 18th century, a leader emerged as the symbol of the Country party—a wealthy landowner known as Viscount Henry St. John Bolingbroke. At the same time, a leader emerged who symbolized the Court Party—the British chancellor of the exchequer, Sir Robert Walpole. In the eyes of Bolingbroke and the Country party, Walpole was the most corrupt of all for having saved the Bank of England from financial ruin with a bit of creative bookkeeping that in turn shifted the nation's wealth from one of land to one of capital. But what was capital compared with land? With land you could grow things, raise sheep and cattle, unearth iron ore and coal. What was capital but a shuffling of paper that yielded dividends, with nothing behind it except the government's promise to pay upon demand? Thanks to Walpole, the tenuous balance between the landed elite and the London moneymen had been significantly altered in favor of the moneymen. In other words, personal property (mainly government stocks and bonds) was now quantitatively as important as real property (land) and qualitatively more so, for it was infinity more mobile and infinitely more dynamic. Under Walpole, vast new quantities of wealth were created, wealth that was financing the Industrial revolution and creating the British Empire.

HONOR vs. VIRTURE

With the influx of wealth came charges of corruption within the British government, and a vast amount of protest literature in the form of pamphlets, party newspapers, even novels and plays. Curiously, the protest literature failed to find an audience in England but did so across the Atlantic, in the British colonies. Thomas Jefferson, for one, had in his library copies of the major writings of Bolingbroke, John Trenchard and Thomas Gordon (writing under the pseudonym of Cato) and James Burgh. These writers had created a language, and indeed an ideology, of opposition to what they saw as the arbitrary and abusive exercise of power by the British ministry. On the other side was a body of literature in support of the British government by the likes of David Hume and Adam Smith. The Founding Fathers read all of these writers, and after the Revolution adopted sides that strongly resembled the principles of the Country party (notably Jefferson) or the principles of the Court party (notably Alexander Hamilton). At the root of the opposing philosophies was how men viewed themselves, as "honorable" (Hamilton) or "virtuous" (Jefferson). According to another British writer from this time, Joseph Addison, honorable men desire the esteem of wise and good men, while virtuous men are motivated by self esteem. The honorable man accepts that there is corruption in the world, but would not stoop to it. The virtuous man shrinks with horror at the existence of corruption, and wants to stamp it out. The honorable man deals with the world as it is, not as he would have it become; the virtuous man seeks to make the world correspond to a utopian vision tied to a mythic past where virtue reigned supreme. Men of both persuasions met in Philadelphia at the Constitutional Convention, and the resulting document was the successful effort of balancing these disparate views. Indeed, James Madison's political views fell somewhere in between, and so it seems fitting that he should be the one to have achieved the balance. Indeed, the U.S. Constitution is a document not of political extremes but of political moderation.

CONSERVATIVES vs. LIBERALS

The idea that the Founding Fathers were one happy band of brothers is as untrue as the tale that Washington chopped down the cherry tree. The Founders quarreled and fought as politicians always do, but somehow managed to set aside their differences and make compromise decisions that created a new nation based on property rights and the rule of law. After the nation was created and its success somewhat assured, they retreated back to their opposing sides, with Jefferson at the head of the Democratic Republic party, and Hamilton at the head of the Federalist party. Today, the Democratic Party looks back to Jefferson as their spiritual leader, and the Republicans to Hamilton as theirs. Yet, to accept this as true is to ignore a great deal of history, and of what constitutes conservative and liberal ideology. From its inception, and up to the presidency of Woodrow Wilson, the Democrats were in fact the conservative party, clinging steadfastly to states' rights, small government, minimal taxes, local militias, no federal bank, and conservative judicial appointments. The party of Hamilton, which would eventually become the Republican Party, was the progressive or liberal party, in favor of a strong federal government and military, a central bank, income tax, ending slavery, activist judicial appointments, and a number of amendments to the Constitution enforcing the civil rights of all Americans.

The change in party ideology that began with President Wilson was completed with the presidency of Franklin Roosevelt, in which the Democratic Party embraced the progressive policies of Alexander Hamilton. At the same time, and possibly as a reaction to FDR's progressivism, the Republican Party become increasingly conservative. And our nation? Where does it stand politically? Judging by the elections, where every four-to-eight years the people oust one party and replace it with a another, this time with Democrats and next time with Republicans, and have done so for most of our nation's 240 years, it's safe to say the majority of Americans are neither liberal nor conservative, but moderate. Yes, moderate, like our Constitution. They work, pay their taxes, have kids, keep their heads, and avoid being drawn in by the extreme elements of either party.

AUTHOR BIOGRAPHY

Washington in New York

by Richard Nisley

Richard Nisley has two books to his credit: a novel entitled *The Ragged Edge*, quasi-self-published by AuthorHouse in 1999, and *If Hemingway Had Written A Racing Novel*, an anthology of stories by various authors that he edited, published by Veloce Press in 2004. Reviews of his books have appeared in *Road and Track* and other magazines. He has written book reviews and articles that have been published in *Car and Driver, Vintage Racecar, Bloomsbury Review, Investor's Business Daily, Racecar Engineering,* and over 500 reviews for amazon.com, under the pseudonym, Ricardo Mio. Also, see Rich's blog: richardnisley.com

Noted authors such as Robert Daley *(Prince of the City, To Kill A Cop)* and William F. Nolan *(Logan's Run)* have praised his novel.

Washington in New York began as a novel but after writing three chapters Nisley started over, writing the story as narrative non-fiction while retaining a novelist's fast-paced, present-tense writing style.

Nisley was raised in Los Angeles, has lived in Chicago, and currently makes his home in Westfield, New Jersey, a suburb of New York City. He graduated from California State University, Northridge in 1975 with a degree in Journalism and worked 18 years for the Firestone Tire and Rubber Company. Among his assignments, Nisley traveled the country giving speeches to Firestone's large sales force on effective customer interaction. He also managed the company's consumer affairs department.

Nisley's two interests are American and British history and international motor racing. He is a member of New York's *Museum of American Finance.*

CPSIA information can be obtained
at www.ICGtesting.com
Printed in the USA
BVHW090857060519
547459BV00022B/2277/P

9 781643 985565